THE WORLD OF

ARCHITECTURE

THE WORLD OF ARCHITECTURE

ARCHITECTURE

PAUL HOLBERTON

CHANCELLOR
PRESS

First published by Mitchell Beazley Publishers in 1988

This edition published in 1997 by Chancellor Press,
an imprint of Reed International Books Limited
Michelin House, 81 Fulham Road, London SW3 6RB
and Auckland, Melbourne, Singapore and Toronto

ISBN 1 85152 996 9

Produced by Mandarin Offset
Printed in China

INTRODUCTION

What is architecture? Is it the shaping of space, the creation of an environment? Is it the technique of building? Is it the expression of an individual's genius, or the spirit of an age? Architecture is above all a tradition. Architects have always learnt from other architects and looked at other architecture, whatever they did afterwards. This book is an introduction to the extent and variety of that tradition.

I have explored here many buildings which have such scale, splendour or richness of decoration that to see them is an experience. But I also wanted to relate the form of the buildings to the use which they serve or once served, which is the particular fascination of architecture. Often this use is or was not simply practical – churches were useful to gather in the community, of course, but the ideas governing their shape and size extended much further. It is these ideas, or ideals, that animate architecture. I am grateful to my friend Alistair Shearer for his contribution on non-western buildings, where a wider knowledge than mine of the cultures that inspired and built them is obviously essential.

It must be remembered that the form of a building is also determined by the materials used and the expertise available for its construction, so that the technical is always relevant and has also been discussed there. Indeed the fulfilment of an ideal often involved the solution of a technical problem: for instance, in Gothic churches the tension structure was evolved to express divine immanence.

The architectural tradition is both a body – of building – and a mind – of ideals. This is true even in contemporary architecture, if one looks for it – though at times one may think the men of the Middle Ages were more articulate about what they wanted to do.

CONTENTS:
PERIODS AND STYLES
OF WORLD ARCHITECTURE

The story of world architecture is told chronologically in this book.
This country-by-country table of contents shows the major periods and
styles of architecture within each country with their relevant page references.

MOUNDS AND MEGALITHS

Before history comes prehistory or proto-history; before architecture there is often a kind of pre- or proto-architecture. Technically, mounds of earth or a circle of standing stones are not buildings, but they share with true architecture first the aim of permanence and secondly the requirement that a large number of people should cooperate in erecting them. At different periods and in different parts of the world we find, quite independent of one another, societies both organized and ready to create monuments, though lacking in technique; frequently the technique, and true architecture, follows shortly afterwards.

For example, in China during the second millennium BC chieftains or "aristocrats" constructed, or had constructed for them after their deaths, increasingly large and well furnished burial mounds (*tumuli*). The practice continued even after the establishment of temples, palaces and cities in the first millennium BC. There was a similar pattern in Japan, which in the early centuries AD had a so-called "Tumulus" period which preceded the arrival of Buddhism and the development of religious and civil architecture from the 7th century. In northern Europe, the construction of *barrows* for local chieftains in the 6th and 7th centuries AD was followed shortly by conversion to Christianity and the construction of churches. Sometimes, however, the transition to architecture is never made: the native American mounds in Ohio have no successors. In other cases, the urge to make monuments led instantly to architecture, as in Egypt, where the pyramids are obviously a direct equivalent in stone to tumuli in earth.

Constructing permanently, or making monuments, is one way of dealing with death, or, more accurately, one way of dealing with afterlife. (The idea that one might perish absolutely occurs only in advanced societies.) Much early architecture, and proto-architecture, is funerary architecture. Alternatively, institutions for regulating the course of life itself, usually called *temples*, are the earliest kind of architecture or proto-architecture to emerge. This seems to be the case in India and Mesopotamia, though the evidence is scanty, and in Pre-Columbian South and Central America Polynesian *marae*, or meeting platforms, are a proto-architectural form of temple.

There are also some isolated and mysterious constructions, such as Stonehenge in England or Great Zimbabwe in the country of Zimbabwe in Africa, which were certainly in some way temples rather than tombs. There is quite a lot of evidence that Stonehenge, in use in the period 1600–1400BC, had some astronomical or rather astrological functions, perhaps equivalent in some way to those of the stone sites constructed by the Olmec culture in Central America 100 years later. Quite probably Stonehenge is a translation into stone of previous similar constructions in wood, and therefore built deliberately for permanence.

STONEHENGE, WILTSHIRE, ENGLAND. There is no need to believe that influence from the Mediterranean lies behind the erection of this circle of megaliths. The mortise-and-tenon joints between stone and stone indicate a native tradition of carpentry. This transition from wood to stone has frequent parallels elsewhere in the world.

MESOPOTAMIA: THE ZIGGURAT

Peculiar to the earliest civilized culture to emerge on the earth (about 3500BC, in the district now mostly in Iraq called Mesopotamia because it was "between the rivers" Tigris and Euphrates) is the *ziggurat*. The word means "high" or "pointed", and the ziggurat was very clearly a manmade mountain serving to make a bond between earth and sky: mountains were the source of all fertility and the bond between earth and sky brought about fertility for the city surrounding the ziggurat. The Tower of Babel (Genesis 11: the first mention of architecture in the Bible) is evidently based on the reality of the great ziggurat at Babylon, intermittently the capital of the region.

The ziggurat at Babylon no longer survives, though it was seen and described in the 5th century BC by the Greek historian Herodotus. However, there are substantial remains of ziggurats at Warka (Mesopotamian Uruk), dating to about 3000BC, Khafaje, of about 2600BC, Muqari'iya (Mesopotamian Ur) of about 2100BC and Choga Zanbil, of about 1250BC, not to mention others. All are built of mud brick (the region is lacking in stone) and rise in a series of terraces to the chamber at the summit. The sloping walls of the terraces were invariably not plain, but buttressed at frequent intervals. The interior and exterior walls of Mesopotamian buildings were usually clad or covered by one means or another, or at least painted: according to Greek sources the seven terraces of the ziggurat at Babylon were each painted a different colour.

These colossal terraces must have served for processions and ceremonies which we can now only imagine. However, sacrifice to the gods, in Mesopotamia as elsewhere, always also involved the consumption by mortals of the left-overs. Sometimes the magazines in which produce was stored have also survived. The god of the ziggurat was believed not only to inhabit it but to own the city in which it stood: he or she was, in other words, a kind of feudal overlord, and the ziggurat was the headquarters of the economic administration. More deeply, it was the focus of communal identity. Something of this emerges in the biblical description: "And they said to one another, Let us make brick, and burn it thoroughly. And they had brick for stone, and slime for mortar. And they said, Let us build a city and a tower, whose top may reach unto heaven; and let us make a name, lest we be scattered abroad upon the face of the whole earth." Herodotus, however, could no longer take the institution seriously, and speaks in his works of taking a rest halfway up to the top and tells stories of the god enjoying women left for him overnight in the upper chamber.

Around 3000BC, shortly after civilization had arisen in Mesopotamia, architecture was also built in independent societies to the west and east. In Egypt, much has survived, but very little remains of the Indus Valley civilization except its engraved seals. But its written language, not yet deciphered, and traces of sewerage and drainage, indicate its importance.

THE SO-CALLED WHITE TEMPLE, URUK (PRESENT-DAY WARKA), IRAQ, is an early ziggurat (dated to about 3000BC) featuring only one terrace. The characteristic in-and-out of the walls—the system of alternating buttresses and recesses—occurs in the earliest architecture both of Mesopotamia and of Egypt. It may well reflect a system of building in wood, before the invention of dowels or nails, when overlapping planks were tied together. At Warka there were also fragmentary remains of cone mosaics: cones of clay dipped in various colours and inset in the walls to create bold geometric patterns. Such colouring and patterning, tiling and cladding of mud-brick walls remained standard Mesopotamian practice.

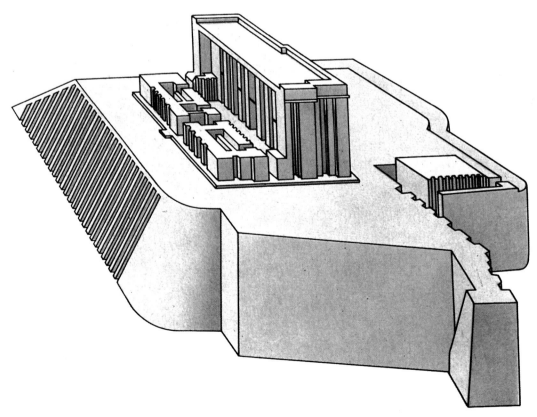

Above RECONSTRUCTION OF
THE ZIGGURAT OF UR, IRAQ.
This was built over an earlier
structure by named kings
(Ur-Nammu and Shulgi) who
evidently deliberately set about
creating a monument to their
glory.
Left PLAN VIEW OF THE TEMPLE
AT KHAFAJE, IRAQ, which is as
old as the ziggurat at Warka
but underwent later
modifications, reaching its final
form about 2500BC. As is not
the case at other sites, much of
the surrounding enclosure has
survived. The round enclosing
wall was built in curved bricks.
The gateways were flanked by
imposing towers (*pylons*), such
as are also found in Egypt.

EGYPT: THE PYRAMID

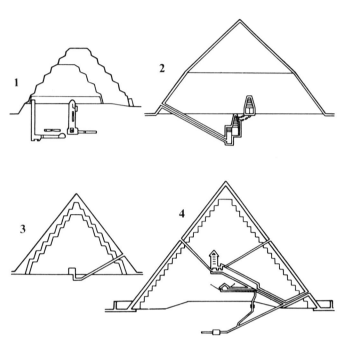

The concepts "house" and "tomb" have one and the same hieroglyph in ancient Egyptian. Death for the Egyptians seems to have been much the same as life, except more permanent and perhaps less demanding. Preparation for the afterlife was often the major enterprise of the King, or Pharaoh's, reign, and Egyptian religion was largely a cult of the dead. Their pyramids were provided with mortuary temples and chapels for the cult of the deified deceased within them.

The beliefs underlying the extraordinary labour given by the Egyptians to funerary architecture are evident at the tomb complex of the Third Dynasty Pharaoh Zoser at Saqqara dating to the 27th century BC, which contains what is probably the first pyramid. The complex translates into stone and eternity the temporary habitation in wood, mud-brick and reed that constituted the Pharaoh's palace. The translation is often very literal: tiles reproduce wall-hangings in matting; even rolled-up matting curtains are reproduced in stone cylinders. And the tomb complex includes not only the mud-brick walls of the palace, reproduced in stone but with blind gateways, but also the ceremonial courtyards and public viewing areas of the Pharaoh to his people in real life.

Originally the resting place of the Pharaoh had been in the form of a *mastaba*, which had a flat or gently curved roof,

and remained the form used by other orders of people. It seems to have been the idea of the Zoser's learned High Priest, Imhotep, to convert the mastaba into a pyramid; hence, Imhotep also became the earliest recorded architect. Undoubtedly the pyramid was in some aspects, like the ziggurat, a symbolic mountain; but the chief Egyptian god was always the sun, and the pyramid was more exactly the mountain-over-which-the-sun-appears.

The greatest and most massive pyramids were those built by a succession of Fourth Dynasty Pharaohs, Cheops, Chephren and Mycerinus, in the 26th century BC at Giza. These are "true" pyramids, with smooth sides, as opposed to the terraced or "step" pyramid of Zoser. (The term *pyramid* is Greek: they named them after a certain kind of bun of the same shape they knew at home.)

After Imhotep's first essay in stone architecture, Egyptian masonry became increasingly skilled, as the perfect joints and interior vaults of the Great Pyramid of Chephren are witness. But already at Saqqara two essential elements of early architecture are present: columns with capitals (imitating reed columns in the natural world) and halls with a central corridor of window apertures overlooking the two sides, known as *hypostyle* ("over-column") halls.

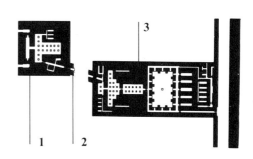

Opposite page, top left DIAGRAMS SHOWING THE DIFFERENT SHAPES, SIZES AND INTERIOR ARRANGEMENTS OF SUCCESSIVE PYRAMIDS. The stepped pyramid at Saqqara (1) is shown in both its original and its enlarged profile. The pyramid at Dahshur (2) is bent because the technique of construction was not yet perfected. It was perfected at Maidum (3), which has a stepped form (enlarged in the course of building) encased in a smooth exterior. The pyramid of Cheops at Giza (4) uses the same technique; the site of the tomb chamber inside was three times changed.

Opposite page, lower left VIEW TO THE TOP OF CHEPHREN'S PYRAMID AT GIZA. The limestone facing has crumbled away except at the top.

This page, above VIEW ACROSS TO THE THREE PYRAMIDS AT GIZA. Cheop's, the largest, is on the left, Chephren's is middle, Mycerinus's on the right.

This page, above right PLAN OF THE MORTUARY TEMPLE ATTACHED TO CHEPHREN'S PYRAMID, the only one to have survived. The entrance part of the temple contained a T-shaped chamber (1), in which were statues of the Pharaoh. This was linked by a causeway or processional route (2) to the main part of the temple (3).

EGYPT: THE TEMPLE

After many vicissitudes and even a period of foreign domination, Egypt entered the period of its greatest ever power in the 16th century BC, the 18th and 19th dynasties of the New Kingdom. This was the period in which the Valley of the Kings was tunnelled, in which Tutankhamun's tomb was stocked and furnished so richly, and in which Ramesses II, also known as Ozymandias, built, to paraphrase the famous poem by Shelley, so as to "dismay the mighty".

Although the Pharaohs now cut rock tombs for themselves instead of erecting pyramids, their fundamental purposes remained the same. Typical is an inscription on a temple built by the 18th-dynasty Pharaoh Amenhotep III: "He made it . . . as a monument for his father Amon (the sun god) . . . making for him an august temple . . . an eternal everlasting fortress of fine white sandstone, wrought with gold throughout; its floor is adorned with silver, all its portals with amber; it is made very wide and large, and established for ever." This was a mortuary temple built on the edge of the desert, but in this period cult temples in the valley of the Nile built in stone appeared also, the greatest of them at Karnak and Luxor.

Central to these temples was the sanctum or *cella* where the god dwelt in statue form. Round about him were numerous offices and so on for the priests, but also a route of corridors and courtyards through which the idol might pass before and after his manifestation to the people during festival. For this purpose he was carried in a model boat, itself housed in a special chamber. The entrance to the temple would be flanked by great *pylons* or gatetowers adorned with flagstaffs, and a processional route extending beyond the temple precinct might also be marked out—for instance, there is an avenue of stone ram/sphinxes at Karnak.

The outstanding architectural feature of the New Kingdom temple is the colonnade, used to flank a courtyard (*peristyle*) or to support a central roofed corridor higher than the surrounding roofs (*hypostyle*). The columns themselves and their capitals took the form of the stem and bud or flower of various plants, among them the papyrus that splays at the top, which had first appeared at Saqqara and is the distant ancestor of the Greek Doric column and capital.

EGYPTIAN COLUMNS AND CAPITALS originally reproduced in stone the forms of the plant material that continued in use in less important or durable buildings. Plant forms continued to inspire capital and column shapes long after stone architecture had been established: the column and capital was envisaged as a stalk and bud or flower. In the examples shown here, a pier from Karnak (1) is adorned with a lotus. At Medinet Habu (2) the column and capital are shaped like a papyrus. From Luxor (3), a column and capital and topmost abacus in the shape of several papyri bound and bundled. The capital from Edfu (4) has the form of a palm. The post-Dynastic, Ptolemaic period capital from Kom Ombo (6) returns again to the papyrus. But the Ptolemaic capital from Dendera (5) uses the head of a goddess, Hathor, rather as Dynastic capitals had sometimes shown Pharaoh heads.

Top left HYPOSTYLE HALL AT KARNAK. The higher central columns create a kind of "clerestory" by which the building is lit.
Middle left THE ENTRANCE FRONT OF A TEMPLE AT ASMAN, showing the processional route or causeway up to it in the foreground.
Bottom left RUINS OF THE TEMPLE AT LUXOR, built by Amenhotep III in the 14th century BC but added to by Ramesses II.
Bottom right PLAN OF THE TEMPLE AT LUXOR, showing the sanctuary uppermost and the entrance court added by Ramesses bottommost. The columns shown in the photograph are those at the narrowest part of the plan, the original entrance building of Amenhotep. The temple is obviously laid out as a "nave" through which processions were to pass.

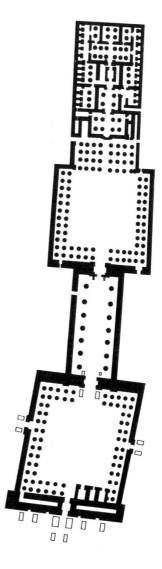

HITTITES, MYCENAEANS, MINOANS

In the 16th century BC two new societies emerged to the north of Egypt and Mesopotamia—the Hittites in Anatolia (Turkey) and the Mycenaeans in mainland Greece. The Hittites were the older, and the Mycenaeans probably learnt from them how to build great walls of fitted boulders, a technique which the Greeks later called *Cyclopean*, since they imagined that only giants could have raised them. Such walls still survive at modern Bogazköy, originally the Hittite capital of Hattusas, and at Mycenae, Tiryns, Athens and other Mycenaean citadels or acropolises in Greece.

Both the Hittites and the Mycenaeans also knew how to arch in these great stones. Proof of it is the great gate at Bogazköy, though the few great stones edge out towards one another (*corbel*) rather than form a true arch. At Mycenae the so-called Treasury of Atreus (in fact a tomb) has a bee-hive-shaped dome constructed on the same principle, though the stones are smaller and built up in regular rows. The Mycenaeans also made corbelled gateways, though they filled in the upper half of the opening and squared off the door.

Inside their citadels, the Mycenaeans built halls of a certain type named from the Homeric word for palace, *megaron*. Its great importance is that it constitutes the prototype for the Greek temple. Its ultimate origin is neither Hittite nor Mycenaean, though it seems to have come from the region of present-day Syria. It is defined as an oblong hall

with a porch in front; the porch is supported by one or more pillars. Often these were built in clusters; they have also been found on the site of Troy in Anatolia.

At the end of the 15th century BC the Mycenaeans overran a third Mediterranean society, the Minoan civilization based in Crete. Though geographically so close, the two cultures appear to have been very different. The Mycenaeans were recent invaders; the Minoans were indigenous. The Mycenaean language and religion would later be Greek; the Minoan language has not been deciphered, precisely because it is not related to Greek. Instead of building Cyclopean citadels, the Minoans built elegant palace complexes without fortifying walls. The central feature of their palaces was not a megaron, but a ceremonial courtyard. Their culture seems most to resemble the kingdoms of Mesopotamia, though they were seafarers.

The Mycenaeans seem to have taken advantage of a volcanic eruption to take over Crete. Further light on the Minoan civilization continues to be shed by the excavations still being conducted in Thera (Akrotiri), an island off Crete buried by an eruption in the 14th-century BC.

Left THE RUINS OF THE ACROPOLIS AT MYCENAE. The beautifully jointed masonry served not a religious but a practical purpose—defence.
Right THE GREAT GATE OF THE HITTITES AT BOGHAZKÖY, with a reconstruction of its original form in the 14th century BC. Quite possibly the Mycenaeans learnt their building techniques from Asia Minor.
Below THE SO-CALLED TREASURY OF ATREUS AT MYCENAE, in fact an anonymous tomb. The similarities to the Hittite gate at Boghazköy are obvious.

ASSYRIANS AND PERSIANS

Though kingship emerged very early in Egypt, the king or Pharaoh seems always to have been constrained by priests. In contrast, the Assyrian kings who conquered and ruled the rest of Mesopotamia from the 9th century BC not only possessed absolute power, they built huge residences in which their military might was intimidatingly expressed.

The palace built by Assurnasirpal II (ruled 883–859BC) at Nimrud seems to have set the standard for his successors. It is not well preserved, but has yielded an enormous quantity of low-relief slabs, originally lining the approaches to the throne room, on which the expeditions and campaigns of the king are narrated blow by blow; there are also some marvellous scenes of the king hunting lions.

Sargon II (721–705BC) set up his capital at Khorsabad, a new town enclosing nearly one square mile within its mud-

Below DECORATIVE MOTIFS OF ASSYRIAN ARCHITECTURE. Many of these motifs resemble or anticipate similar forms in Greek architecture. For instance, the central meander of the frieze from Nimrud (1) was taken over directly into Greece. Some of the motifs appear on glazed bricks, for the Assyrians continued the Mesopotamian tradition of ceramic decoration. Some were found at Nimrud, others at Khorsabad. The alabaster relief of the king hunting lions, now preserved in the British Museum, London, is from Nineveh, a single item from an enormous series.

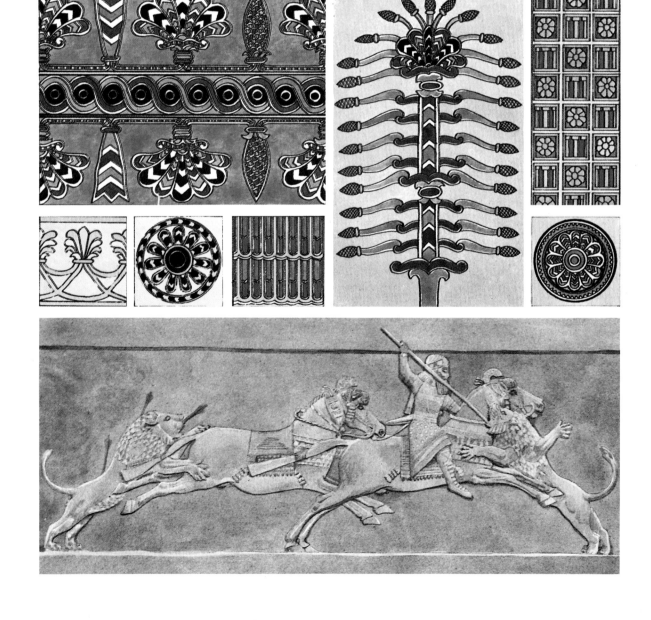

brick fortifications. It was dominated by the palace complex, which included in one corner the ziggurat: the king had the god in his pocket. Once again there was an awe-inspiring approach, including great winged bulls flanking the gateways. Subsequent kings moved to Nineveh, which remained the capital till the fall of the empire in 612BC.

In the aftermath Nebuchadnezzar II (604–562BC) established a new state, the so-called Neo-Babylonian empire. Though the ziggurat at Babylon has entirely disappeared, Nebuchadnezzar's Ishtar Gate, with its towers or pylons decorated with glazed moulded bricks in rows of animal reliefs, was retrieved from the ruins.

Following further disruption, Cyrus the Great (559–530BC) founded the Achaemenid dynasty and the Persian empire. His palace at Pasargadae retained some Assyrian features, such as the huge winged bulls flanking gateways, but also had splendid colonnades, porticoes and hypostyle halls, dependant ultimately on Egyptian and other foreign precedent.

The palace at Persepolis built from 518BC onwards by Darius and his son Xerxes again had an international character, employing materials and craftsmen from all parts of an enormous empire. These kings held sway not only in modern Afghanistan, Iran, Iraq, Syria, Palestine, Yemen and Egypt but also Turkey, or Asia Minor, where there were by this time Greek cities. There is considerable Greek influence at Persepolis. Attempts by Darius and Xerxes to subjugate mainland Greece failed, however, and a century and a half later, in 330BC, Alexander the Great of Macedon entered Achaemenid Persepolis and burnt it.

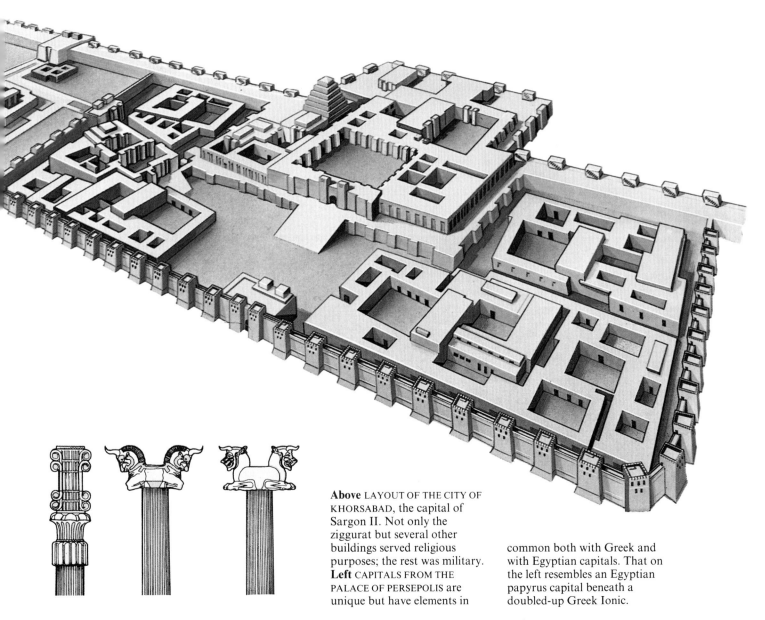

Above LAYOUT OF THE CITY OF KHORSABAD, the capital of Sargon II. Not only the ziggurat but several other buildings served religious purposes; the rest was military.
Left CAPITALS FROM THE PALACE OF PERSEPOLIS are unique but have elements in common both with Greek and with Egyptian capitals. That on the left resembles an Egyptian papyrus capital beneath a doubled-up Greek Ionic.

THE GREEK TEMPLE

In the course of the 12th century BC the Mycenaeans succumbed to a new society, the invading Dorians. There was an interval, a "Dark Age". Then a new civilization sprang forth with extraordinary and accelerating vigour at the end of the 8th century BC. This Greek culture was rooted in its Mycenaean heritage, but initially nourished by contact with mainland Asia and Egypt, passing through a so-called "orientalizing" period. One product of this period of assimilation was the Greek temple, which was built according to a more or less uniform design derived from the Mycenaean megaron or porched hall, but indebted to Egypt for its colonnades and masonry and to Asia for its ornament.

Like Persian cult, Greek religion was centered on an open-air altar. Here animals were sacrificed (in Homer, 100 at a time) and of course eaten. The Persians seem to have built no temples at all, but the Greeks provided a house for the god a short distance away, in essence no more than a sanctum or cella where the cult statue resided. It was fronted and backed by porches, raised on a platform, and surrounded by a ring of columns to carry the eaves of the roof. But the glory of the Greek temple is its symmetry. These temples were built by the people who also invented logic and pure geometry, who devised the theory of the atom, and who first conceived of something existing without having a body. They transformed architecture into something more than building: they evolved a sense of form.

Partly the "form" resulted simply from the standardization of building elements. The Greeks built in uniform blocks of tufa or marble, and analyzed their design and ornament into a fixed system involving a limited number of units. But all architecture has repeating elements. The Greeks had rules. They built ideal buildings, in which design took over from mere function.

Two rules or systems became dominant, the Doric order and the Ionic order. The more severe Doric order prevailed in mainland Greece and the western colonies (Sicily, Italy); the Ionic order, more ornamental and more variable, prevailed in the eastern Mediterranean, where the tendency to "orientalize" was naturally stronger. The Ionic only took definitive form in the late 5th-century BC buildings of the Athenian Acropolis. The Doric was established by the end of the 6th century.

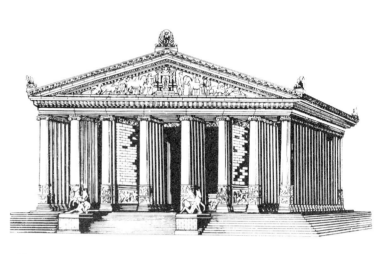

Above RECONSTRUCTION OF THE TEMPLE OF ARTEMIS AT EPHESUS, of which only fragments now survive. It has most features in common with mainland Greek temples, but different are the decorated lower shafts of the columns and their greater number. The order used is the Ionic.

 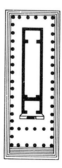 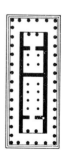

Middle PLANS OF GREEK TEMPLES. The first is one of the earliest known, the 8th-century BC Heraion at Samos. It has the distinctive form of the Mycenaean megaron with its front porch, but the single row of central columns was soon expanded to two. The much larger Temple at Selinunte in Sicily, dating from the 6th century, has something of the same elongation. The "classic" plan is represented by the temple of Apollo at Corinth (on the right), also 6th-century: note the division of the central sanctuary into porch, pronaos or antechamber, naos or cella, and opisthodomos.

Below, bottom THE TEMPLE OF HERA AT OLYMPIA. The Greek guide-writer Pausanias reported that this temple still had in his time (2nd century AD) one wooden column; the rest had been replaced piecemeal in stone. This was clear proof that Greek stone architecture was a translation into stone of timber forms: the column was originally a tree-trunk.

THE TEMPLE AT SEGESTA, SICILY. Dating from the 5th century BC, the Doric temple of the little hill-top town was never fully finished, so that the knobs by which the blocks were hoisted into position are still there, and the local stone never received its plaster coating to make it resemble marble. In its ruined form (the central cella is missing) it is one of the most impressive surviving Greek temples, and in design is very similar to the Parthenon in Athens.

THE ACROPOLIS AT ATHENS

After the defeat of the Persian kings Darius and Xerxes at Marathon (490BC) and Salamis (480BC), the independent Greek states created a league in order to liberate their kin still under Persian rule in Asia Minor. Athens, the victor of Marathon and Salamis, was naturally leader of the league. Gradually the contributions of ships and troops by other members were commuted to contributions of money, and when the Athenians found an excuse to transfer the treasure of the league from Delos to Athens in 454BC, the league became an Athenian empire.

The magnificent temples of the Athenian acropolis were partly built with this money, partly they were this money in

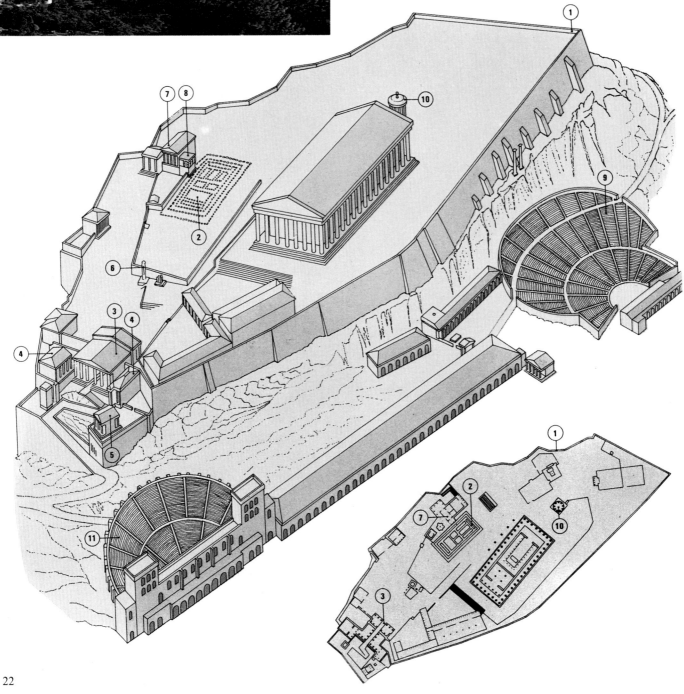

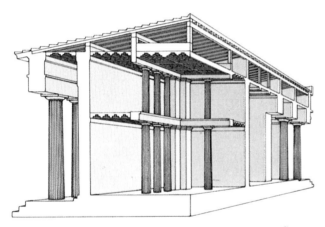

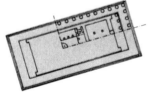

Opposite page, top left
GENERAL VIEW OF THE
ACROPOLIS AT ATHENS, seen
from the centre of the old city.
Opposite page, left LAYOUT OF
THE ATHENIAN ACROPOLIS. The
encircling wall (1) recalls its
original defensive as well as
religious importance. However,
in the first Persian War the
Athenians chose not to defend
it, and the old temple of Athene
(2) was burnt by the Persians.
Under Pericles, the temple was
rebuilt beside it as the
Parthenon. New
embellishments included the
gatehouse or Propylaea (3),
with side-wings (4). The temple
of Athene Nike, or Victorious
Athene (5), was built soon after
(c. 438BC). Once famous was
the statue of Athene
Promachos, or Protective
Athene (6). The ancient shrine
of the Erechtheion (7)—actually
several shrines in one, hence its
irregular shape—was next

rebuilt. On its south side the
porch (8) was supported by
female column-figures called
caryatids. The theatre of
Dionysus (9) was below, on the
south flank. In Roman times a
small temple of Rome and
Augustus (10) and the Odeion
or concert hall of Herodes
Atticus (11) were added.
This page, above REAR VIEW
AND CUTAWAY
RECONSTRUCTION OF THE
PARTHENON. Note the two tiers
of columns inside the cella (at
the end of which was once
Phidias's colossal statue of
Athene) and the wooden roof.
This page, above right A VIEW OF
THE EXQUISITE IONIC TEMPLE
OF ATHENE NIKE.

bankable form. The colossal cult statue of Athene, the goddess of the city, which almost reached the roof of the greatest
of the temples, the Parthenon, was made by the sculptor
Pheidias in gold and ivory in such a way that she could be
"stripped" if necessary. An additional room (*opisthodomos*)
behind the cella seems to have served as a strongroom.

The bank itself, however, the Parthenon, was hardly
reconvertible; nor was its unprecedentedly large programme
of sculpture, filling both pediments, not, as was usual, just
one; adorning all the panels (*metopes*) between the columns,
not just those at the short ends of the building; and providing
an extra frieze in low relief running all the way round the
outside top of the cella and opisthodomos. Moreover, the
fabric of the building was all marble, not partly in marble but
mostly in tufa plastered over; the building was unusually
large, being eight columns wide instead of six; and the joint-
ing of the masonry was not only so fine as to be invisible but
also accommodated a subtle curvature.

The Parthenon was built in the Doric order, though the
four internal columns of the opisthodomos may have been
Ionic. The Propylaea or entrance gate to the Acropolis, built
during the same period (447–432BC) certainly combined
Doric exterior columns with Ionic ones inside. Two other
buildings on the Acropolis, much smaller and built in the last
years of the 5th century BC, the Erechtheion and the temple
of Athene Nike, were entirely Ionic. These are exquisite; their
ornament is wonderfully exact, bold and delicate. Altogether
the Acropolis achieves a "classic" balance of Doric majesty
and calm with Ionic liveliness. The achievement was not
inevitable: the Doric temple of Zeus Olympios at Akragas
(Agrigento) in Sicily, the so-called Temple of the Giants, is
contemporary, but by comparison it is a monstrosity.

The Acropolis temples are only one sign of the flowering of
Athenian culture. On the south slope of the hill the plays of
Aeschylus, Sophocles and Euripides were performed in the
Theatre of Dionysus, and concerts held in the Odeion (or
Odeum) of Pericles, a square building supported by a forest
of columns resembling to some extent the audience hall of
Xerxes at Persepolis. From the 5th century BC onwards such
civic amenities became commonplace throughout an increas-
ingly Greek-influenced world.

HELLENISTIC GREECE

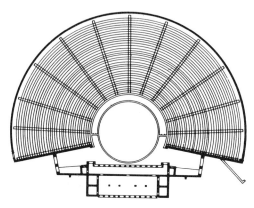

Above PLAN OF THE THEATRE AT EPIDAURUS IN GREECE, one of the best preserved Greek theatres. It dates from the 4th century BC. **Right** VIEW OF PART OF THE THEATRE AT EPIDAURUS TODAY. It is still used for the staging of Greek drama. **Far right** VIEW OF THE THEATRE AT THE SANCTUARY OF APOLLO AT DELPHI; the remains of a temple are visible behind.

The defeat of Athens by Sparta in 404BC ended its "Golden Age", but did nothing to halt the progress and dissemination of Greek culture. The Athenian Plato's greatest pupil was Aristotle, who came to Athens from Macedonia, hitherto a "barbarian" society; Aristotle returned to Macedon to tutor Alexander the Great. The Macedonian army, trained in the Greek pattern, now conquered Greece (338BC); but Alexander by 330BC had also conquered the Persian empire, pushing the West the furthest East it has ever reached. The influence of *Hellenistic* art in the Indian kingdom of Gandara is quite clear. Hellenistic is the term given to the art and architecture of the succession of kingdoms into which Alexander's conquest was divided and redivided.

In new form, Greek colonization continued unabated. Alexander founded towns wherever he went. Already in the 6th century BC town-planning had been the subject of treatise and discussion. Hippodamos of Miletos advocated a grid plan, and organized the city round its essential elements: the *acropolis* ("high city"), the fortifiable and sacred "centre" of the city; the *agora*, both market and meeting-place, with its adjacent social, political and commercial buildings; fountain-houses; the *palaestra* or sports ground; the theatre, shaped out of some convenient hillside; perhaps also a stadium and hippodrome; and of course the residential quarters, in which the larger houses were built round a courtyard. There were no gardens as such, though flowers were cultivated.

The agora and palaestra were flanked by *stoae*, long passages open on one side through a colonnade. The equivalent of cafés (as the musculature of their statuary shows, Greek men seldom sat down), or lecture rooms ("Stoic" philosophy took its name from the stoa in which it was taught), stoae served also many other activities not yet institutionalized. One such stoa at Delos, dating to about 210BC, was lit internally by a corridor of taller columns, in the manner of the earlier hypostyle hall; it is also probably an ancestor of the Roman *basilica*.

Some individual Hellenistic buildings achieved great fame, such as the lighthouse at Alexandria in Egypt; the tomb of King Mausolos of Caria in Asia Minor; the Great Altar of the city of Pergamon, also in Asia Minor.

Urban expansion continued unabated even after the Hellenistic kingdoms had fallen in before the Roman empire. Some ancient centres, such as Ephesus, were "redeveloped"; the Romans also founded new towns, like Philippi. It has been remarked that Athens was at its most beautiful as a provincial university town in the late 2nd century AD, when it was restored and endowed by the Emperor Hadrian and the millionaire Herodes Atticus.

Classical

Above left
RECONSTRUCTION MODEL OF THE SANCTUARY AT PERGAMON IN ASIA MINOR, the showpiece of the powerful Hellenistic Pergamene kings. The stupendous Altar of Zeus, now housed in the Pergamon Museum in East Berlin, was only one element of the complex: it is the colonnade surrounding an open square with two projecting wings over steps, visible on the right.

Above right THE STOA BUILT BY ATTALOS II, King of Pergamon, for the Athenians beside the Agora or civic square-cum-market of their city has been reconstructed in this century.

Left VIEW OVER RUINS AT DELOS dating from the 2nd century AD. Houses of this date at Delos are exceptionally well preserved and very informative about the lifestyle of the middle classes in the eastern Mediterranean under the Roman empire at its height.

VITRUVIUS AND THE ORDERS

According to tradition, Rome was founded in 753BC by two robbers, Romulus and Remus. But like the Macedonians, whom the Greeks had regarded as "barbarians", the Romans, too, became Hellenized, and began to use the Greek word *barbari* on others. Like the Macedonians, the Romans became fully Hellenized only when they had conquered Greece and Greek Asia Minor, which took place during the 2nd century BC.

The development of a distinctly Roman architecture does not occur until the 1st and 2nd centuries AD. Under their emperors, the Romans made advances in building form and technique that went far beyond the Greeks. But in the republican period, and even under Julius Caesar and the Emperor Augustus (d. AD14), Roman architecture differs from Hellenistic architecture in style only.

The Etruscan civilization, extending rather further south than modern Tuscany, was a dominant influence on the developing city. The Etruscans were themselves heavily influenced by the Greeks, though they lacked their talent for logic and symmetry. They made greater use of wood and terracotta and less use of stone. What survives of their architecture (apart from tombs) is massive but rather squat. But they knew how to build arches and had their own version of the Doric order, the so-called *Tuscan*.

The assimilation of Hellenistic architecture involved above all learning the orders. The rules of their use and handling, together with a great deal of other useful information, is contained in *On Architecture* by Marcus Vitruvius Pollio. Vitruvius was an architect in the service of Augustus, to whom his work is dedicated. This is the only such treatise to have survived from antiquity (though Vitruvius refers to several Hellenistic books on architecture).

By Vitruvius's time Doric and Ionic had been joined by the Corinthian order, though the Corinthian, as Vitruvius says, is really only a variation on Ionic. He also has a brief description of the Tuscan order. Vitruvius explains the use of the orders for the free-standing columns of temples, an attitude that soon became rather old-fashioned. The Romans came to use the orders predominantly in *applied* form, that is, as decoration for a wall, and without any real structural purpose. Vitruvius also describes what he calls a *basilica*, which is recognizably a hypostyle hall, though it has two storeys flanking the high toplit corridor of columns. Unlike the Greek stoa, it is enclosed on all sides by a wall. Increasingly walls and arches would come to take the place of columns and beams, though the columns were preserved as a facing.

A magnificent sample of Roman architecture just after Vitruvius's time is provided by the extraordinary survival of the town of Pompeii and the smaller neighbouring suburb of Herculaneum, engulfed by volcanic lava in AD79. These were not merely provincial towns but fashionable coastal resorts (overlooking the Bay of Naples, the beauty of which the Romans appreciated). The streets, squares, tombs, houses, shops, temples - all is laid out for our view, and helps to make the Romans seem closer to us than the Middle Ages.

Above left ETRUSCAN TOMBS AT CERVETERI, ITALY. The Romans inherited much from the Etruscans: these round domed tombs show that the Etruscans were skilled masons with knowledge of the arch, and were the source of the Roman tradition of round, central-plan burial monuments.

Left THE ETRUSCAN ARCH AT PERUGIA, ITALY. Only the arch itself is Etruscan, of the 2nd century BC. The superstructure of the arch is Roman, of the 1st century BC, and the loggia on the left is Renaissance.

Above right THE MAISON CARRÉE (SQUARE HOUSE) AT NÎMES, FRANCE, once stood by the forum of the Roman city. It shows the typical deep portico of Etruscan and Roman temples, leading directly into the cella. Its columns, free-standing in the portico and "applied" round the walls, are of the Corinthian order, much favoured by the Romans. The temple dates from the 1st century BC.

Right VIEW OF A STREET IN HERCULANEUM, 1st century AD.

THE SIGHTS OF ROME

Above and below VIEW AND PLAN OF THE PANTHEON, ROME. The Pantheon consists of a temple portico conjoined somewhat awkwardly to an enormous round chamber. The plan reveals clearly the alternating niche-and-pier construction of the domed part.

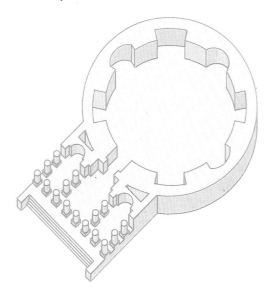

The Emperor Augustus boasted that he had found Rome a city of brick and left it a city of marble, but the architectural transformation made by subsequent emperors in the first centuries AD was even more dramatic. The difference in size between the old *forum* or "centre" of the city, the Forum Romanum, and the imperial fora laid out so grandly beside it expresses this change. While the old sacred spots of the city are small and cramped, the new temples, basilicas, markets, libraries and so on are imposing even today.

The greatest surviving Roman building is the Pantheon, built on low-lying ground to the north of the Forum by the Emperor Hadrian in the years 120–124. It is still an extraordinary experience to stand beneath its dome, partly because it is exactly the same height, 43m (142ft), as its width, and makes a perfect half sphere inside; outside the dome is almost flat. It was built upwards and inwards in decreasing rings of brick held in concrete, with an opening nearly 9m (30ft) wide left in the middle (it is remarkable that very little rain seems to come in). The dome is supported not on a uniform round wall but on a ring of six arches closed off by columns on the inside and a thin brick wall on the outside. This alternation of open niche and massive pier is typical of imperial Roman construction.

Still more famous is the Colosseum. This amphitheatre enclosing an oval arena is a structure of arches and vaulted

corridors in great blocks of tufa, but it also has a facing of *applied* half-columns. The Doric order is used at the bottom, Ionic in the middle, Corinthian at the top. The tiers of arches carry the load; the superseded system of column and beam or *entablature* has become a form of decoration.

The Colosseum was built by the Emperor Titus about AD70–80 on the site of the ornamental lake of Nero's "Golden House". A vast country estate abutting the Forum, the "Golden House" had been created on expropriated land cleared by a fire in AD64 during which Nero is reputed to have fiddled. This was one of Nero's most unpopular excesses, and succeeding emperors made amends by replacing his pavilions with public buildings—the Colosseum, and the Baths of Titus. These, too, had great vaults, but were dwarfed by the later Baths of Caracalla and of Diocletian erected in the 3rd century—amenity complexes with sequences of rooms each nearly the size of the Pantheon.

Between the Forum and the Colosseum several basilicas were erected, culminating in the 4th-century Basilica of Maxentius, the last emperor before the Christian Constantine the Great. This still had the shape of a hypostyle hall, a long central space rising above flanking lower spaces, and still had internal columns, but the roof was vaulted in brick and concrete and most of its load borne by great brick piers behind the columns. Between the piers the thin "curtain" walls were

cut away into arch-shaped windows in a pattern that recurs in the final triumph of this development in vaulting, the Hagia Sophia in Constantinople.

Above left ONE OF THE STREETS, WITH TWO STOREYS OF SHOPS, OF TRAJAN'S MARKET IN ROME. Inside, the shops are barrel-vaulted.
Above ASPECTS OF THE COLOSSEUM, ROME. The photograph shows the substructure of the arena, from which the floor has vanished. The artwork shows the system of arches supporting the spectators' seats and the Orders used on the outside.
Below CUTAWAY VIEW OF THE BATHS OF CARACALLA, ROME.

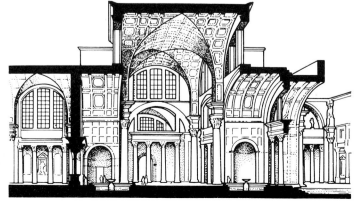

SIGNS OF EMPIRE

The invincible Roman armies that conquered first the rest of Italy, then the south of France, Spain, North Africa, Greece and Asia Minor, then the rest of France, Britain, parts of Germany, and the Balkans, were not only better disciplined and equipped than their "barbarian" or Greek opponents, but every brigade had its attached engineering corps. The Romans conquered not just with the sword but, more lastingly, with the spade.

The signs of this are everywhere apparent in the legacy of straight Roman roads that have been superseded only by the construction of motorways since World War II. Roman bridges continued to be used through the Middle Ages and beyond. In southern Europe some spectacular stretches of aqueduct survive, and Roman plumbing and sewerage systems are reputedly still in use in some places. And most of the old towns in Europe are Roman foundations, many of them still retaining a Roman grid in their street-plan.

These feats of engineering were the infrastructure of the Roman empire, facilitating communication and in the west imposing an urban hierarchy on tribal, peasant or even nomadic subject peoples. Also certain visible symbols of Roman authority became embedded in European culture rather as Roman constructions became embedded in the landscape. The Roman basilica, the space where the governor or the Emperor himself held audience or gave judgement, came to determine the shape of the Christian church. The eagle of the Roman legions became a universal symbol of empire; and so on.

One symbol of military might that took on particular importance was the triumphal arch. Originally temporary structures erected along the route taken through the Forum and up to the Capitol by a general celebrating a victory in a "triumph", triumphal arches became permanent memorials in stone under the Emperors. A comparatively early and simple one is the Arch of Titus in Rome, with reliefs showing his triumph, including the spoils of his sack of Jerusalem being led in procession. The Arch of Trajan in Benevento is outside the town, commanding the road that leads on to Brindisi (Brindisium), the port for Greece. There is a four-way arch built by Septimius Severus at Lepcis Magna in Africa, as well as his Arch in the Forum at Rome.

Another "triumphal" form was the single free-standing column. Trajan's and Antoninus's columns in Rome celebrated their victories, with the events of their campaigns being recorded in the reliefs that spiral upwards. This rarer and more expensive symbol also has its modern progeny – Nelson's column in Trafalgar Square in London and Napoleon's column in the Place Vendôme in Paris.

Classical

Opposite page, left THE PONT DU GARD, FRANCE, is one of the best preserved and largest Roman aqueducts. Such scale was possible because the Romans realized that arches were as strong as walls, and obviously much lighter.

Opposite page, lower left THE ARCH OF SEPTIMIUS SEVERUS IN THE FORUM, ROME. It is situated on the route taken by triumphant generals up to the temple of Jupiter on the Capitol Hill.

This page, left THE MAGNIFICENT ROMAN GATE AT TRIER (TRÈVES), GERMANY, a major capital of the late empire.

This page, lower left and below THE COLUMN OF TRAJAN, ROME, AND A DETAIL OF THE BASE OF THE COLUMN. The reliefs are a pictorial narrative of the military campaign against the Dacians in modern Romania in the first decade of the 2nd century AD. It once stood beside a library (ruins of which are visible in the foreground), from which its upper parts were better legible.

DOMESTIC AND IDIOSYNCRATIC

A significant section of Roman society was leisured and affluent. Quite apart from the millionaires, many private individuals possessed the means to adorn their (one or more) houses splendidly, to donate or contribute to civic monuments, and to build themselves fine tombs. There was an efflorescence of this kind of architecture in the outlying "new towns" of the later Roman empire perhaps even in greater degree than in Rome itself. At this level of society, the eastern and southern regions start to set the fashion even before Constantinople became the new capital in 330. This is true in architecture as it is in religion.

Since they were no longer load-bearing, the orders could be manipulated more freely for decorative ends. The most imaginative or extreme variations are found in the east. In round temples the entablature carried by the columns had necessarily been curved, but at Baalbek we find not only convex but concave, in counterpoint. Gables or pediments also become curved instead of straight, and the cross-pieces are "broken" or interrupted in various ways. These and other "mannerist" variations were perhaps limited in appeal, but one fundamental shift became universal: instead of supporting an entablature or beam, columns bear arches.

Also it became usual to import or revive old styles, or to mix different elements in the creation of "eclectic" buildings. The Emperor Hadrian's villa at Tivoli is a pleasure garden of quotations from the past (for instance, the *caryatids* or female column-figures copied from the Erechtheum on the acropolis at Athens, which here stand around a pond), adorning buildings and spaces of novel creation. A wide variety of architectural forms is employed in Diocletian's palace complex at Split on the eastern Adriatic coast. The villa at Piazza Armerina in Sicily, which may also have been imperial, is remarkable more for its mosaics than its architecture, but is the best surviving example we have of the Roman self-contained country estate or *villa*.

The architecture of the more moderate or less wealthy sections of society has survived to a lesser degree and is naturally less eye-catching. Some tenements or apartment blocks of the kind inhabited by the majority of townspeople are well preserved at the port of Rome, Ostia. Descriptions of life in their villas by writers such as Horace, Cicero or Pliny remained an ideal of cultivated civilization long after their bricks and mortar had crumbled.

Left THE MASK IS FROM THE THEATRE AT OSTIA, the port of Rome at the mouth of the Tiber. The tenement block (insula) is a reconstruction of ruins also at Ostia. Shops to the same design as those in Trajan's Market (see p. 29) occupy the ground floor. Though such blocks so closely resemble modern examples, they did not include plumbing. Only the richest had their own baths and lavatories. But public lavatories were provided (see bottom right below).

Left and above VIEW OF THE PRESENT RUINS AT HADRIAN'S VILLA AT TIVOLI, OUTSIDE ROME.
Above RECONSTRUCTION MODEL OF HADRIAN'S VILLA COMPLEX AT TIVOLI, extraordinary for the diversity of its architecture.

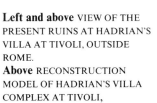

Above right THE ROMAN PUBLIC LAVATORY SURVIVING AT OSTIA, NEAR ROME.

THE EARLIEST CHURCHES

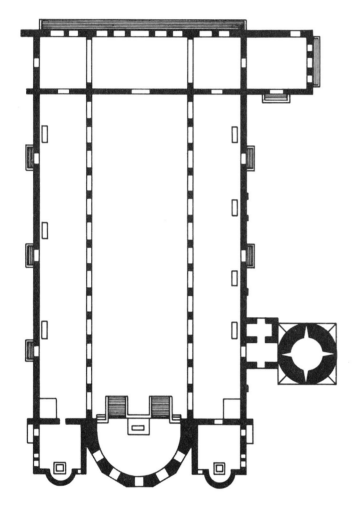

Top PLAN OF THE CHURCH OF SANT' APOLLINARE IN CLASSE, RAVENNA: note the apse and at the entrance end the narthex. **Above** VIEW DOWN THE NAVE OF SANT' APOLLINARE NUOVO, ALSO IN RAVENNA, and very similar in design. It was very common to place mosaics, as here, or paintings between arcade and clerestory.

Even when they were not being persecuted, Christians at first celebrated the rite of the Mass in private houses, or, equally privately, at the site of a grave. The simple installation involved is shown by the oratory of a 3rd-century house at Dura Europos in Asia Minor (the oldest surviving Christian *church*), or by the "chapels" of the Roman catacombs. The 5th-century church of Santi Giovanni e Paolo at Rome is built over a complicated succession of conversions from the original private house. But most churches, after Constantine had made Christianity the official religion in 330, were erected over or beside saints' tombs. The catacombs were not so much places of refuge as spiritual dormitories constructed all round a shrine—for the best effect as close as possible.

The form used for the new public churches was naturally the basilica, designed, unlike the pagan temple, to accommodate large numbers of people and already sanctioned by official use. However, certain specifications were introduced in accordance with Christian cult. Only the initiated could witness the central rite of the Mass, but those under instruction could listen outside: a portico (*narthex*) or courtyard (*atrium*) was provided for them. Within the church, men and

women were often segregated; various chambers were required as offices and so on for the clergy. The clergy became strictly demarcated from the laymen and in basilicas a structure was erected to screen them off just short of half way down the church. At the centre of this enclosure, the tomb or relic of the holy personage to whom the church was *dedicated* was housed under or in front of the altar in what would become a *crypt*.

Once the basilica had been adopted, the Christian liturgy could be standardized and institutionalized within it. Its development was partly influenced by the secular ceremonies such buildings had previously housed: Christ received the same sort of respect as the emperor. One significant new idea was the succession of entrances into the building—from outside into the forecourt or atrium; from the atrium into the church; from before to inside the choir-screen. These entrances were enacted in processions, and caused the older system of columns running both up the long sides and across the short sides to give way to the now familiar system of nave and aisles.

Opposite page, right EXTERIOR AND INTERIOR OF THE BASILICA AT TRIER (TRÈVES), GERMANY. This secular basilica may be compared with the basilica churches illustrated.
Above VIEW DOWN THE NAVE TOWARDS THE APSE OF SANTA SABINA, ROME, the least altered of the many Early Christian basilica churches surviving at Rome. It dates from the early 5th century.

THE CENTRAL-PLAN CHURCH

Above EXTERIOR AND INTERIOR VIEW OF THE CHURCH OF SANTA COSTANZA, ROME, built in the 4th century. It is a typical central-plan memorial church, except that it is unusually richly decorated and well preserved. It was built outside the city walls to commemorate the daughter of the Emperor Constantine in the 4th century.

The *longitudinal* church with nave and aisles developed from the basilica, the stoa and ultimately the hypostyle hall that had been known to the earliest civilizations. The origin of the round or polygonal church symmetrical on all sides about its centre is probably equally old, but less easily traceable. Round temples or, better, shrines, were certainly common among the Greeks. However, centrally planned buildings were usually small until the perfection by the Romans of the kind of vaulting used for the Pantheon, which is much larger than anything that could be built in wood and does not require the clutter of internal supports.

The "perfect" dimensions of the Pantheon, with its width exactly equal to its height, suggest that central-plan buildings already had a numerical symbolism in Roman times. Symmetrical buildings could serve as scale models of the universe as it was in those days conceived, that is, with four corners, composed of four elements, and so on: the symbolism involved was made clear by the rituals performed inside.

This kind of thinking was also dear to the Judaic tradition, witness the minute description in the Bible of the Temple of Solomon. It was developed still further by Christians. For example, we know that the octagon of the Church of the Nativity built by the Emperor Constantine at Bethlehem was meant to symbolize the seven days of Creation plus an eighth for Christ's Nativity, the day of human regeneration.

There was also a tradition that tombs should be built round or central-plan, which the Romans seem to have taken over from the Etruscans, and which the Christians inherited from the Romans. The most beautiful and famous example of such a central-plan tomb is the tomb of Galla Placidia at Ravenna, in which the original mosaics and sarcophagi are still preserved. This is cross-shaped; the mausoleum of the Visigoth King Theodoric the Great in the same city is a round example.

The case of Theodoric is only one among many in which the "barbarian" invaders of the decaying Roman empire continued and developed Roman traditions rather than destroyed them. It may have been Theodoric who began the harmonious and exquisite octagonal church of San Vitale in Ravenna, which the Emperor Justinian completed and adorned when he temporarily reconquered part of northern Italy for the Roman empire in the 6th century. Both monarchs would have looked to the famous "Golden Octagon" built by Constantine in the 4th century at Antioch, in just the same way that Charlemagne, King of the Franks, looked to San Vitale when he built his own octagonal palace chapel at Aachen in the early 9th century.

Similarly when the Muslim armies invading the Byzantine empire from the south in the 7th century came to build, they adopted both the basilica (in the Great Mosque at Damascus) and the central plan (in the Dome of the Rock in Jerusalem) for their religious architecture.

Above and left VIEWS OF SAN VITALE, RAVENNA, justly the most famous central-plan building to survive in Italy from before the Renaissance. It has superb 6th-century mosaics, which the building was built to bear; outside, its plain brick surfaces have no pretensions. It has vaults of hollow terracotta tiles, so light that the walls remain thin, just as they do for wooden-roofed churches. There are also basilica churches in Ravenna of the same date, but San Vitale marks the beginning of an increasing Byzantine preference for central-plan churches.

HAGIA SOPHIA, CONSTANTINOPLE

So many early churches visitable today retain no more than their bare structural necessities—so that the sense of mystery they were designed to induce is absent. Increasingly from the 4th century onwards, the altar and chancel enclosed by the choir-screen were a privileged, entirely secret realm to which the ordinary participant could never penetrate. Church furnishings, moreover, could be exceedingly rich, in materials, decoration and symbolism. Wrought in marble and mosaic, the greatest of these churches were designed to shimmer and glow, to reflect and diffuse a coloured, flickering light by which the eager participant would be suspended in trance. He or she would strain to perceive the Almighty, in the words of St Paul, "through a glass darkly".

The most stupendous of these churches was (and partly still is) Hagia Sophia (Holy Wisdom) in Constantinople, built to be in effect the cathedral of the Empire. Roman techniques of vaulting in brick were developed still further, though the use of concrete was discontinued. The Emperor Justinian appointed for its construction two distinguished scientists, Anthemios of Tralles, who had written on the geometry of cones, and Isidorus of Miletus, an expert specifically on vaulting. They began work in 532, and the church was consecrated only five years later. It is a basilica, with a *narthex* or portico at the west for those under instruction, and an altar framed by an apse at the east, but the nave is vaulted by a great dome, 33m (109ft) in diameter. Though this is smaller than the dome of the Pantheon, the dome is only the centre of a series of vaulted spaces and the overall effect is even more impressive. The system by which the "thrust" (the tendency to push the walls outwards) of the dome is contained and transmitted is much more delicate and complicated. Its supports are hardly apparent, and it seemed to contemporaries "to hover in the air".

Hagia Sophia embraces and combines several types of church in one. It is a basilica, but also takes the form of a cross with a central dome: it has a *domed cross* plan. The dome rests not on a ring (like the Pantheon) but on four arches in a square. *Pendentives* or curved triangles effect the transition between the circle of the dome and the square it covers. Increasingly Byzantine churches were built on the domed cross plan, that is, round a large square space with subsidiary spaces around it from which the lay community looked in on the central performance. The basilica, in which movement had been comparatively free and lighting natural, gave way to an enclosed, more dimly lit design more strictly determined by ritual functions.

VIEWS OF HAGIA SOPHIA,
CONSTANTINOPLE (ISTANBUL).
The inset on the extreme left
shows the thin wall, opening
into large and frequent
windows, between the massive
piers that bear the thrust and
weight of the vaults. The view
of the interior immediately
above reveals the kind of light
this method of construction
makes possible within. The
exterior view shows the massive
buttressing required without.
The building is now surrounded
by four Turkish minarets. The
cutaway view reveals the
sequence of domes and
half-domes over screens of
columns shaping the interior.

SYRIA AND ARMENIA

Byzantine architects, continuing Roman tradition, built in brick and enriched in marble and mosaic. However, in Syria and Cappadocia on the eastern border of the Empire, and in the independent but Christian kingdom of Armenia, it was traditional to build in stone. Remarkably beautiful and original churches were erected in these regions in this medium between the late 5th and the late 7th century, when the Muslims conquered the area (and in Armenia also afterwards).

The late 5th-century pilgrimage centre of St Simeon Stylites, now an impressive ruin at Qal'at Si'man, consisted of an octagon abutted by four basilicas, forming a cross; at the midpoint was the column on which St Simeon had spent the second half of his life. There are several precedents for the design and ornament, except for the rich moulding that runs continuously round both the outside and the inside of the building, looping up over windows and doors, stringing or roping all the parts together. This moulding is in essence an entablature, of the type that had bent and curved in the architecture of the eastern Roman empire, but it has run off from its columns. The Orders have expired; a new idiom, specific to masonry, has emerged.

At the contemporary church, also now ruined, at Qalb Lozeh, there is another new element, twin towers flanking the entrance to the basilica. Though it is not clear where these came from or what they mean, they undoubtedly lent an imposing air and framed off the façade in an emphatic way. It was a kind of emphasis alien to the Romans, but recurrent in the Middle Ages.

Syrian ideas were taken up in neighbouring Armenia, though the more common form of church was the Byzantine domed cross. These parish churches are generally small, though built in massive blocks closely set and finely finished, so that they have a clear compactness. In order to mount the dome over the square nave of the church, *squinches* or bridging arches were laid across the corners; it would have been difficult to reproduce the Byzantine "pendentive" in masonry, though the domes are built in shaped stone blocks.

From the 7th century stones in alternating colours and from the 10th century a flat relief reminiscent of Persian carpet designs were used to enliven the exterior. A sign of the prestige of Armenian masons is the fact that an Armenian, Trdat, was called in to repair the dome of Hagia Sophia in Constantinople in 989.

Opposite page THE CHURCH OF THE ARMENIAN KING GAGIK OF VASPURAKAN, on an island in Lake Van in present-day Turkey. Early 10th-century, it has superb masonry and anticipates many features of European Romanesque.

This page, left THE CHURCH OF ST GREGORY AT ANI, the capital of 10th-century Armenia. Note, for instance, the blind arcading and polygonal tower, also widespread in Europe a little later.

This page, below THE LATE 10TH-CENTURY CATHEDRAL AT ANI, now missing its central dome. Its architect was Trdat, who was later called to Constantinople to repair Hagia Sophia.

ISLAM: THE BEGINNINGS

It is a considerable irony that the Arabs, who were to weld the religion of Islam into such an imperial and cultural power, had no architecture of their own. But they did have a dynamic and aggressively proseletyzing religion with clear ritual requirements. To serve these, the nomadic desert dwellers looked to whatever models they could find. The early builders drew on two well-established traditions: brick and stucco in Mesopotamia, and stone construction in Syria. From such humble beginnings, the architects of Islam were in time to create some of the finest buildings ever seen.

The ritual requirements were simple: a wall to indicate the direction of Mecca, and an area in which the faithful could assemble. Such assemblies were from the first social and political as well as religious. The mosque (*masjid*: "place of prostration") was in fact where the community gathered on all important occasions. Unlike the Hindu temple, Buddhist *stupa* or Christian church, the mosque housed no deity, commemorated no historic event, contained no sanctuary and was served by no formal priesthood.

The community gathered behind the *qibla* wall, facing Mecca, into which was set the arched niche (*mihrab*) that actually indicated the holy city where the Prophet was born (AD570). The shape of the *mihrab* may have come from the blade of a spear that Muhammad stuck haft down in the sand to show the direction of Mecca: it may be derived from the apse of Egyptian (Coptic) churches or a liturgical niche in certain contemporary synagogues. To the right of the mihrab in a congregational mosque, stands the *minbar*, a pulpit recalling the three steps from which Muhammad addressed his followers. A railed enclosure (*maksura*) protected the rul-

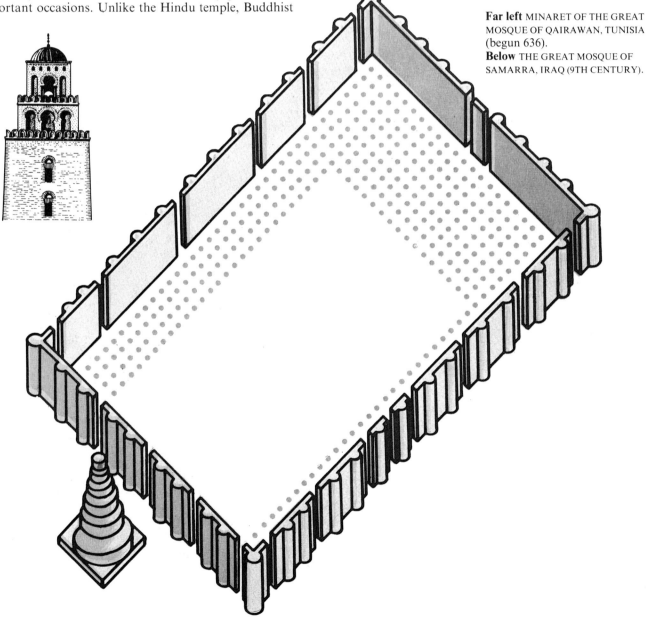

Far left MINARET OF THE GREAT MOSQUE OF QAIRAWAN, TUNISIA (begun 636).
Below THE GREAT MOSQUE OF SAMARRA, IRAQ (9TH CENTURY).

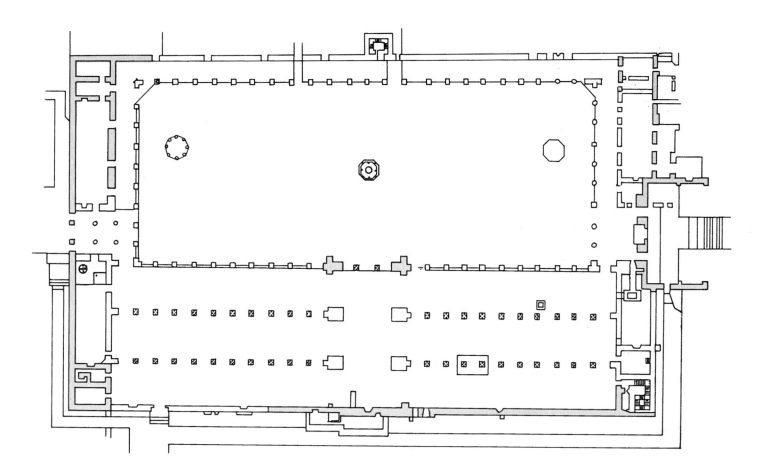

ing caliph or his representative when leading prayers. Ritual ablutions were performed in a tank or basin (*hauz*). The *minaret*, from which the muezzin sounds the call to prayer five times a day, was usually raised on the far side of the mosque to the qibla wall.

The 7th to 11th centuries witnessed the building of many great congregational, or Friday, mosques (*ulu Jami*). These had greatly extended open courtyards (*sahn*) to accommodate huge numbers. They were surrounded by flat-roofed porticoes, usually two or three rows of arches deep. The qibla wall end of the *sahn* would have four or more rows so many worshippers were under cover. This design was realized for the first time in the rebuilding of the Great Mosque at Kufa in Iraq in 670. Influences on it came from earlier eastern synagogues, themselves influenced by Hellenistic buildings, and possibly from the forum complex of such Roman cities as Kremna and Smyrna in Asia Minor. Another model was the house of the Prophet himself at Medina, which had porticoes.

The Great Mosque at Damascus, one of the most important early congregational mosques (706–715), incorporated existing Hellenistic buildings, including corner towers, which became Islam's first minarets. The original structure had a wooden dome, and, as can still be seen, was

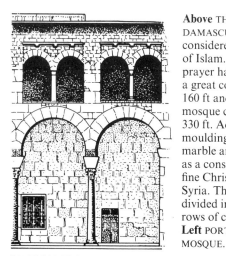

Above THE GREAT MOSQUE OF DAMASCUS, (706–15) is rightly considered one of the marvels of Islam. The porticoes and prayer hall together marked out a great court of some 400 × 160 ft and altogether the mosque covered an area 520 × 330 ft. Adorned with rich mouldings and Byzantine-type marble and mosaics, it was built as a conscious rival to the many fine Christian basilicas then in Syria. The prayer hall was divided into three naves by two rows of columns.
Left PORTICO OF THE GREAT MOSQUE.

adorned with a moulding set high over marble panelling and numerous mosaics of Byzantine type. Though badly damaged by fire, these mosaics, with their lack of all human or animal imagery, point to a style of decoration that was to become the hallmark of Islamic architecture.

ISLAM: DEVELOPMENT

The formative period of Islamic architecture is indissolubly linked to the dominance of the Umayyids, an off-shoot of the Quraysh tribe to which the Prophet had belonged. This dynasty established the institution of the caliph ("deputy") and organized the Arab tribes to lay the basis of the Islamic state. Their art is known to us primarily in Syria, where there had already been fertile contacts between the Semitic and Graeco-Roman worlds.

A good example of their hybrid fusion is Islam's earliest monument: the Dome of the Rock in Jerusalem (685–705). Built on a site long sacred to both Jews and Christians, the shrine shows strong Byzantine influence, and is in some ways a Muslim version of the Christian central-plan church. The dome is raised over a colonnaded octagon, just as it was in many parts of the Christian world.

Little remains of early Islamic secular architecture, of which the most important category was the "desert palaces" of the Umayyids. These seats of government (*dar al-imara*), often the residence of the caliph, incorporated features from Persian architecture: Persia had fallen to Arab armies by 642. About 100 years before this, the Sassanian overlords of Persia had built the splendid Palace of Ctesiphon near Baghdad with an imposing arched gateway (*iwan*) serving as an audience hall. At Kufa, the first Muslim *dar al-imara* (670) developed the Persian example further in its courtyard faced by four *iwans* on the axes of a cross. The focal point is here the *iwan* leading into a domed hall, an arrangement that is to play a crucial role in subsequent Islamic buildings.

An extremely rare example of an urban complex of this time (early 8th century) is Anjar on the Beirut-Baalbec road. Abandoned after the fall of the Umayyids, this town has distinct Roman echoes. Its square surrounding wall is pierced by four gates. These serve two main colonnaded streets intersecting at the centre at right angles. The place has a central court with audience halls on its short sides and apartments on its long sides. Near the north gate are the public baths.

As desert dwellers, the Arabs loved and valued water, and Muslim builders were soon constructing reservoirs. The great reservoir at Qairawan in Tunisia (862) is a fine example. A polygon with 48 sides and a diameter of some 128m (425ft), its central platform once housed a small pleasure pavilion.

Long Mesopotamian tradition was still alive in the palace of Lashkari Bazaar (999–1030) near Bust in Afghanistan. Built primarily of compressed mud and unbaked brick, the walls are lined and strengthened at stress points with baked brick. The palace is quadrangular, with four *iwans* of varying size on the central court. The two largest are the two most important: the main entrance and the one leading to the throne room. The embellishment is of brickwork interweaving geometric and arabesque motifs with ornamental calligraphy, with stucco and painting as well.

After Saladin had unified Syria and Egypt at the end of the 12th century, Islamic building entered a new phase. At Aleppo, in Syria, the citadel's main portal, dated 1209, cut in sharp angles and sturdily corbelled, is an assured masterpiece.

Right THE DOME OF THE ROCK, JERUSALEM, begun *c.* 684 on the site of a Jewish temple, is Islam's earliest monument. The sumptuously decorated building has a harmonious geometrical plan: dome and clerestory are supported on a circular colonnade of piers, while the outer lower storey is a double octagon. The exterior is swathed in multipatterned ceramics; the dome has an inner glazed surface and an outer shell of wooden ribs covered by boarding and gilded lead.

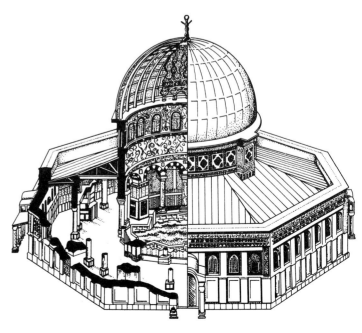

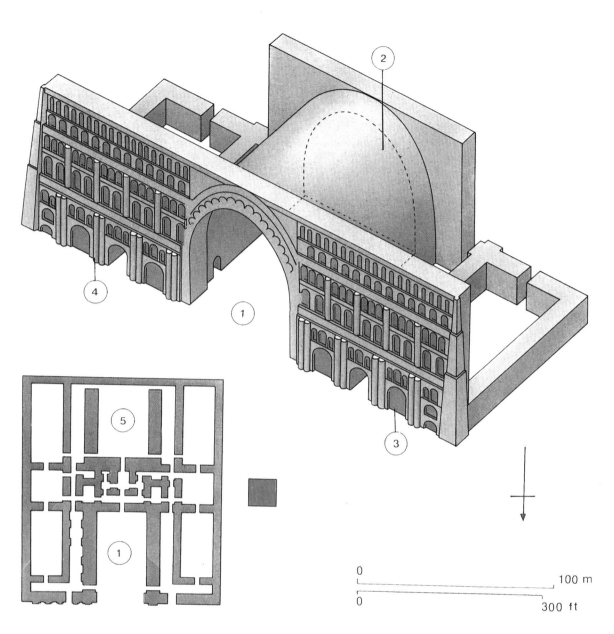

Above THE PALACE OF CTESIPHON, on the banks of the Tigris, near modern Baghdad, is usually attributed to the Sassanian King Chosroes (AD531–79) but may be earlier. The huge audience chamber (iwan) (1) is open on one side and has a vault (2) of kiln-baked brick 120 ft high with a span of 83 ft. There are blind arches in the Roman manner (3) as part of the decoration of the enormous brick facades, of which only one (4) remains. The open-fronted iwan later became a standard feature of Muslim architecture, as did the lateral halls and corridors. The purpose of the chambers behind (5) is not fully understood.

0   100 m
0   300 ft

THE ROCK-CUT SANCTUARY

The rock-cut sanctuary or *chaitya*-hall was crucial in the development of Indian architecture: the cave had an importance without parallel anywhere else in the world. More than 1200 of these chaitya caves have been discovered in all parts of the subcontinent, excavated by Hindus, Jains and Buddhists. They were worked in the period between the 3rd century BC and the 10th century AD.

Cave temples continued to be created long after the construction of free-standing buildings had been perfected. The cave was very practical, being cool in summer, warm in winter and needing virtually no maintenance. Over and above this, it seems as if the cave served a particularly Indian spiritual need that had been felt with peculiar intensity ever since the Vedic ascetics had dwelt in caves in about 1500BC.

The chaityas are the most ambitious examples of monumental stone carving in the flowering that followed Alexander the Great's invasion into northwest India in 325BC. There seems to be no stylistic connection to Greek art, but the influence of such prototypes as the tombs of the Achaemenid kings of Persia at Naqsh-i-Rustam with their carved facades is hard to deny.

The earliest Indian sanctuaries belong to the Hinayana, or early, school of Buddhism. They were replicas of the sect's first temples of wood and thatch, an element of the rainy season retreats (*viharas*) used by the monastic communities, and they enshrined some cult object. In some of these pillared halls (e.g. Bhaja, 1st century BC) wooden transverse beams were actually affixed to the vault. In others (e.g. Ajanta, Cave no. 10, 2nd century BC) this wooden ribbing was mimicked in stone. The columns of the Bhaja interior are staggered inwards, so that the top is almost 15cm (6in) out of alignment with the base, just as the wooden originals would have been staggered to support the weight of the roof. By the time of the magnificent chaitya-hall at Karli (AD100–125), such nostalgic mimicry of wooden structures had disappeared, but one feature that did remain widespread was a wooden frontis-piece to the cave. This screen followed the curve of the vault at the top, dividing the space into a number of semicircular openings, while its lower half shielded entrances to the nave and aisles.

The sanctuaries were hollowed out from the top downwards, starting at the intended height of the vault, to avoid the need of scaffolding. Quarrying, dressing, finishing and carving were carried on simultaneously. There is some resemblance of these sanctuaries to the classical or early Christian basilica, and their purpose was similar. It was to provide access for pilgrims to the cult object and to house the assembly of the monastic community.

Some of these structures are veritable cathedrals in stone, sophisticated examples of an architecture of pure mass. Those belonging to the Mahayana school (dating after AD100), display the Indian stonecarvers' consummate skills in their decorative exuberance. Their interior murals, especially those of the Gupta period at Ajanta (6th century AD), established standards of perfection that helped to shape the Buddhist art of all of southeast and eastern Asia. Of the surviving Hindu cave temples, the most impressive are the Temple of Shiva on Elephanta island, off Bombay, and the contemporary Cave no. 16 at Ellora. For this cave, also dedicated to Shiva, over 200,000 tons of rock are estimated to have been excavated.

Opposite page KAILASHANATHA TEMPLE, CAVE 16, ELLORA, was built by Krishna I, of the Rashtrakuta dynasty, from AD765, largely in the Dravidian style.

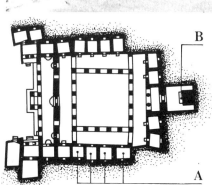

Above CAVE 19, AJANTA, dating from the 5th century AD. A Mahayana chaitya fronted by buddhas and divine beings, with a portico of fluted Dravidian columns with "cushion" capitals.
Top right CAVE 19, AJANTA, INTERIOR, with elongated Mahayana stupa.

Middle right CAVE 9, AJANTA dates from the 1st century BC and is a Hinayana chaitya. Note the *chaiya window*. and the same motif in miniature on the door.
Bottom right CAVE 1, AJANTA, dates from the 6th century AD. It is a Mahayana *vihara* with dormitory cells (A) and Buddha shrine (B).

EARLY INDIAN PALACES

The most impressive example of early freestanding architecture in the Indian subcontinent are the remains of the Royal Palace at Pataliputra (near modern Patna in Bihar). This was the capital of the Mauryan dynasty, which ruled over a united empire stretching from the Khyber to the Deccan, from 322 to 185BC. The Mauryan emperor Ashoka (d. 232BC), the first and most influential imperial patron of Buddhism, was a great builder and promoter of the faith, sending envoys and missionaries both to the Hellenistic courts of the West and south to Sri Lanka.

Pataliputra owes an obvious debt both to earlier Indian and to ancient Middle Eastern precedents. The latter influence was brought to India by Alexander after his conquest of the Achaemenid empire and the destruction of the line of Xerxes and Darius in Persia with the sacking of Persepolis in 330BC. As in the Middle Eastern civilizations, walls, towers and numerous pavilions were constructed of brick or baked clay and wood, while great attention was paid to the laying out of parks, reservoirs ("tanks") and pleasure areas. Megasthenes, a Greek ambassador to the Mauryan court, tells of Pataliputra's 560 towers and a wall pierced by 64 gateways.

Unfortunately, little of this remains today, but we can visualize the former glory of the palace not only from contemporary descriptions but from carved panels, such as those at Sanchi in central India, which show cities like Kapilavastu, home town of the Buddha. These portray cities surrounded by moats and protected by railings. These railings, which the excavators of Pataliputra have shown to be of teak, clamped by iron dowelling, are a type of fortification that harks back to Vedic times (1500–500BC). The gateways (*toranas*) also echo Vedic prototypes; these flat archways with three crosspieces, such as can still be seen at Sanchi itself, were to influence greatly the *torii* of Japan.

The palace combined enormous scale with detailed variety on the battlements and balconies. These balconies were topped by barrel-vaulted roofs terminating in windows of the kind seen in contemporary Buddhist rock-cut sanctuaries. The marvellous effect of this design is confirmed by the Chinese Buddhist pilgrim Fa Hsien, who, when visiting Pataliputra in AD400, remarked that "the walls, doorways and the sculptured designs are no human work".

Excavations at the Mauryan capital seem to suggest that there was a pillared cloister structure running the length of the ramparts, with a wooden floor and roof supported by wooden columns 4.5m (15ft) high and almost the same distance apart. It is not clear whether this enigmatic structure was a tunnel within the ramparts or would have been filled with earth as a strengthening bulwark.

A huge audience hall existed within the palace area itself, fronted by a series of platforms of solid wood, recalling the ziggurats of ancient Mesopotamia and Iran. Presumably the platforms supported stairways, balustrades and pavilions, rising to the audience hall. Here, 80 massive sandstone pillars once supported a wooden roof, in a pattern repeated in the Mauryan-influenced city of Anuradhapura in Sri Lanka. The pattern is clearly reminiscent of the arrangement of the "Hall of a Hundred Columns" in the Achaemenid palace at Persepolis.

Early Oriental

Opposite page AN ASHOKAN LION PILLAR AT LANRIYA, PROVINCE OF NANDAN GASH. Such pillars date from the 3rd century BC and are certainly influenced by Persian forms (compare the Persian columns illustrated on p. 19).

This page RELIEF SHOWING TYPICAL MAURYAN ARCHITECTURE, FROM A GATEWAY OF THE STUPA AT SANCHI. Note the distinctive round-topped chaitya windows over the balcony.

INDIA: THE STUPA

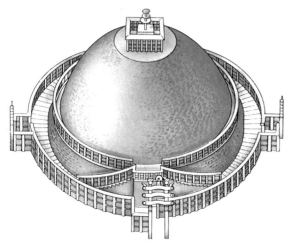

Above and below THE GREAT STUPA, SANCHI, dating from the 3rd century BC, was rediscovered in 1818 after 600 years, and restored by John Marshall from 1912 to 1919. The dome's height is 54 ft, its diameter 120 ft; railings and gateways are yellow sandstone.

The *stupa* ("mound or heap") is the principal contribution of Buddhism to world architecture, and is found wherever that religion took root. Basically, the stupa is a hemispherical dome containing the relics of a great teacher or patron of the faith. The stupa was modelled on the funerary tumulus in which Indian kings and chieftains had been buried since neolithic times. This practice is, of course, to be found independently in many parts of the world, for example in the so-called barrows of Celtic Britain.

According to the *Mahaparinirvana sutra*, an early text, the Buddha was asked how his remains should be treated after his death. He replied that, after a royal cremation, his followers were to construct "a tumulus for the bones at a cross-roads, and honour it with parasols, victory banners, flags, scents, garlands, incense, coloured powder and music". Furthermore, they should have "a great festival, honouring, venerating and worshipping it". Thus, whereas early Indian tumuli had been placed in isolated spots far from habitation, the Buddhist mounds were built in accessible places, often already holy, and frequently visited on pilgrimage. A memorial to the dead was transformed into an inspiration for the

living.

The first stupas contained the Master's remains after his death (*c.*550BC), but none of these exist today. The best preserved early stupa is the Great Stupa at Sanchi, in central India, built in the 3rd century BC by the Mauryan emperor Ashoka. The weight of the mass is concentrated downward (like the pyramids, ziggurats, and Aztec temples) to ensure stability for a construction of essentially inflexible material. The solid dome (*anda*), of burnt brick and mud mortar, was originally 9m (30ft) high and 21m (70ft) in diameter. It enclosed a chamber in which relics were placed, probably encased in urns within a box, both receptacles of precious metal. About 150BC, the structure was enlarged to its present height of 16m (54ft) and 36m (120ft) diameter. Such enlarging of stupas was a common practice, believed to confer much religious merit on the patron.

Other additions were made at the same time: the sandstone railings (*vedika*) surrounding the mound, for example, that enclosed a circular paved path. These were built in imitation of wooden fences, with octagonal uprights with cross-bars mortised into them and massive crowns, rounded at the top.

A railed terrace (*medhi*) was added halfway up the dome to provide a second level walkway. The magnificent sandstone gateways (*toranas*) at the cardinal points were added about 75BC. They are profusely carved in high relief with episodes from the Buddha's life and previous incarnations. Here Indian sculptors adapted a technique perfected previously in wood and ivory into the more durable but more demanding medium of stone. The top of the mound is truncated, crowned by an umbrella-shaped finial (*chattra*) within a railed enclosure (*harmika*).

The stupa provides a fascinating example of how a building evolves to suit the historical and doctrinal needs of the religion it serves. The dome (*anda* or "egg") reminds the devotee of the mythical Golden Egg from which the universe was born. The chattra finial recalls, historically, the sacred parasol under which the king held court. At a religious level it signifies the actual *bodhi* tree at Bodh Gaya under which the Buddha attained enlightenment. And at a mythical level, the chattra is the *axis mundi* joining heaven and earth, the Cosmic Tree or Tree of Life in whose branches all the worlds are supported.

Left SANCHI, NORTH GATE (*c.* 75BC): panel depicting devotees worshipping.
Right EAST GATE (SAME DATE): YAKSHI, female tree-spirit personifying bounteousness of nature.
Below NORTH GATE, architrave showing worship of the *bodhi* tree and the defeat of the armies of Mara.

THE STUPA IN BUDDHISM

The development of the *stupa* was dictated by two factors, doctrinal changes within Buddhism, and the aesthetic and cultural style of the countries it colonized. About AD100 a new school emerged, the Mahayana. This transformed the early, or Hinayana, Buddhism from a rational and contemplative monastic life to a fully-blown popular religion. The pantheon of divine figures, colourful mythology and subtle transcendental philosophy of the Mahayana was reflected in the increasingly ornate form of its main architectural structure.

Sri Lanka's first stupa, or *dagaba* ("relic-womb") as it is called there, was the Thuparama at Anuradhapura (3rd century BC). It is believed to enshrine the right collar bone of Buddha, sent from India when Hinayana Buddhism came to the island. As befits the luxuriant fertility of the place, the dagaba was shaped like a heap of rice, which became the model for many later structures.

In Nepal, a unique mixture of Hinduism and Buddhism created a distinctive stupa style. Here the harmika has become a solid square support for a greatly extended chattra, composed of 13 levels. The *chorten* in Tibet and Ladakh followed the general pattern of extending the chattra and diminishing the dome. Further east, in Burma and Thailand followers created *pagodas* and *chedis* shaped by the love both those countries have for graceful, elongated forms. In China and Japan, the pagoda became a free-standing tower of several stories.

The supreme development of the stupa is at Borobodur, in Java (8th century AD). This massive structure is no less than a replica of Mount Meru, the cosmic mountain at the centre of the universe in Indian mythology. Like the holy mountain, the stupa has 9 levels, each depicting increasingly abstract subjects as the pilgrim ascends to the peak. The buried basement level portrays the realms of desire, carved in a lively and realistic fashion to represent the ceaseless flow of action in the world. The next 5 levels are walled-in terraces or galleries on a rectangular plan. The first two illustrate stories from previous lives of the Buddha, the third is devoted to a text about Maitreya, the Buddha of the future in Mahayana teaching. The fourth depicts Samantabhadra, the last Buddha of the Future.

At each stage the carving becomes more classical and stylized and we move further away from the realistic portrayals of everyday life. The next 3 levels are round, open to the sky, and have 72 miniature stupas, each containing an image of the Buddha in teaching posture. These structures are not closed in, but latticed, to suggest that we are moving now from the realm of form towards the ultimate reality of the Mahayana, the formless Void (*shunyata*).

The whole structure is crowned by a single sealed stupa at its centre and summit. This represents both the actual man who built Borobodur, the god-king Shailendra ("King of the Mountain") and, more abstractly, the one spirit that unites all creation and exists eternally. This unity is expressed through the 72 smaller Buddhas, which probably represent the fact that, as the ancients knew, every 72 years marks a change of one degree in the precession of the equinoxes. Borobodur shows an architecture based uncompromisingly on the values of religious symbolism and not merely on technical expedients.

Right KUMBUM STUPA, GYANTSE, TIBET (11th century AD) with Gyantse fort in the background. The spire (vasti or chattra) shows strong Nepalese influence. The whole building is designed as a representation of the universe.

Far right CHATTRA OF THE GREAT STUPA OF BODNATH, NEPAL (AD500). The brick and masonry dome is 300ft in circumference and 125ft high; the copper-gilt plated spire rests on a harmika base on which are painted the "all-seeing eyes of supreme buddhahood"—a uniquely Nepalese feature.

Top THUPARAMA DAGOBA, ANURADHAPURA, SRI LANKA (3rd century BC), is the oldest stupa in the country. It served as a model for its successors, and was originally surrounded by a covered walkway and surmounted by a protective dome of copper-gilt tiles on wood. Such a structure, unique to Sri Lanka, was called a vatadage.
Above BOROBODUR STUPA, JAVA (AD c.800). A huge stone buddha figure was enclosed in each of the 72 bell-shaped stone stupas on the top three circular terraces that represented the higher levels of abstract truth.

THE HINDU TEMPLE

Right TYPICAL ORISSAN-STYLE TEMPLE, with tall curvilinear sanctuary (deul), shorter stepped pyramidal audience hall (jagamohana) and four ancillary shrines at the corners. The whole complex was usually walled.
Bottom right MUKTESHVARA TEMPLE, BHUBANESHWAR (10th century AD).
Below DETAIL OF MUKTESHVARA SPIRE'S CARVING.

The Hindu temple is above all a building serving metaphysical rather than physical needs. It is the dwelling place of the gods on earth, and houses the images into which the deities deign to descend when correctly invoked by priestly ritual. Unlike church, mosque or chaitya, the temple was not designed for congregational worship, but for the individual's encounter with the divine energies. Temple interiors are often cave-like—dark, introverted places that mimic, and facilitate entrance into the hidden realms of the psyche. Symbolically, the temple is the *axis mundi* providing the connection between the world of the gods and our own—a miniature of the Cosmic mountain and the home of the gods.

The design and building of a temple was an immensely sacred affair. At each stage of construction, priests performed purification rites to ward off harmful influence. Ideally, the site was near water and trees, and the material used was stone. The building was entrusted only to certain families and sub-castes who were the traditional guardians of the science of building. This knowledge was set down in the *shilpashastras*, or architectural texts. From these we learn that the ground-plan of a temple was considered a representation of the universe in the form of the body of Purusha, the Cosmic Man. The complex was divided into a squared grid. The *Brihat Samhita*, an important 6th-century text, recommends 64 squares, but we know from other texts that no less than 32 types of ground-plan were permissable. Each square was assigned to the deity governing the corresponding part of the universe. The general proportions, the images and their positions were all established by a mathematical standard not unlike the central-plan architecture of the European Renaissance. The essentially sacred nature of the Hindu temple (*mandira*: "reception hall for gods"; *vimana*: "the well-proportioned") must be borne in mind if we are to appreciate an architecture in which esoteric considerations both determine and transcend what we call style.

In the north, very few really old temples remain. This is due not so much to the extremes of the Indian climate, but to the wholesale vandalism perpetrated by the Muslims. It continued virtually unabated for 500 years from their establishment in the subcontinent at the end of the 12th century. As a result, what remains are the creations of minor provincial rulers in those parts of the country where the Muslims did not penetrate, that is Bundelkhand, Orissa, Rajasthan, Nepal and the Himalayan foothills.

Fortunately, the south remained relatively intact. Early structures date from the 7th and 8th centuries AD. These can be divided into two broad categories. The northern (Indo-Aryan) style is characterised by a spire or *shikhara* ("mountain peak") that is conical and convex, usually topped by a vase shaped finial, the *kalasha* ("pot containing elixir of life"). In many later temples, this spire forms the entire roof of the sanctuary. In the southern (Dravidian) style, the spire is less vertically emphasized, being more of a pyramidal tower ascending in a series of horizontal terraces to a finial shaped like a rounded cone or miniature stupa. As time progressed, the Dravidian spire became less pronounced, but was surrounded by a series of monumental entrance gateways, or *gopurams* ("city of light").

Top KAILASHANATHA TEMPLE, KANCHIPURAM (8th century AD), built by the Pallava dynasty. One of the earliest extant Hindu temples.
Above MAHABALIPURAM, THE FIVE TEMPLES (RATHAS), PALLAVA (7th century AD), are embryonic models of later Dravidian, or southern, temple styles.
Below KANDARIYA MAHADEVA TEMPLE, KHAJURAHO, (AD1030), a classic example of the Indo-Aryan, or Northern, temple style, with ascending peaks and rich carving.

LATER EASTERN TEMPLES

The norms for temple building established in the Gupta period (4th century AD) were followed no matter how grandiose the temple. Indian builders used "dry stone" construction with the blocks jointed together with iron dowelling. Spaces, whether doors or ceilings, were spanned by the post-and-beam system. Lime mortar, along with the true arch was a Muslim import.

Whether as a demonstration of political power or religious fervour, the temple was sometimes enormous, including whole areas of residences, shops and businesses within its precincts. At all times it was very much the centre of the community, a large landowner, and an employer of labour—such as priests, musicians, craftsmen, gardeners, garland makers, cleaners, and cooks who prepared the food for offerings. The temple was also the provider of education and entertainment, in the form of religious music, dance and drama, as well as being the focus for social life. The scale of the ceremonies could be huge. Even today, there is an annual festival at Tirupati in the south of India at which 32 types of flowers, together weighing 2,450 kilograms (2.4 tons), are offered to the presiding deity, an image of Vishnu.

The 13th century Sun Temple at Konarak in Orissa must have been one of the most impressive Northern-style temples. The whole complex was conceived as the sun god Surya's chariot, that crosses the sky each day. It followed the developed Northern pattern in having a main sanctuary with a massive shikhara joined to a porch with pyramidal roof and faced by a detached hall for dance. The porch and sanctuary, the latter now sadly gone, were flanked by 24 intricately carved stone wheels, representing the 12 months of the year, each having a light and dark lunar phase according to Hindu astrology. The chariot-temple was pulled by seven massive horses, symbolizing the days of the week and the seven celestial sages who govern the movement of the heavens.

A few miles from Konarak is the Jagannatha temple at Puri. Here many thousands of pilgrims gather each July to see the main images being pulled around the city in a huge cart (from which we get our word "juggernaut").

There is great regional variety in temple style, as local dynasties developed and dictated their preferences. A general feature, however, is a fondness for carved ornamentation both inside and out, which often tends to blur the distinction between architecture and sculpture. Major and minor deities, archaic fertility spirits, animals both naturalistic and fantastic, and episodes from the great epics, the *Mahabharata* and the *Ramayana*, are the preferred subjects. At the Jain temples on Mount Abu, for example, extremely detailed and delicate carving reduces the white marble surfaces to almost translucent tracery.

Indian culture spread to most of southeast Asia. Burma, Thailand, Indo-China and Indonesia all produced their own versions of Indian architectural forms. Generally, the court and aristocracy adopted the classical Indianized culture, while the common people continued with their age-old beliefs and customs. The supreme example of the Hindu temple in Greater India is the complex of Angkhor Wat in Cambodia. Built by the Khmers in the 12th century, the sandstone temple is dedicated to Vishnu, and is probably the largest religious structure in the world. The approach road crosses a moat some 187m (625ft) wide, and enters by a magnificent triple gateway that leads, through cloistered galieries, artificial lakes and library buildings, to the steep steps up to the elevated platform of the main buildings. Overall, Angkhor Wat reflects Khmer cosmology, as mounting terraces of diminishing size are crowned with five towers symbolizing the peaks of Mount Meru, home of the gods. The whole structure, including the roofs, is covered with low-relief narratives that perfectly complements the architectural lines.

Above THE GOPURAM OF THE MEENAKSHI TEMPLE, MADURAI, built by Tirumala Nayak (1623–60). It stands 152ft high, and is completely covered in brightly coloured reliefs depicting divine beings.
Right GOPURAM OF THE BRIHADISHVARA TEMPLE, TANJORE, built by the Chola king Rajaraja the Great (985–1014), is typical of the early Dravidian gateway.

Early Oriental

Left JAGANNATHA TEMPLE, PURI (1198), showing sanctuary (left) and audience hall (right).

THE CHINESE OUTLOOK

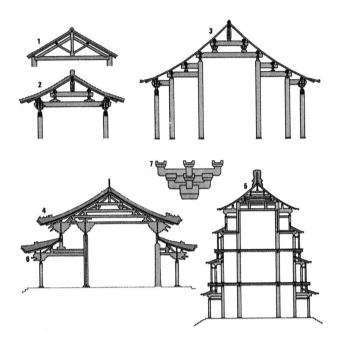

In China, architecture was never a spectacular branch of the arts, figuring little in painting or in the development of a pervasive ornamental style. This was not because the Chinese were uninterested in building as such, but because they established early on a system that, with their typical practicality and conservatism, they felt met their building needs adequately. The history of architecture in China is the history of the modification of this original system.

Early building in the north was characterized by the semi-subterranean dwellings found along the Amur river, while in the south, extending into southeast Asia and the islands, there existed a tradition of wooden buildings on piles that can be seen even today. But it is in the Yellow river valley, cradle of Chinese civilization, that we find, from the Han period (200BC–200AD), a system of pillar and beam construction that was to become the model for Chinese and all eastern Asian building. A fascinating glimpse into the beginnings of this tradition is provided by the pottery tomb models of the later Han period. These show miniature palaces, towns and farmhouses, and also the brick towers with wooden roofs that were to be the indigenous model for the Buddhist pagodas of the 11th century onwards.

Most Chinese buildings differ little in their basic layout from the simple peasant accommodation of a cluster of buildings surrounded by a rectangular walled compound. The differentiation comes not so much in design as in the building's material, scale and height. The height is determined by the size of the podium, number of storeys and intricacy and grandeur of the roof.

Generally speaking, brick and earth were used for poorer structures or for functional ones such as the gatehouses, corner towers and observation posts that punctuated the for-

Above THE CHINESE SYSTEM OF ROOFING. The Chinese system (2) is contrasted with the European truss system (2). In the Chinese way there are no diagonals: theirs is a post-and-beam system. But it is capable of elaboration to create buildings and spaces of large scale (3, 4, 5). Outside, there usually appears an extended overhang (6). The key element in an elaborate roof was the cluster of supporting brackets, or tou-kung (7). **Below** ROOFING EAVES, DETAIL OF A BUILDING IN THE THOUSANDS HILLS PARK NEAR ANOSHAN, PROVINCE OF LIAONING.

tified walls of a city. Wood was scarce in central China, and was reserved for the most important buildings, palaces, temples or halls of justice. But also in houses pine or cedar pillars were used, widely spaced. Houses were built on a rectangular plan, divided by light walls of plaster, bamboo matting or lattice.

In all Chinese buildings of note, the eye is drawn irresistibly upwards to the roof, silent proclaimer of the status of the structure beneath. Because triangular trusses were not used, it was necessary to ensure a vertical thrust on the pillars by multiplying the points of support under the rafters. An increasingly complex bracketing accompanied ever larger and many-storied roofs. It soon demanded a unit of measurement from which the overall proportions could be calculated. This modular unit was established in AD1103, with the publication of Li Chieh's *Methods and forms of architecture*, a treatise adopted throughout the vast, yet centralized, empire. This basic unit was the vertical thickness of the bracket arm (*ts'ai*). This persisted as the official measure until the Ch'ing dynasty introduced the horizontal thickness of the bracket arm as the new module in the 17th century. Li Chieh's work also deals with carved ornament in both animal and floral designs, panelled ceilings and the use of lattice for screens, doorways and windows. These constitute features that add lightness and elegance to buildings which might otherwise become merely solemn.

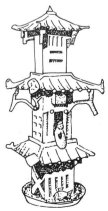

Above A TYPICAL CHINESE PAGODA. A stone foundation supports the wooden structure. The form of the roof is repeated in each storey, having an overhang supported by brackets. Sliding doors give access.

THE JAPANESE SYNTHESIS

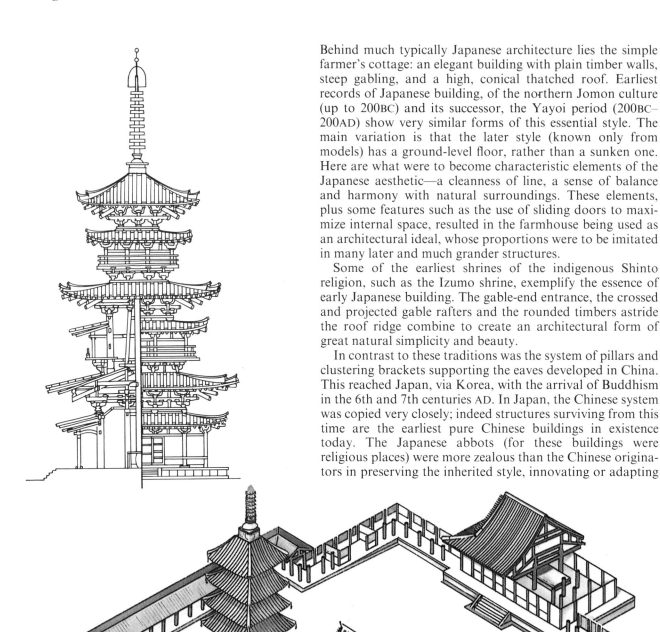

Behind much typically Japanese architecture lies the simple farmer's cottage: an elegant building with plain timber walls, steep gabling, and a high, conical thatched roof. Earliest records of Japanese building, of the northern Jomon culture (up to 200BC) and its successor, the Yayoi period (200BC–200AD) show very similar forms of this essential style. The main variation is that the later style (known only from models) has a ground-level floor, rather than a sunken one. Here are what were to become characteristic elements of the Japanese aesthetic—a cleanness of line, a sense of balance and harmony with natural surroundings. These elements, plus some features such as the use of sliding doors to maximize internal space, resulted in the farmhouse being used as an architectural ideal, whose proportions were to be imitated in many later and much grander structures.

Some of the earliest shrines of the indigenous Shinto religion, such as the Izumo shrine, exemplify the essence of early Japanese building. The gable-end entrance, the crossed and projected gable rafters and the rounded timbers astride the roof ridge combine to create an architectural form of great natural simplicity and beauty.

In contrast to these traditions was the system of pillars and clustering brackets supporting the eaves developed in China. This reached Japan, via Korea, with the arrival of Buddhism in the 6th and 7th centuries AD. In Japan, the Chinese system was copied very closely; indeed structures surviving from this time are the earliest pure Chinese buildings in existence today. The Japanese abbots (for these buildings were religious places) were more zealous than the Chinese originators in preserving the inherited style, innovating or adapting

only in response to changes of fashion reported from the Chinese mainland.

This Chinese influence was even stronger after the 670s, when Korea ceased to be the intermediary between the two countries. From then on, architects, sculptors and tile-makers all flocked to the imperial Japanese court seeking patronage. To Chinese forms the Japanese brought what was in fact a superior tradition of woodworking, partly the result of having to create buildings for a court that was always on the move until it was finally fixed at Nara in AD710. Thus the Japanese handling of the imported system was always deft and pleasing to the eye, combined with a certain austerity.

Most notable of these early buildings are the main parts of the magnificent Horyuji temple at Nara (7th century). Here the Main or Golden Hall, the Five-storied Pagoda, Gate House and Cloistered Gallery are the earliest representatives of east Asian wooden architecture. The Main hall (*kondo*) is a development of a form seen in China from Han times (200BC–200AD). From outside it appears to have two storeys, but in fact only a lovely latticed ceiling separates the image platform with its bronze statues from the roof. The use of brackets is simple and without the elaborate joinery of later buildings. The pagoda, the east Asian form of the Buddhist stupa, which shares with it the symbolic role of *axis mundi* or Tree of Life, is now a free-standing building enshrining a

Far left EAST PAGODA OF THE YAKUSHIJI TEMPLE, NARA (AD680). The only surviving building of the complex, it differs from other towers of the period in having three roofs instead of five (compare the Horyuji Temple). From the ground to the *hosho*, or crowning sacred jewel, is 103ft.
Left and above HORYUJI TEMPLE, NARA (7th century AD), earliest extant representative of east Asian wooden architecture. The pagoda stands to the west and the kondo (main hall) to the east of the main north-south axis—a position unique to the temple.

relic. The Gate House (*chu-mon*) has a double façade to match the Main Hall, while the Cloisters' outer row of pillars are in-filled with lattice. The whole complex is thoughtfully set out with trees of varying size to offset the buildings and allude to both their material and their symbolic origins.

EARLY WESTERN MONASTERIES

Renouncing the world and devoting oneself body and soul to God are eastern ideas, though they have a long western history. The Greeks were familiar with the holy men of India, whom they called "gymnosophists" or "naked sages". St John the Baptist, "making straight the way of the Lord" in the wilderness, had numerous Christian successors, particularly in the deserts of Syria and Egypt. Individual hermits were besieged by followers eager to learn or simply to bask in their sanctity. One example among many is St Simeon Stylites, who lived atop a column partly in order to escape his followers. The impressive church and pilgrimage centre at Qal'at Si'man, which took shape around it, is mentioned on previous pages.

A similar ascetic fervour animated the early Christian monks of Ireland. Several beehive-shaped cells survive at Inishmurray which testify to the comfortlessness of their existence. Elsewhere within this movement men such as St Basil in the east, St Martin of Tours in France and St Benedict in Italy stressed the virtues of communal existence. The latter exalted brotherhood and charity over mortification and penitence. Benedict's ideal of a self-contained community whose members practised farming and crafts, and also taught, was a Christian version of the old Roman "villa", though it was now geared to the glorification of God in chant.

Conditions were not yet ripe, however, for the building of

monasteries. Benedict's settlement at Monte Cassino, founded in 529 on the eve of Justinian's conquest of Italy, was destroyed at the end of the 6th century by Lombard invaders. Such devastations continued until Charlemagne, King of the Franks, crowned Holy Roman Emperor by the Pope in 800, united and stabilized Europe. Charlemagne had Benedict's rule copied and circulated throughout his realm, in which, just after his death, more than 1,200 monasteries are recorded. The remarkable plan of an ideal monastery preserved in the library of St Gall in Switzerland dates from about 820.

The St Gall plan, however, is not the earliest surviving evidence for the architecture of these monasteries. A mid-8th century description of the abbey of Jumièges on the Seine details "the cloisters wrought in stone" with their "arcades, and a variety of decoration to delight the spirit, and a girdle of running water". Previously monasteries probably had no settled or characteristic plan. Now they possessed a cloister, square in plan, which was placed to the south of the church, and off which opened the dormitory and refectory. The abbot had his own house to the north of the church, where he could entertain. There were further buildings for novices, for the sick and for visitors. The library and treasury, like the sacristy, were beside the main altar of the church, though later the library and a writing-house (*scriptorium*) were often situated off the cloister. However, the chapter house, situated usually on the east side of the cloister, was a feature introduced probably in the 10th century at Cluny. Until then, the chapters (of the monastic rule) were read in the cloister itself, by the door into the church.

Left VIEW OF A LAVRA, OR MONASTIC COMMUNITY, ON MOUNT ATHOS, GREECE. Neither Eastern monastic leaders (such as St Basil) nor St Benedict himself in the West made architectural recommendations for the monks who followed their rule. In the East the monastery buildings were grouped amorphously in no fixed pattern, but in the West a pattern had emerged by Carolingian times.

Right THE ABBEY CHURCH OF CENTULA, SAINT RIQUIER, BELGIUM. In plan and profile Saint Riquier is typical of the churches of the great Carolingian monasteries. Note the two transepts, and particularly the number of turrets. The monastic cloister and its essential buildings—dormitory, refectory—abutted the wall between the two transepts.

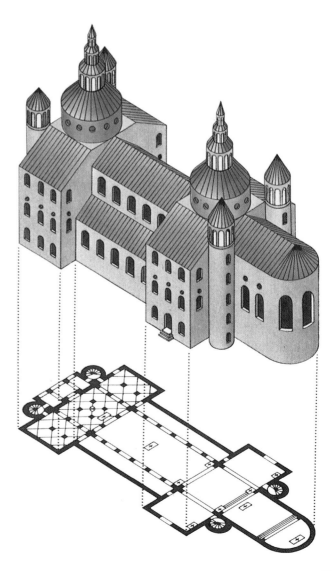

CAROLINGIAN AND OTTONIAN

Charlemagne, recognized as Holy Emperor by the Pope in 800 and as Emperor of the West by Constantinople in 812, undertook a "renovatio" or renewal of western society, chiefly carried through by the monasteries. This deliberate renewal had enormous implications. It meant that instead of simply developing the resources of contemporary culture, Celtic (in Britain) and Byzantine, Charlemagne looked elsewhere, back to early Christian or even pagan Rome. He initiated the idea of the recovery of something lost. He was responsible for the ideal of *classicism* by which the west would long be haunted.

Some of his acts of "Romanization" were superficial, such as the transport back to Aachen of Roman columns and capitals. More profoundly, Carolingian and later Ottonian architecture was imitative. Charlemagne's palace chapel and cathedral at Aachen imitated San Vitale at Ravenna. Carolingian and Ottonian churches in Flanders, the Rhineland and elsewhere in Germany imitated Early Christian basilicas: colonnades divide nave and aisles, above the colonnades there is a large expanse of blank wall (in the originals for the display of mosaic or painting), there are small windows (the *clerestory*) and a wooden, not a vaulted roof. These characteristics persist even against the current of the Romanesque style developing elsewhere in Europe from the 11th century. Paradoxically, the imitation also creates some striking differences—chiefly because the German walls are stone, not brick. Compared to San Vitale, with its slender terracotta vaults, Charlemagne's chapel at Aachen is sturdy, plain and stolid; the German basilicas are massive while the Italian ones are airy.

Carolingian and Ottonian churches also possess new elements. Not infrequently the east ends of 4th and 5th century basilicas had been extended north and south outside the line of the aisle walls, but these Holy Roman churches are firmly patterned in a T. Also, the main apse often protrudes some distance beyond the arm of the T. Thus the *transept* and *crossing* (at the meeting of transept and nave) became established in the 9th century.

Towers, usually six in number, adorned these churches. Probably they were not bell-towers originally (the casting of large bells seems a later invention: the earliest known bell-towers, at Ravenna, are dated to the 10th century). Rather they recall the towers of Roman fortifications, like those that survive in the 4th-century German capital of Trier. No connection to the twin towers of Syrian basilicas has been proved. The towers were more likely introduced together with the *Westwerk*, a distinctive feature of Carolingian and Ottonian architecture. The east transept was balanced by a western one, containing an upper gallery reserved, it seems, for the emperor. This position does not correspond to Byzantine ritual, in which the emperor sat in the south arm and joined the clergy on the ground floor. But commonly in western architecture the ruler has an apartment on an upper floor between two towers, so that he is secure, and can watch literally and symbolically over his subjects.

Above TOWER OF HEILIGE MARIA IN CAPITOL, COLOGNE. The city of Cologne is rich in early medieval churches. Though the tower has been renewed since the building of the church in the 11th century, it demonstrates faithfully enough the massiveness of both bulk and detailing in early Holy Roman Empire architecture.

Below RECONSTRUCTION OF THE PALACE COMPLEX AT CHARLEMAGNE'S CAPITAL, AACHEN. Only the chapel, shown in cutaway on the right, survives, with alterations not shown here. A mosaic crowns the vault of the central space. Note the grouping of the slender columns between weighty piers, continuing in essence the system used for Hagia Sophia in Constantinople.

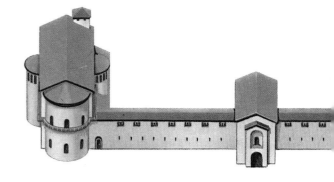

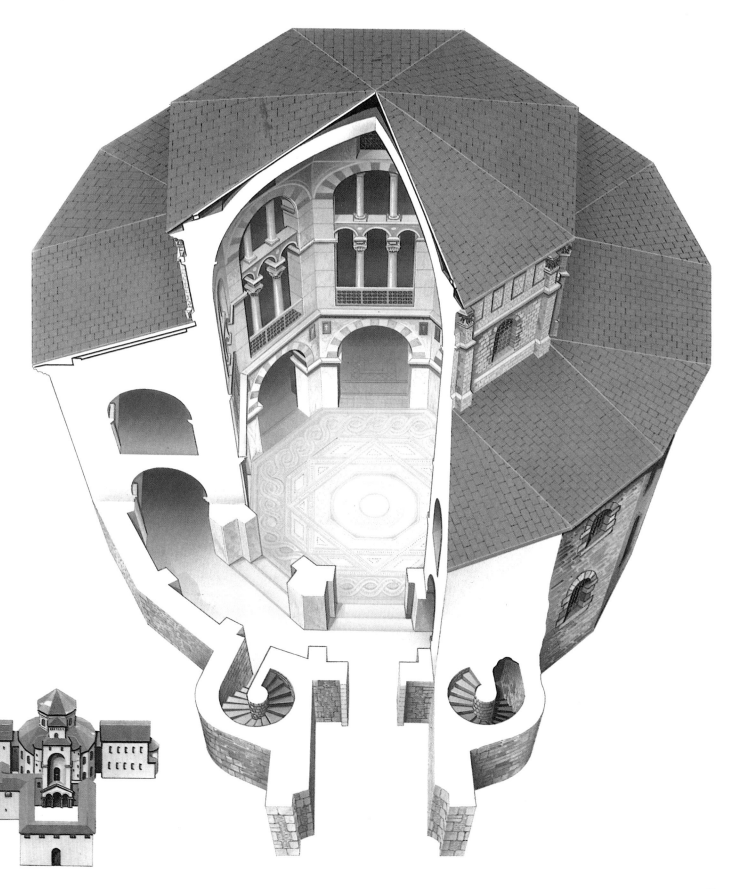

PRE-ROMANESQUE IN EUROPE

In France, Italy, Spain and Britain, outside the heartland of the Holy Roman Empire, there was no equivalent of the "renewal" programme of the Carolingian monasteries, and building was generally on a small scale, even in the Mediterranean regions. There the architectural tradition was sometimes unbroken (for instance in Rome) or was nourished by contact with Byzantium (not in Rome, for the popes were deliberately conservative). In Spain there was influence from Islamic architecture; however, the stilted or horseshoe arch, which certainly became Islamic, seems to occur there first before Islam, under the Visigoth rulers. In Britain, the Anglo-Saxons built churches with a single tower and had the nave open on to the aisles (if there were any) through doors and windows rather than an arcade. The use of columns, piers and arches was limited and crude, or nonexistent.

Even in Britain, however, the use of columns, piers and arches, which was the fundamental grammar of the Roman tradition, persisted. Long arcades, however, were rare. Instead, the working unit became two, three or four columns set between piers. This development had first taken place in Byzantine architecture, as Hagios Demetrios in Thessaloniki, from the 6th century, clearly shows. It even affects German building, as at St Michael, Hildesheim, built at the turn of the 11th century.

The typical western pattern is clear in San Miniato, built in the 11th century on a hill above Florence. The nave is divided into three sets of three arches over column, each set being divided by a pier. Here, as elsewhere, this pier is linked across to its correspondent on the other aisle by a cross or *diaphragm* arch. This arch has no structural necessity, since the roof is wooden; instead it reveals the builders thinking in terms of cubes of space. It is as close as Italy came to the recurring *bay* unit of developed Romanesque architecture.

This cube or bay is felt insistently only when the church is vaulted. The demand to vault basilica churches (as opposed to central-plan churches, which had usually been vaulted) arises first in the region encompassing northern Italy, southern France and northern Spain (Lombardy-Provence-Catalonia), which was closely knit in the Middle Ages. From the middle of the 10th century we find small churches with *barrel* or semicircular vaults over the nave. Such vaults do not derive from Roman or Byzantine architecture, indeed, they are primitive in comparison, and use a different technique (rubble and mortar rather than brick). Arches standing proud divide up the nave and aisles. These divisions are repeated in buttresses on the outside of the church, where something analogous to the pier-and-set-of-columns system is also found. Between the vertical strips dividing up the wall a set of little arches (*Lombard arcading*) runs across at the line of the eaves.

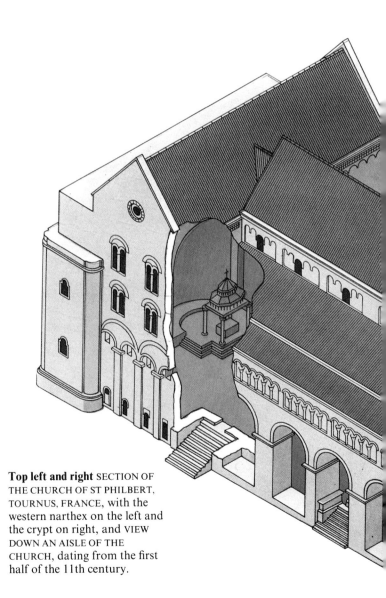

Top left and right SECTION OF THE CHURCH OF ST PHILBERT, TOURNUS, FRANCE, with the western narthex on the left and the crypt on right, and VIEW DOWN AN AISLE OF THE CHURCH, dating from the first half of the 11th century.

Left SAN NICOLA, BARI, was originally a Byzantine governor's palace but was converted into a Romanesque church, essentially by dividing it into bays. Its original function explains its unusual east end (middle right above).

Above right THE FACADE OF SANT' ABBONDIO, COMO, ITALY, showing the typical Lombard arcade at the roof line.
Above bottom THE CLOISTER OF THE ABBEY OF SANTA MARIA, RIPOLL, SPAIN, as so often, with richly decorated capitals.

CLUNIACS AND CISTERCIANS

One reason for preferring a vaulted to a wooden nave may have been its acoustics. Certainly one of the most important influences on the Romanesque style of architecture in Europe was the Benedictine abbey of Cluny, whose monks spent eight hours a day in choir. Their chant must have echoed magically beneath the great vaults of Cluny III, which, until its destruction after the French Revolution, was the largest church in Christendom except for New St Peter's.

Cluny III was the third church on the same valley site in Burgundy. Cluny I was rapidly replaced by Cluny II, built by Abbot Majeul (954–994). Majeul was an intimate of the Emperor Otto the Great, and the church had a *Westwerk* and transept after the German pattern, but it also had a barrel vault of the Lombard type. It had apses of the Lombard type as well, but more of them: they extended not only off the choir but also off the arms of the transept. This was probably in order to provide more altars for those monks who were priests.

Cluny II may very well have presented the developed Romanesque *bay* system, in which there is a strict logic. Every vaulting element must have a support. The pier therefore becomes a cluster of shafts, some of which support the arches down the nave, across the nave, and over the aisles. All the parts of a Romanesque church are interlocking, creating a joyous harmony.

If this was already so in Cluny II, Cluny III presented no great advance, except in size. Built between 1088 and 1130, it had two sets of aisles, and three storeys to the nave (ground arcade, *gallery*, and *clerestory*). It had beautifully carved capitals, some of them an accomplished classical Corinthian, and much other sculpture, painting and ornament of which there are superb reflections all over Burgundy, for instance at Vézèlay. The arches spanning the nave were slightly pointed—an indication that Romanesque architecture develops instantly into Gothic. Cluny III also had buttresses protruding above the roof of the aisles, like Gothic *flying buttresses*.

At the height of its glory Cluny housed about 1,200 monks and controlled about 1,500 lesser monasteries. Even in the 12th century, however, there was vigorous reaction to it. St Bernard of Clairvaux condemned both the luxury and the excessive choir duty of the Cluniacs, and championed the newly founded (1112) monastery at Cîteaux, also in Burgundy, (1112) dedicated to physical work and to austerity as well to singing. By the end of the 12th century there were more than 500 Cistercian monasteries. The Cistercians were the first order to regulate a standard design for a monastery, in a pattern based on Cluny but stripped of all ornament.

Far left, above THE SOLE
REMAINING TRANSEPT OF THE
GREAT CHURCH OF CLUNY IN
BURGUNDY, with its octagonal
tower. This is not the crossing
tower, which would have
bulked still larger beside it. In a
fully developed Romanesque
style, the abbey of Cluny also
displayed some classical
ornament and a clear
knowledge of Byzantine
architecture.

Far left, below THE CONVENT
CHURCH OF PARAY-LE-MONIAL
not far from Cluny shows all its
characteristics on a smaller
scale, intact. The classical
ornament includes classical
fluting on the piers, and the
Byzantine knowledge is evident
in the squinches used for the
crossing tower.

This page, above THE
CISTERCIAN ABBEY OF
FONTENAY, COTE D'OR. The
absence of ornament is
distinctive. The use of the
pointed arch for the
barrel-vaulted nave was taken
over from the Cluniacs.

This page, below THE CLOISTER
OF THE ABBEY. It was statutory
that Cistercian abbeys should
be founded in remote valleys
just beneath a supply of water,
which could then be piped into
the monastery: hence the
fountain in the cloister.

NORMAN CHURCH-BUILDING

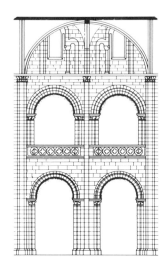

Above left THE RUINED CROSSING TOWER AND NAVE OF THE ABBEY CHURCH OF JUMIÈGES, NORMANDY. A major feature of the church was the passage running round the church at the clerestory level, which necessitated unusually thick walls. This became standard in England as well. The clerestory passage is shown particularly in the view on the opposite page, lower left, of Winchester.

Above right SECTION OF THE NAVE OF ST ETIENNE, CAEN, NORMANDY, which also has a clerestory passage. The vaults shown were added in the later 12th century, just over 100 years after the church was built. Prominent is the large and well-lit middle gallery, which also became usual in English buildings, particularly in East Anglia.

Like Charlemagne before them, the Norse overlords of northwest France called in monastic leaders to their aid. William of Volpiano, who arrived from Dijon in 1002, clearly brought with him knowledge of Cluny II. From the early 11th century the Normans were building developed Romanesque buildings of three storeys, though the middle storey, between nave arcade and clerestory, was not always a gallery; sometimes it was *blind* (not lit by a window), and is called a *triforium*. William the Conqueror, aided by his first Archbishop of Canterbury, Lanfranc, then carried this style across to England, although the Saxon king Edward the Confessor had already adopted the Norman style for his new cathedral at Westminster (since rebuilt).

Between 1066 and the end of the 11th century Romanesque churches had also risen at Canterbury, St Albans, Bury St Edmunds, Ely, Norwich, Lincoln, Durham, York, Winchester, Gloucester, Worcester—to name only a few. According to Norman policy, following that of Charlemagne, cathedrals were often also abbeys. All display the superb clarity of Norman Romanesque: some, like St Albans, built unusually of brick, remained bare; others, for instance Ely, received wonderfully rich and dense sculptural decoration. Norman Romanesque has a distinct repertoire, including notably interlacing arches along walls and chevrons round arches.

Nevertheless, the serene perfection of some of the smaller buildings (such as Romney in Hampshire or Lessay in Normandy) belies a continuous grappling, particularly with problems of vaulting. The collapse of the central tower at Ely (later replaced in wood) indicates the ever-present risk of failure. Large churches in which modifications are not introduced during construction are rare. This is true not least at Durham, which illustrates once again how the same impulse fires both Romanesque and Gothic.

Durham is famous for presenting the first example of the *rib* vaults that were to be an essential constituent of a Gothic church, though the experiment had no immediate successor in England. The leap forward was partly a result of backwardness. Instead of having each pier identical and all bays equal, Durham, following the major mid-11th-century rebuilding of Jumièges abbey in Normandy, grouped every two bays between major or *strong* piers. This habit resembles the pier-and-set-of-columns system of pre-Romanesque. The church is divided not into bays but into two-bay boxes. At Durham, the strong piers guarantee the structure. The experiment takes place in the area between them.

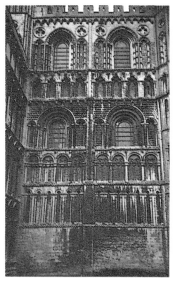

Top left, VIEW OF THE TRANSEPTS OF WINCHESTER, one of the most important Norman cathedrals in England; the rest of the church is rebuilt. **Above left** VIEW INSIDE THE TRANSEPTS AT WINCHESTER.

Top right THE TWIN-TOWERED FAÇADE OF THE CHURCH OF THE TRINITY, CAEN, NORMANDY. **Middle right** DETAIL OF THE WEST FRONT OF ELY, of the later 12th century. **Lower right** A VIEW DOWN THE NAVE OF NORMAN NORWICH CATHEDRAL.

SICILY AND VENICE

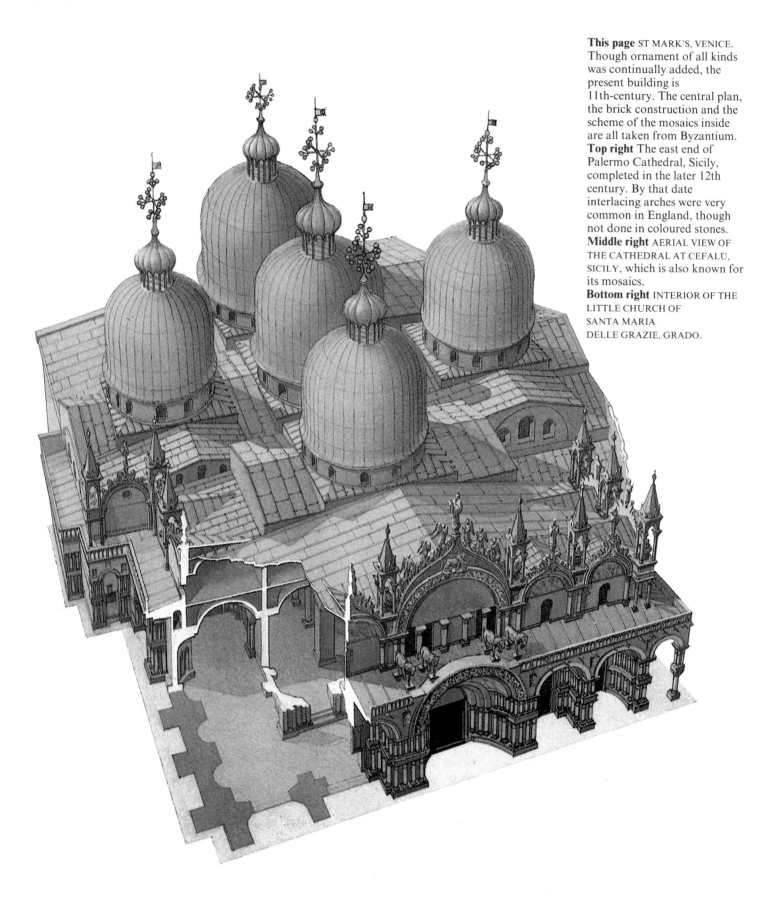

This page ST MARK'S, VENICE. Though ornament of all kinds was continually added, the present building is 11th-century. The central plan, the brick construction and the scheme of the mosaics inside are all taken from Byzantium.
Top right The east end of Palermo Cathedral, Sicily, completed in the later 12th century. By that date interlacing arches were very common in England, though not done in coloured stones.
Middle right AERIAL VIEW OF THE CATHEDRAL AT CEFALU, SICILY, which is also known for its mosaics.
Bottom right INTERIOR OF THE LITTLE CHURCH OF SANTA MARIA DELLE GRAZIE, GRADO.

Charlemagne had conquered Italy from Desiderius, King of the Lombards, but the Lombard kingdom did not include either Venice, protected by its lagoon, or southern Italy, variously under Byzantine, Arab, independent Lombard and autonomous rule. During the course of the 11th century Norman adventurers, made unwelcome in Normandy itself, took over southern Italy. Roger II was crowned King of Southern Italy and Sicily in 1130. Meanwhile Venice had prospered by trade and by exploiting the Crusades: the Latin sack of Constantinople in 1204 ended the city's nominal subjection to the Byzantine emperor.

Early in their history Venetians had built parish churches in the Byzantine domed cross pattern as well as with nave and aisles, but only the plan survives through the later rebuilding, except at Santa Fosca on the remote island of Torcello. Byzantine influence on Venetian art and mosaics can be overestimated. For all its trading links with the east, Venice was a western city.

However, Venetians and Normans alike were concerned to legitimize their independence from both pope and Holy Roman emperor. Not by chance, San Marco in Venice, housing the body of St Mark, is an 11th-century copy of the 6th century Holy Apostles in Constantinople (now lost). Holy Apostles had also housed apostolic relics, and was an imperial church. San Marco implicitly claims a rank equivalent to the tomb-church of St Peter in Rome. Though it was not a cathedral, but the doge's palace chapel, its magnificence, and the numerous ceremonies it hosted, marked it as the state church. The doge sat in the south arm, just like a Byzantine emperor.

In a comparable way the Byzantine emperor proved a useful model for the Norman kings of Sicily, whose subjects included large numbers of Greeks and Arabs. The Norman kings fostered religious freedom and kept out the pope, echoing some of the religious functions of the Byzantine emperor. Good relations with Constantinople, despite the bitterness aroused by the Crusades, enabled Roger II to import Byzantine craftsmen to adorn his palace and palace chapel in Palermo. The same craftsmen also decorated the church of the Martorana in the same city, built by Roger's admiral, George of Antioch, for the Greek Orthodox rite. Otherwise, however, Norman churches in Sicily were clearly Romanesque in plan and character, despite their mosaics or the occasional appearance of a bare round dome. The interlacing arcades that adorn the cathedrals of Palermo and Monreale are probably derived not from Islam but from Norman England. The splendid mosaics of Monreale are by local craftsmen, and have better parallels in western manuscript illuminations than in Byzantine art.

POSTMILLENNIAL BYZANTINE

Above THE KATHOLIKON, HOSIOS LUKAS, GREECE, dating from the early 11th century. The incorporation of decorative patterns into brickwork had been an element of Byzantine architecture since the 4th century, but is here pronounced. The detail of the window may well recall Islamic architecture of the same period. Also the interior of the church is beautifully preserved.
Opposite page, left THE CHURCH OF THE MONASTERY AT GRACANICA, YUGOSLAVIA, dating from the 14th century. Though its form is Byzantine, it was built under the independent Serbian empire.
Opposite page, right ST BASIL, MOSCOW, was built in the mid-16th century, but retains an essentially Byzantine plan and structure. The typically Russian onion-shaped domes are justified by the need not to let the snow settle in too great quantity. They were further embellished in the 17th century.

In the 9th and 10th centuries there had been a revival in Byzantium: territory lost in Asia Minor, the Balkans and even Italy had been regained and there was a new impetus in the arts and literature. Yet the architectural achievement in the area had been limited and no great new buildings went up. The church of Holy Wisdom at Kiev, built from 1037 following the conversion of the Russians 60 years before, was larger than any new building at home.

In the second half of the 11th century Constantinople once again came under severe threat, this time from the newly arrived Seljuk Turks. The Emperor Alexius I was compelled to ask for western aid, which arrived, unwashed and increasingly unwelcome, in the form of the First Crusade in 1091. Byzantine refinement, treasures, holy relics and arts were the object of great, and rapacious interest; but the Venetians based San Marco not on a contemporary but on a 6th-century church, Holy Apostles, built by Justinian. The Normans, though they hired Byzantine mosaicists, built in Romanesque, and so also did the Crusaders who founded the Latin kingdom of Jerusalem in Palestine.

Nonetheless parish churches of great charm, sometimes equipped with superb mosaics, were built both in Constantinople and in the provinces of the Empire, particularly Greece, in the Byzantine postmillennium (after AD1000). These churches are invariably central-plan, but lack both the proportions and the spaciousness of the domed cross plan evolved in the 6th century. They are smaller, more intimate and often cramped. Even where marble columns and carved capitals feature, the arches between them are timid in their span. The effect is dominated by the varied, colourful patterns of the brickwork and the rather outsize mouldings. The play of many small domes increases the complexity inside and out.

Such churches continued to be built after the fall of Constantinople to the Fourth Crusade in 1204, and especially in the period between the Greek recapture of the city in 1261 and the loss of most of Greece in the mid 14th century. Perhaps Mistra in the Peloponnese, which did not finally fall until 1460, preserves the spirit of the last years better than Constantinople, which fell in 1453 but was transformed into a new Ottoman capital.

Nevertheless the new rulers permitted the continuance of Christian worship. The monasteries of Mount Athos in Greece are said still to be fragrant with the air of antique Byzantium. This is not the case in Christian Russia, though the Russian tradition was founded on Byzantine models, and Byzantine advisers continued to be called in until Constantinople fell. After it had fallen, the advisers were Italian, from as early as 1475. Russia is therefore untouched by Gothic, but it is not easy to discern foreign influence until the 18th century. Russian churches have distinctive *onion* domes, and their own motifs of wooden decoration. In their general conception, however, and in plan, there is no reaction against the Byzantine heritage.

INTERNATIONAL ROMANESQUE

There was a sharp spirit of renewal abroad in the 11th century, more powerful, more widespread and less backward looking than the Carolingian renaissance. The term *Romanesque* is a great misnomer, because the interest of the period was not in antiquity but in the present. Romanesque architecture has about as much to do with Rome as romance literature, which also came into being at this time. It was called Romanesque because to the 19th century observer it looked closer to Rome than Gothic, having round, not pointed arches, but organically it is almost the same as Gothic.

One main principle of Romanesque architecture is the pier, and the box of space, a set of piers, defines the *bay*. The pier is as it were the gene of the space: all the parameters of the space can be read off or decoded from the clusters of shafts that surround the pier. Each shaft sets off to a defined destiny (except that in some Norman churches the great main shaft of the pier ends untopped.

Also in Norman churches shafts spring from mid wall as if they were afterthoughts; however, a *console* or footing is always provided. In French churches, both in the pilgrimage churches plotting the way through central France to the goal of Sant' Iago de Compostela in northern Spain, and in the various regional "schools" of Romanesque architecture, the logic of the pier is strictly observed. The same logic is fundamental to French Gothic.

In Italy, where there is no "true" Gothic, there is almost no "true" Romanesque, either. The truest Romanesque are the churches built by the Normans in Sicily and southern Italy, and Cistercian monasteries built to the standard

design. The magnificent cathedral at Pisa, begun in 1063, was built with diaphragm arches and a wooden roof by a Greek architect, Busketos. Both in Tuscan and in northern Italian examples, such as San Zeno in Verona, the walls and arches define the space only loosely, and there is no insistent rhythm of piers. Colourful marble cladding or striped stones or decorative "dwarf" colonnades often adorn these churches, also distinctive porches with columns resting on the backs of animals, but their façades are seldom organized or logical.

It is largely true that also in Spain the Lombard patterns of pre-Romanesque continue, except where there is French influence, along the route to Compostela. In the 12th century, however, there are some interesting decorative developments in Mozarabic architecture (Christian architecture under Muslim rule or influence). But these do not relate to the mainstream, or not to the emergence of Gothic, at least.

Romanesque also appears in central Europe, superseding Carolingian forms in Germany, and shaping, influencing or at least relating to buildings further afield, for instance Scandinavia (Denmark and Sweden) or Czechoslovakia. The 12th-century stave churches of Norway show a comparable coherence and discipline.

Romanesque is not only not Roman, it is distinctly not Byzantine either. The Great Schism between the Roman Catholic and the Greek Orthodox Churches in 1054 had been germinating for some time. While the Greek rite held to a central-plan church, the *Latin Cross* plan became established in Romanesque. For liturgical reasons the nave remains

Far left TWO VIEWS OF THE BUILDINGS AT PISA—the façade of the cathedral (above) and the Leaning Tower, begun in 1174. **Centre** VIEW PAST THE BAPTISTERY AT PISA, of the mid-12th century, to the Cathedral, of the mid-11th century, to the Leaning Tower. **Above, left** EAST END OF WORMS CATHEDRAL, GERMANY. Dating from the early 11th century and comparatively well preserved, it conserves certain Carolingian traditions though much of the ornament is Romanesque in type.
Above, right THE REMARKABLE "STAVE" CHURCH AT BORGUND, NORWAY, of the 12th century. **Above** NÔTRE DAME, POITOU, a splendid Romanesque church in this important centre of medieval France.

long, rendering complete symmetry impossible. However, the church takes on a cross plan, and the two arms of the transept and the choir are symmetrical.

THE FIRST GOTHIC CHURCH

Above THE PLAN OF ST DENIS. Abbot Suger's work was at the west end, first, then at the east end. The nave and transepts were rebuilt in the 13th century. **Right** THE WEST FAÇADE OF THE CHURCH AT ST DENIS. In its bulk it is still firmly Romanesque, but the style of its original sculpture (now lost) and the rib-vaulting over pointed arches are Gothic. **Far right, opposite page** VIEW OF THE EAST END OF THE CHURCH AT NOYON, which closely reflects the original scheme at St Denis. Note the still modest flying buttresses and the undulating wall of the protruding chapels.

Abbot Suger (1081–1151), abbot of St Denis outside Paris, belongs to a tradition of builder-abbots going back to Carolingian times (when one Abbot Ratger of Fulda had brought about his own dismissal because of his building mania). Abbot Suger was more politic, indeed was also a considerable statesman, serving as Regent of France while Louis VII was on the Second Crusade, 1147–49. However, having built the first church in the Gothic style, Suger also, fascinatingly, left an account of his stewardship in which he justifies it.

The prime reason Suger had for rebuilding the old abbey, the tomb church of the French kings, was the crush of the devout who had come to pray, "with floods of tears", at the holy relics of St Denis, the national saint of France. Accordingly he concentrated on the west front, with its two towers, its portals and its *narthex*, and on the east end, where the tomb was housed. He re-designed and amplified the west front to make it a better setting for processions and as a kind of "bible of the illiterate", to express the sacredness and symbolism of the church. While its sculpture introduces the Gothic style in representative art, its vaulting is the first developed example of Gothic engineering. Within each bay, a complex of shafts shoots off the pier according to the Romanesque system. But the shafts include two that cross the square of the bay diagonally. Since these are round, the ones on the sides of the square must necessarily be pointed. In fact the diagonal *ribs* determine the disposition of the entire structure, with potential consequences for the shape

and appearance of the whole building. This new principle sets St Denis apart from Durham, though Suger, who states that he called in the best craftsmen "from diverse parts", certainly knew of Durham.

Having finished the west end (except the towers) in 1140, Suger rebuilt the east end by 1144. It may already have been round, with radiating chapels. To facilitate circulation, Suger cut away the walls between the chapels to create in effect a second *ambulatory*. The vaulting involved uniting a series of little, differently shaped spaces into a single harmonious one, which was extremely complicated, and would have been impossible without exploiting the flexibility of the pointed arch. The space he created must have resembled a central-plan church of Byzantine inspiration (for instance, Charlemagne's chapel at Aachen). He "Byzantinized" it further by providing large stained glass windows that darkened and coloured the light, and set off the glitter and iridescence of the central tomb of St Denis, newly gilt and inlaid with precious stones by Suger. Though his techniques in architecture, sculpture and stained glass were novel, Suger's inspiration was partly Constantinople. This is also shown by the (lost) mosaic he placed above the west end portals, even though, as he says himself, this was contrary to Romanesque custom. Suger thanked God that He had permitted him to build this church, which meant more to him, he says, than the treasures of Constantinople, hitherto the greatest religious objects known to man.

EARLY FRENCH GOTHIC

Romanesque churches can be found in abundance in north-west, central and southern France, but are rare in north-eastern France. Precisely in this area, and around the capital, Paris, there is a sudden upsurge of building in the second half of the 12th century. In these buildings the early Gothic style is developed and consolidated, giving way at the end of the 12th century to "High" Gothic, of which the first great monument is Chartres Cathedral.

Most of the early Gothic churches retain the double-bay *strong* and *weak* pier system seen at Durham. The diagonal *rib* of the vault crosses from strong pier to strong pier, not between each pier. The square, or nearly square, area between the strong piers is the same as that of the crossing (the meeting point of nave, choir and transept), so the church has greater uniformity. Following on Suger at St Denis and the prototype of Cluny II, there is a desire to make the eastern part of the church a perfect, central-plan element in itself. The choir screen, which in this period was set some way down the nave, would mark off this *Greek Cross* within the *Latin Cross* of the whole. Processions up and down the

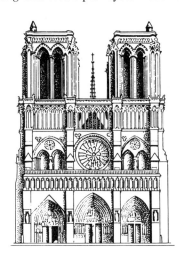

Above THE WEST FRONT OF NÔTRE DAME, PARIS, on which work continued well into the 13th century. It may be compared with the west front of St Denis (previous page) or with the west front of Rheims (see p. 84). Taller and more clearly organized than St Denis, it is not so slender and bulkier than that of Rheims. The central rose window (at St Denis it was arched) becomes standard, not only at Rheims but very widely.

Right VIEW INTO THE DOUBLE AISLES OF NÔTRE DAME. The vaults still bear rather thick ribs.

church, with ritual stops, would transform these patterns into religious symbols.

Thus the length of the choir equals the length of the transept arms, and at Noyon and elsewhere these arms even receive round ends to match the choir. However, the original design of Nôtre Dame in Paris introduced a further development: the choir was made equal to the nave, and the transept set in the middle of the church. At Laon, starting in the east, they built the choir equal to the transept arms. But then, having finished the nave to the west, they went back to the east and built out a larger choir, equalling the length of the nave.

Still more impressive than these changes in plan are the changes in elevations. The heights, and also the proportion of the height to the width, rise rapidly. One obvious means of achieving this is to jack up the nave arcade. In addition, an extra storey was sometimes added, and the cathedrals at Noyon and Laon have both a gallery and a triforium between ground arcade and clerestory. In the original design for Nôtre Dame in Paris, a row of rose windows took the place of the triforium. It was the development of this area that was most important. The clerestory windows grew larger and larger, rising high into the roof between the ribs of the X-shaped vaults and extending down to absorb one of the intermediate storeys. Nôtre Dame in Paris clearly anticipates the arrangement at Chartres, where the row of rose windows is now above, not below the clerestory. Like Chartres, it also had *flying buttresses*.

On the border between early and "high" Gothic is Bourges Cathedral. Geographically it is also on the fringe, the southernmost of the great French Gothic cathedrals. Bourges has the new flying buttresses, but it has the old strong pier system.

Above VIEW FROM THE SOUTH OF SENS CATHEDRAL, showing especially the transept, of which the end wall is given over increasingly to window.
Below VIEW FROM THE SOUTH EAST OF BOURGES CATHEDRAL, with its ranks of flying buttresses over double aisles.

EARLY ENGLISH GOTHIC

English churchmen seem to have been unaffected by the French mystic desire to build high and to build logically. After the cathedral building campaign immediately following the Conquest, there were fewer major undertakings. The most important foundation of the early 12th century was Reading Abbey, favoured by Henry I, but now lost. Undoubtedly, however, its accent was on rich and dense decoration, such as is found rather sporadically on numerous buildings from this period, except in the austere Cistercian monasteries of Wales and Yorkshire.

Gothic arrived rather suddenly in England as a result of an accident. In 1170 St Thomas à Becket had been martyred by soldiers of Henry II in Canterbury Cathedral. In 1174 a fire in the wooden roof of the new choir burnt the cathedral down. The rising cult of the martyr made possible a spectacular new building, for which a French mason, William of Sens, was called in. Though he built in the latest French style, he followed the old plan, and included other compromises. Still, in England it was now regarded as necessary to vault, and to do so in the Gothic manner. His most important innovation otherwise was the use of black Purbeck marble for the clusters of shafts round the piers, windows and blind gallery.

Wells Cathedral, started only a little later, ignores Canterbury and is fully English. Although the repeating elements not only repeat but begin to fuse, as in the French cathedrals, this homogeneity has no vertical thrust, and no absolute grandeur. Instead, Wells has a number of different striking effects, such as the magnificent display of its west front.

Lincoln, rebuilt from 1192 after what was passed off as an earthquake, does have grandeur, but it is the grandeur of a spacious basilica. Lincoln reconciles Wells and Canterbury. It has the flat-ended chapels that Wells had adopted and the Purbeck marble shafts of Canterbury. In the vaults, the logic of Gothic rib vaulting is disregarded: the number of ribs is increased, they are no longer strictly diagonal, and they meet at a central horizontal *ridge rib*. The innovation recalls the early cross vaults at Durham. It is half-structural, half-decorative; it has an immense future, which was unfortunately not followed up. It is not followed up, for instance, at the next great new cathedral, Salisbury, built from scratch on a new site because the site of the old cathedral was too small. The restrained use of Purbeck shaft clusters, the disciplined grouping of *lancet* windows, the monotonous straight edges and right angles, and the fact that it was built all in one campaign give Salisbury a remarkable homogeneity. It is a remote ancestor of the English *Perpendicular* style of late Gothic.

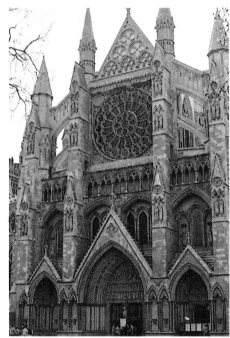

The building of a new Westminster Abbey by King Henry III from 1245 brought to England French "high" Gothic, the Gothic of Amiens and Rheims. Westminster was the tomb church and the coronation church of the English kings, and so combined the function of Rheims and St Denis. It is constructed in symbolic geometry round the relics of St Edward the Confessor, whose cult was fostered by Henry. The logic and the geometry again made little headway elsewhere; but the new large rose windows and the use with them of stone *tracery* were taken up enthusiastically.

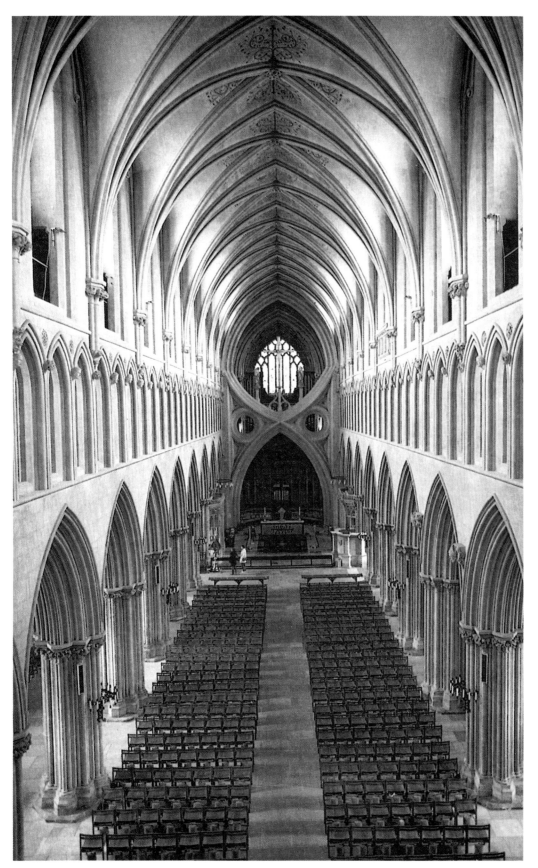

Opposite page, above
SALISBURY CATHEDRAL, built swiftly in one campaign from 1220 to about 1260. The only major subsequent modification is the spire over the crossing tower. Typical is the way its buildings extend across the ground loosely, rather than being gathered into a compact mass as they would be in a French church.

Opposite page, below THE SOUTH TRANSEPT OF WESTMINSTER ABBEY. New from France are the rose window and the flying buttresses.

This page, left VIEW DOWN THE NAVE OF WELLS CATHEDRAL. The moulded X-form was added in the 14th century in order to buttress the crossing tower. With this there, and the typically thick walls of the nave arcades, the nave is a self-enclosed space—an effect without parallel in French churches.

This page, right THE "ANGEL CHOIR" OF LINCOLN CATHEDRAL, showing the ridge rib running down the middle of the vault.

FRENCH HIGH GOTHIC

The work done by Abbot Suger at St Denis had been instantly appreciated by Chartres, as the west front of about 1145 survives to prove. The Cathedral which was rebuilt on the old foundations from 1194, when a fire swept through the building, is a perfect achievement of Suger's stated aim, to make the immaterial light of God material in his church. The inscription Suger set upon his doors is still the best introduction to the soaring experience that Chartres induces:

> The noble work shines out: but let the work that shines nobly brighten our minds, leading us truly through its lights to the true light . . . (the work) makes clear how Christ is inside in these lights: the dull mind rises through the material lights to the truth, the sunken mind floats up again once it has seen this light.

The logic of the piers, shafts and ribs, the symbolic geometry, the transfusion of coloured light through the enormous windows, the exquisite calculation of the external buttressing, the height, all this is purposefully unified to achieve transcendance. The extraordinary combination of simplicity and endlessly complicated division and subdivision has been compared to the "scholastic" systemizing of medieval theology and philosophy.

Technically, the provision of *flying buttresses* has made it possible to lighten the actual structure of the church still further, so that the walls are just a light scaffolding hung with glass. Church walls had always had outer buttressing, but it had usually been concealed under the aisle roofs. For such an enormous building this was no longer possible, nor felt to be desirable (by contrast to England, where flying buttresses were not liked, and the walls remained thick).

Not yet at Chartres, but later, the buttresses would be capped with pinnacles. Though these also had a structural, stabilizing function, they were decorated and affect the appearance of the building considerably. They are part of a deep change in taste, of which the 12th-century spire on the south tower of the west end at Chartres, the earliest in France, is also symptomatic.

The most important means of expression for the new taste begins to be exploited in the 13th century rebuilding of Rheims Cathedral. This is *tracery*. The windows at Rheims, like those at Chartres, are the size of the nave arcade. However, to obviate the wind, it was necessary to strengthen the window by "nerves" of stone, which would be mapped into larger and larger, more complicated patterns.

Still these buildings rose ever higher, at Amiens and at Beauvais. At Amiens the clerestory windows come right down behind the triforium, which is reduced to a screen of tracery. At Beauvais the limits were reached, and the enormous transept gives on to a tiny Carolingian nave. From the mid 13th century the emphasis shifts to adornment: though incomplete, Beauvais is magnificently adorned in the lacy late-Gothic flamboyant style. The 13th- and early 14th-century west front of Rheims, though dirty and marred by the absence of its intended twin spires, is already almost fuzzy in outline: apart from the firm horizontal of an upper range of sculptured kings, voids give way to solids and solids give way to voids so that neither seems to exist, and all point to the sky.

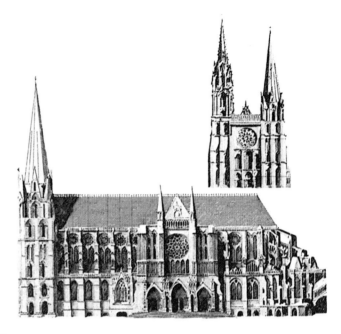

Above CHARTRES FROM THE SOUTH AND THE WEST. The achievement of unity, uniformity, harmony in the Gothic style.
Below THE WEST FRONT OF RHEIMS, with a detail of its column-sculptures and a plan. Even from the plan one has a sense of the flowing space inside the massive vessel.

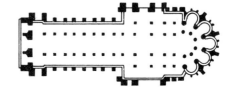

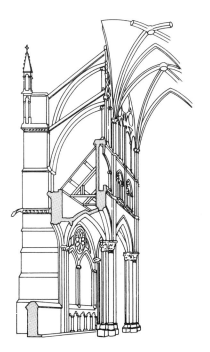

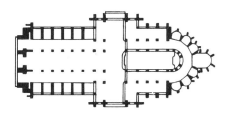

Above AMIENS CATHEDRAL.
Here the soaring height to
which these French cathedrals
aspire is at its most soaring. But
the plan (immediate left) is not
so satisfying as that of Rheims,
and the sculpture (a king, below
left) is not so distinguished.
Far left THE PRINCIPLE OF THE
FLYING BUTTRESS. The buttress,
instead of being contained
within the aisle roof, as in
Romanesque buildings, stands
free above it. Instead of a thick
wall and pier in the nave, as in
Romanesque, the massive aisle
pier supports the building. The
flying buttresses transfer the
thrust of the nave vault to this
great anchor.

CASTLES

The world-beating skills of the Roman army sappers were not permitted to decay by the Byzantines, who continued to have much need of them. They developed the arts of defence and attack further: "Greek fire", or burning naphtha expelled through tubes, fought off the Saracens from Constantinople in the late 7th and early 8th centuries.

Town defence continued otherwise unchanged from Roman times. High thick walls with towers protruding at intervals to extend visibility could be manned by the citizens in case of need. Such walls were laid out in the 5th century round Constantinople, and in addition a smaller forward wall and a moat. However, the Byzantines did not build castles in the later European sense. They built fortified camps in the old Roman pattern, though they placed them in strategic positions and built them of stone.

In Europe the classical systems of defence were lost. The standard means of defence was earthwork and a wooden palisade. By the 11th century, however, the *motte and bailey* had evolved. In fact the bailey was nothing new: just a palisade mounted on an earthwork surrounding a space where people, animals and property could be grouped. Inside the bailey, the motte, a wooden or square stone tower on a steep mound, was a more secure refuge. Numerous such Norman keeps survive in Britain; the earliest and finest is the White Tower of the Tower of London. From the 12th century both motte and bailey might have stone walls.

With the Crusades, and the establishment of the Latin kingdom of Jerusalem in 1099, Europe went back to school in the art of fortification. Though the keep is adequately defensible, it does not make it possible to keep the enemy in view or to stop him getting up to such tricks as sapping, digging under a wall or tower to make it collapse. (Stopping this is the prime purpose of a moat.) Projecting round towers were introduced and forward walls to protect the main ones. Essentially, the principle of Byzantine town defences was applied to the keep or fortress. In the Holy Land, a shortage of manpower encouraged reliance on massive, very solidly constructed walls, as at Krak des Chevaliers.

These ideas were brought back to Europe and they were applied notably by Philippe Auguste (1160–1223) to defend the conquests he had made against the Normans in France. The Normans in England used them for the castles they built against the Welsh. Similar castles again were built by Frederick II Hohenstaufen to defend southern Italy against the Pope.

In practice, these castles fell mostly by treachery or by the gates being forced. In the 14th century the gatehouse receives particular attention, with loopholes and sightlines in every direction (including inwards). The idea of a bent or double gateway in which the intruder is forced to expose himself to fire on his vulnerable, right flank and back is as old as the fortifications of Mycenaean Tiryns, but continued to be used by the Crusaders. The 14th century also saw the introduction of cannon, which for the first time would give the advantage to the besieger.

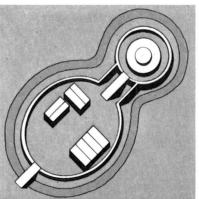

Left THE WALLS AT AVILA, CASTILE, showing perfectly town fortification as evolved in the late classical period. The round protruding towers make it possible to attack from the side any enemy coming right up to the walls.

Inset far left THE NORMAN WHITE TOWER IN THE TOWER OF LONDON. The masonry technique is just like that used in churches. The inner floors were more commonly constructed in wood than in stone.

Inset centre left THE NORMAN KEEP AT ROCHESTER. The classical system of protruding towers is not known: the defenders are powerless against an enemy at the foot of the walls. In fact, once the enemy had got that far, the next recourse was to remove the ladders between the floors. For this reason stairs in stone are never found.

Inset right A DIAGRAM OF THE "MOTTE AND BAILEY" SYSTEM. The motte, usually more or less round, is at one end of the compound.

FREDERICK II AND THE COMMUNES

The portal sculptures of Rheims Cathedral include several clear quotations from classical sculpture. How can this be, in the midst of the full flower of Gothic? Quite simply, because in the 13th century there was no opposition between Gothic and classical. In the 16th century, Italian critics identified Gothic with the "barbarian" invaders who had "destroyed" Rome, and in the 19th century English moralists denounced classical in favour of Gothic, but their enthusiasms have little to do with the state of things in the 13th century.

The "castle" of Frederick II Hohenstaufen at Castel del Monte in Puglia is another 13th-century example of a harmony between Gothic and classical. Its portal has a gable that is also a pediment. Flanking the pointed arch of the door are jambs with the fluting and capitals of the Corinthian order. The external windows have a trefoil pattern under a pointed arch, the windows looking on to the courtyard are oblong beneath a round arch with a classical moulding, and so on. But Castel del Monte is an outstandingly coherent building. The solid abstract perfection of its octagonal shape remains, though the exquisitely coloured marble with which its interiors were once sheathed has mostly been looted.

The reign of Frederick II Hohenstaufen (1194–1250), Holy Roman Emperor, King of Sicily, King of Jerusalem, is pivotal. Frederick's court was conversant with the Greek, Latin and Arab traditions, and Frederick himself wrote of things "as they are", in empirical spirit. Politically, Frederick aimed to restore the Holy Roman Empire to the state of the old Roman Empire, and in particular to re-unite Italy and Germany. In this he was opposed by the Pope, but what actually prevented him was the new independence of the Italian towns, the "Communes". While Frederick displayed the purple regalia of the old Roman emperor, the Italian towns saw themselves as new Roman republics. (Siena even adopted the emblem of the wolf suckling Romulus and Remus.) The classical past became part of the living rhetoric of Italian politics and society.

Frederick II's architecture was designed deliberately to impress. This is evident from his Entrance Gate at Capua, on the border between his own and the Pope's territory. It consists of two massive towers, originally with a balcony between, like a Carolingian Westwerk but without the church. His castle and palace at Foggia is now lost, but it is recorded that he brought down prisoners from resistant Milan to see it, with the conviction that its magnificence would persuade them to submit.

The impression of the Milanese is not recorded. But the Communes themselves took over the idea, and would begin to build in order to express patriotic pride, often looking back to classical example when doing so. At first, however, they built chiefly strongholds—for instance the Bargello (justice hall) and Palazzo Vecchio ("old palace") in Florence. Even though they successfully established their independence, they were bedevilled by internal strife: hence the numerous towers, which at San Gimignano in Tuscany survive in original numbers. The family town "palace" served as the family stronghold in these unpoliced times. Domestic architecture continued to echo the fortress air of the town chancery into the Renaissance.

Far left THE ENTRANCE PORTAL OF FREDERICK II'S CASTLE AT CASTEL DEL MONTE, combining Gothic and classical elements.
Top near left AERIAL VIEW OF CASTEL DEL MONTE. The exact purpose of the building is not known. Its location indicates a hunting lodge (Frederick II wrote a treatise on falconry). Passage is not free between all the rooms, and they were evidently designed to serve different functions—as private, reception and ante-chambers—even though architecturally the perfect symmetry of the exterior is continued inside. The view to and from the castle is unchanged from Frederick's time.
Near left centre VIEW OF THE FAMILY TOWERS OF SAN GIMIGNANO, TUSCANY—a defensive necessity of the time.
Near left, bottom THE CASTLE BUILT BY FREDERICK II AT BARI, PUGLIA. The bastion in the foreground is a later addition. Frederick built a series of such castles by the harbours of his southern Italian towns; they were for defence by both land and sea.

ISLAM: THE WESTERN REACHES

Within the fold of Islam, the Maghreb (consisting of North Africa and Spain) represents a cultural unity with very much its own characteristics. These began to take shape from the second half of the 11th century, with the rise of such dynasties as the Almoravids and Merinids, both Berber nomads converted to Islam. These were called into Spain—which already had thriving cultural centres at Cordova, Seville and Toledo—to repel the Christians. The fusion of Spanish Umayyad and Muslim Berber on a terrain already cultivated by Roman and Visigoth influence gave rise to many splendid buildings. Severity of line, clarity of composition and use of volume are features of the style. Decoration was in sculpted stone, baked brick, moulded plaster and ceramics. Later, faïence mosaic in many colours is found widely, in both interiors and exteriors.

While the Maghreb boasts many fine mosques (those at Cordova, Algiers, Tlemcen, Fez, for example) it is the palace-fortresses that attract our attention. Chief among these in Spain is the Alhambra in Granada (1333-1391). Many consider this "red citadel" the most perfect example of Islamic architecture. Within a sober and austere exterior of bright red burnt brick lie salons, courtyards, pavilions, fountains and shady loggias, all of which combine to recreate the Muslim idea of Paradise on earth. Noteworthy are the arches, either horseshoe or with delicate columns supporting fretted stalactite work (*muqarna*) into which the ceiling dissolves. The Alhambra exemplifies the term *arabesque* in its fullest sense: a realm of airy space carved into form by flowing stucco ornament, lustrous tiling and variegated marble.

Egyptian architecture of the 9th to 14th centuries is also distinguished. Because of its geographical position, Cairo was immensely rich for much of this period. The ruling Fatimid dynasty took advantage of the new mercantile activity of the Italian maritime cities. Because Cairo was spared destruction, its medieval buildings are unequalled in their variety and number.

Much Fatimid building has a classical flavour in its handling of volume and decoration. Ornament serves to exploit and enhance architectural function. The entrance façade and judicious use of muqarnas in the al-Aqmar mosque (1125) illustrate this tendency. The Fatimids also favoured funerary architecture. The basic shape was a cube surmounted by a dome (often lobed), with niches enlivened by *muqarnas*. An innovative building, drawing on Seljuk and Mesopotamian types of arch, capitals and cornices is the tomb-mosque of Emir al-Juyushi near Cairo (1085).

The *madrasa*, a teaching mosque or theological college, occurs very frequently under the Ayyubids and their successors the Mamluks, who ruled Egypt until it joined the Ottoman Empire in 1516. The madrasa of Sultan Hassan (1356–62) is the outstanding example. It has a cross plan, the arms being four iwans with immense pointed arches. There is a minimum of decoration, which adds to the ordered serenity. Always technically excellent, many Mamluk structures have a stiff and formal feel. A late and creative exception is the madrasa of Quait Bey (1496).

THE ALHAMBRA,
GRANADA, dating from
the 13th and 14th
centuries.
Left THE COURT OF THE
MYRTLES.
Far left VIEW OF THE
INTERIOR. The
Alhambra is made up of
three separate units each
joined around a central
court, and is mainly
attributable to Yusuf I
(1333–54) and his
son Muhammed V
(1354–91). Overlooking
the ancient city of
Granada, a medieval
centre of learning, the
curiously irregular
design of the palace may
well owe something to
North African models.

GOTHIC DIFFUSION

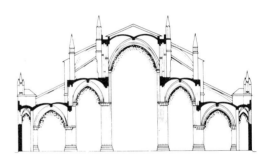

Above THE CATHEDRAL AT BURGOS, SPAIN, the earliest Gothic church in Spain. In scale and grandeur it rivals the greatest French cathedrals. The artwork shows the patterned ribs and bosses of one of its vaults.

Above right, top THE CATHEDRAL AT LEÓN, SPAIN, has magnificent stained glass in its enormous windows.
Above right A SECTION OF THE NAVE OF TOLEDO CATHEDRAL, showing its double aisles like those of Bourges in France.

Gothic architecture spread from France into Germany to the east, to Spain to the west and to Italy in the south more gradually than to England in the north. The four-storeyed cathedral at Limburg-an-der-Lahn, begun about 1220, reproduces the pattern of French churches such as Noyon or Laon, begun 50 years or more earlier. Cologne Cathedral, begun in 1248, follows Amiens, begun in 1218. Cologne is even larger, and was not finished until the 19th century.

The prototype for Gothic building in Spain was Bourges Cathedral, the closest of the great French cathedrals geographically. Bourges was taken up as a model for the cathedrals at Burgos, begun in 1222, and Toledo, begun in 1226. Although León Cathedral, begun in 1255, introduces the Amiens pattern, Bourges, with its giant arcade, remains the model also for later cathedrals.

The Gothic rib vault was used widely by Frederick II's architects, though they might set it over classical-looking columns. It was also adopted by the Franciscans, first at the first Franciscan church, San Francesco at Assisi, begun in 1226. In the 13th and 14th centuries Italian churches hardly smaller than the great French cathedrals were built widely, but they always had only two storeys, nave arcade and clerestory, and frequently had wooden, not vaulted roofs. Gothic decoration was not general in Italy until the 14th century.

Cologne Cathedral in Germany, Westminster Abbey in

England, and León Cathedral in Spain show French "High" Gothic to have been assimilated generally by the mid 13th century. The rest of Europe had learnt how to handle not only Gothic building techniques but also Gothic decoration, above all window tracery. France was no longer the pioneer, though Paris remained the capital of European fashion.

However, certain new needs, largely irrelevant to monarchs' courts, determine the form of many late Gothic churches. The Latin Cross plan was well adapted for cathedrals and churches served by monks, whose numbers, rituals and singing required a large choir and transepts and an echoing vault. Franciscan and Dominican friars, on the other hand, set out to gather the people in and preach to them. They required a building more like a hall, or like a basilica. Accordingly friars' churches in Italy have broad, long naves and wide arcades, opening out the nave into the aisles, and other churches, including the cathedrals, follow suit. A similar development occurs in Germany, where *hall churches* become increasingly popular from the mid 14th century. A hall church has no clerestory rising above the aisles; instead the aisles have very high windows or have two tiered windows and reach the same or almost the same height as the nave. Circulation between nave and aisles is very free; slender supports take the place of wall-like arcades. An important early hall church is St Elizabeth, Marburg, begun in 1235.

Above SAN FRANCESCO, ASSISI, façade and interior view. In the rest of Europe the advent of Gothic resulted in a dramatic change in the appearance of the building: in Italy the shape remained much the same. The walls were painted, not given over to stained-glass windows; San Francesco has a most important early cycle of frescoes.

FRENCH RAYONNANT GOTHIC

In the 13th century we find the first concrete evidence of people communicating about architecture. Although it is obvious that they had done so before, nothing like the sketchbook of Villard de Honnecourt, dating to the 1230s, survives. This widely travelled master mason's teaching manual includes the earliest surviving formal architectural drawings, used not only by architects, but also used by building committees. A surviving design for the façade of Strasbourg Cathedral by a German named Erwin was filed in 1277, though never used.

The more frequent use of paper as a design tool very probably assisted the increasing complexity of Gothic design. Structural problems no longer dominated or hampered the architect's imagination. Building became a display of ingenuity and skill; increasingly the names of masons are recorded, especially the king's mason. Richard I Lionheart took a special interest in his castles, and Frederick II Hohenstaufen may have designed some of his buildings himself.

The development of new decorative effects in late Gothic architecture is charted by tags—*rayonnant* (starry) and *flamboyant* (flamelike) in France, *decorated* and *perpendicular* in England. Fundamental to all of them is the term *rayonnant*, referring to the tracery introduced into French churches in the mid 13th century. The typical feature of a rayonnant building, or part of a building, is a rose window. All the oddments of area around the rose are also filled with tracery, creating a flat wall of glass. The tracery also spreads to the wall proper, and sometimes open tracery sets a kind of fretwork screen against the glazed tracery behind it.

The Sainte Chapelle in Paris is a rare building wholly in this style. It has no aisles, and completely envelops the worshipper in a warmth of coloured glass. The chapel was built by the devout King Louis IX (St Louis, as he soon became) to house relics from Constantinople, including thorns from the Crown of Thorns. It is interesting that the chapel also had a private oratory: the shift of interest from vast structures to decorative effects accompanies signs of increasing private devotion among the laity.

The Sainte Chapelle had considerable influence, even 100 years after it was built (for instance on the architecture of the Emperor Charles IV), but it was the last important Gothic church built in France. The buildings which followed it were small in scale and limited in variation. Work still continued on the great cathedrals, however; from the 14th century the intervals between the buttresses of the nave were usually filled with private chapels (these increase also in England and Italy).

Towards the end of the 14th century rayonnant gives way to flamboyant, but the change is slight: flamboyant refers only to a flamelike or teardrop-shaped motif of tracery decoration, usually acocmpanied by *ogee* arches (arches with a similar in-and-out curve) and additional ribs, between the ribs, on the vault (*liernes*). All these forms had been anticipated in English decorated Gothic at the beginning of the 14th century.

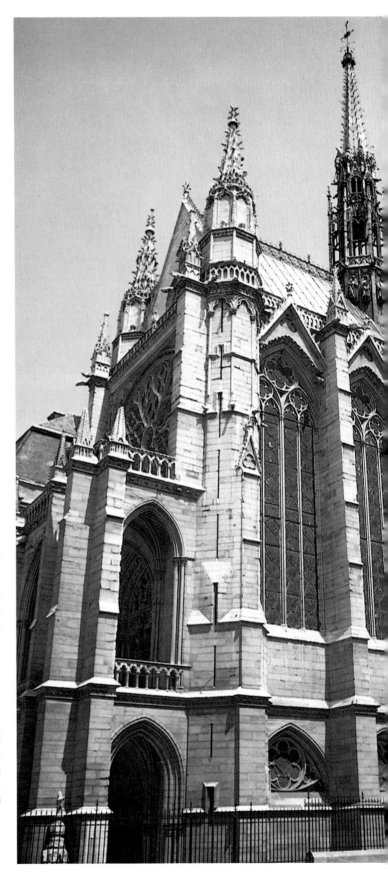

1. Before tracery   2. "Plate" tracery, 12th century   3. "Bar" tracery, 13th century   4. Intersecting, 14th century   5. Reticulated, 14th century

6. Curvilinear, 15th century   7. Flamboyant, 15th century   8. Perpendicular, 14th century   9. Perpendicular, 15th century

Left THE SAINTE CHAPELLE, PARIS. It has two storeys; on the upper one, the whole wall is given over to window. Also the vault is richly painted.
Top right THE EVOLUTION OF TRACERY FORMS. The crucial development is from "plate" to "bar" (the English equivalent of Rayonnant).
Above THE FACADE OF ST OUEN, ROUEN, with a typically Flamboyant window, gables and pinnacles.

ENGLISH LATE GOTHIC

The *decorated* phase of English Gothic, just before and just after 1300, is the most inventive in the entire history of the style. Its varied experiments produced what later became the national *perpendicular* mode; they produced flame-shaped or ogee arches of the kind characteristic of French flamboyant; and they produced novel patterns of vaulting ribs that would later be taken up in the Holy Roman Empire.

The decoration of English decorated involves not only the windows and walls, exploiting the rayonnant tracery of French "high" Gothic, but also the ribs of the vault. At Lincoln Cathedral, English masons had already shown themselves willing to play around with the bits that the French regarded as holding the building up; the English, however, regarded the walls as performing this function, and would never thin them down to a mere scaffolding, as the French did. At Lincoln a ridge rib running down the ceiling had appeared, and the number of cross ribs had multiplied; at Exeter, begun before 1280, the multiplication continues, and is matched by a multiplication of the mouldings of the arcade below. The development of *liernes*, or ribs between the ribs, followed rapidly.

Several shapes and dispositions of the ribs were then tried, in which the dominant cross ribs and ridge rib give way to an all-over net pattern. This in turn was harmonized with the tracery of the windows and triforium: this is the basis of perpendicular, a regular, all-over pattern or coating of tracery in which, on the walls and windows, the uprights tend to predominate. The first perpendicular building was probably St Stephen's, Westminster (1290s), burnt down with the Houses of Parliament in 1834; the classic statement of the style is now the choir of Gloucester Cathedral, dating from the early 14th century. The first examples of the *fan* vaults of developed perpendicular are found in the cloister at Gloucester.

The vision of English masons was formed not only by the choir, nave and aisles of the church, but also by the chapter house, the administative meeting-place of the monks. Round chapter-houses appear in England in the 12th century. During the 13th century the application of Gothic techniques to a perfect symmetry produced wonderful results, such as the chapter house at Wells, a Roman candle of ribs rising from a central column. Undoubtedly these visual effects also influenced what was attempted in the church proper, or in the "lady chapels" that were added to the east end of many cathedrals in the 13th century.

The decorative effects achieved at St Augustine's, Bristol, begun before 1306, and in the octagon over the crossing and in the "flowing florid floss" of the Lady Chapel at Ely, of the 1320s, are different again. For the Ely octagon, carpenters were called in where masonry could go no further. Such "sham vaults" are quite common in England in the 14th century, and indicate eloquently the English outlook. So does a small chamber at St Augustine's, Bristol, in which the ribs are free-standing beneath an independent ceiling.

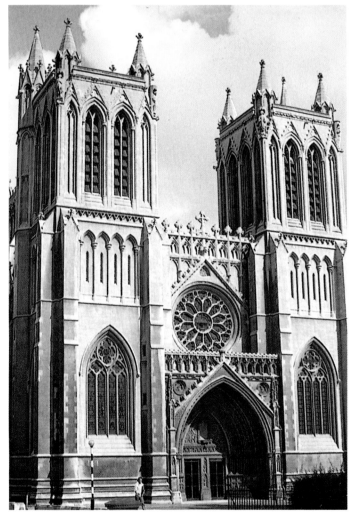

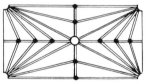

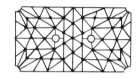

Opposite page, above YORK MINSTER. An important example of English use of the French Rayonnant style.
Opposite page, below THE FAÇADE OF ST AUGUSTINE'S, BRISTOL. At the end of the 11th century a distinct West Country "school" of architecture had appeared, and made an individual contribution also in the 14th century.

This page, above The multiplication of vaulting ribs. The left-hand artwork and diagram shows Exeter Cathedral's nave, of the later 13th century. The ridge rib (A) taken over from the Angel Choir of Lincoln Cathedral (see p. 83), knits in most of the ribs, but a further rib at right angles to the ridge rib forms a collecting point for others. All the ribs start from the top of the shaft or springer (B) at the corner of the bay. At the new nave at Canterbury, of the 14th century, additional ribs, liernes, springing off from ribs in the middle of the bay create a net-like effect.

This page, above THE OCTAGON AT ELY replaced the Norman crossing tower in the 14th century. It is in two stages, the first of masonry, the second of wood.

This page, left VIEW DOWN THE AISLE OF ST AUGUSTINE'S, BRISTOL, with ribs that seemingly descend from the ceiling.

A NEW CAPITAL: PRAGUE

The Hundred Years' War with England dislodged France from its pre-eminence in matters artistic. In the middle of the 14th century the lead shifted to central Europe, to Germany and the eastern territories of the Holy Roman Empire, in particular to Bohemia and its capital, Prague. The transformation took place under the Holy Roman Emperor Charles IV (1316–78), whose favoured residence was Prague. While war preoccupied the two nation states, Charles succeeded in pacifying dissension in Germany and healing the long-standing quarrel between emperor and pope.

Usually the masons responsible for the new buildings are known to us by name. Heinrich Parler was the architect of the *hall church* of Heiliges Kreuz (Holy Cross) at Schwäbish

Gmund, which set the pattern for similar churches all over Germany and the Baltic regions. It is lofty and airy but does not reach for the sky like a "high" Gothic church. Only slender supports, stripped of their multiple shafts, mark the lines of nave and aisles. The nave and aisles share one roof, which resembles an umbrella, leading us to look around in these churches, not up. The sacred place is well lit, clear and simple, though with outbursts of elaborate decoration within defined areas, for example the ribs of the vault. The clean, clear, human order anticipates Protestant purity.

Heinrich Parler's son Peter was called by Charles IV to direct the work at Prague Cathedral, which had been begun by a French architect. The French architect, Matthieu d'

Near right THE CATHEDRAL AT ERFURT, IN EASTERN GERMANY, is a spectacular building in a French Gothic style, dating from the 14th century.
Far right THE CATHEDRAL AT PRAGUE. In exterior aspect it is not so different from French Gothic cathedrals, but the disposition inside, the space, the decoration, is more original.

Arras, had laid out a standard "high" Gothic cathedral. Peter Parler, taking over in 1352, cut off the rise of the great shafts with a firm parapet over the arcade. Parler seems to have wanted to make the church more like the Sainte Chapelle, to bring things closer down to the prayer stool and an earthly sanctity. The Sainte Chapelle was also the model for a new choir Charles IV added to the old Carolingian palace chapel at Aachen.

In other respects Peter Parler and architects after him were more interested in English decorated architecture. St Augustine's, Bristol, is the first church in which the shafts rising to the vault are pared down to such a degree that they lose their capitals. This becomes normal in the Holy Roman Empire, and is an important contribution to the effect of the church. In particular, German architects shared with their English colleagues a delight in making complex patterns, and at first adopted ideas and specific moulding forms and rib patterns from them. The idea of spinning out the ribs free in space had been tried on a very small scale once at Bristol, but is taken up with more audacity in the Holy Roman Empire. Peter Parler tried it in the south transept arm of Prague Cathedral; a later, spectacular instance is in the church at Annaberg in Saxony. The geometry and cutting of these ribs were extremely sophisticated; and, unlike the English, who had turned to the carpenters, the Germans did it in masonry.

GOTHIC SECULAR BUILDING

During the periods of Romanesque and Gothic architecture, the economic and social advance of Europe continues unabated. The inability of either the Holy Roman emperor or the pope to govern Italy left the way free for the rise of the Communes, the independent city states of Italy. Netherlandish towns, at the intersection of the English, French and German powers, were able to work free as well. Subject towns also grew more significant and more powerful, but the most spectacular buildings expressing new-found political and commercial self-sufficiency are in the Low Countries and in Italy.

These buildings were first and foremost meeting places, in which councils, courts and guilds could take or witness joint decisions. They are oblong but otherwise rather formless, except that the main hall is usually on the second floor and storerooms are underneath. The large span of the hall meant that it was roofed in wood, and might be a considerable feat of carpentry—the enormous shell of the Palazzo della Ragione (Palace of Justice) at Padua, or the hammer-beam roof of Westminster Hall are famous examples of this. Also, however, these halls were given towers, not only for security but also for bells and to be visible. The Torre del Mangia of the Palazzo Pubblico in Siena is completely out of scale with the building; so is the tower of the Cloth Hall in Bruges.

The earliest of these halls is the Cloth Hall at Ypres, begun in about 1260. A spate followed in the later 13th century, and they were built, rebuilt or embellished throughout the 14th and into the 15th century. Fairest of them all is the doge's palace in Venice, of the mid 14th century.

The papal consistory, or council, also required a hall, and this was one of the first buildings to be erected when Pope Benedict XII decided in the early 14th century to settle at Avignon, under the protection of the French king. Benedict also built himself private apartments, including not only a bedroom but also a study, the earliest surviving study anywhere. Of course monks had had cells, kings had had treasure rooms and many persons of rank had had private bedrooms, but studies as such were new. These private rooms, as always, were set in a tower, or in two towers, as in the case of Avignon. One could look at the view and at life going on below, as well as think. In the apartments at Avignon the painted decoration survives in two rooms.

Libraries were still generally the preserve of monasteries, though universities now existed. The first had been founded at Bologna in the late 11th century. Universities long remained linked to and similar to monasteries, though in England, first at Merton College, Oxford, in the 14th century, the cloister becomes a *quad*. Hospitals and hospices were also the preserve of monasteries, at least until the 15th century. The magnificent hospital at Beaune in Burgundy was built in the mid 15th century by the chancellor to the duke of Burgundy, then the leading court in Europe. Jacques Coeur, "surintendant" to the King of France, built himself a fine "palace" that survives at Bruges.

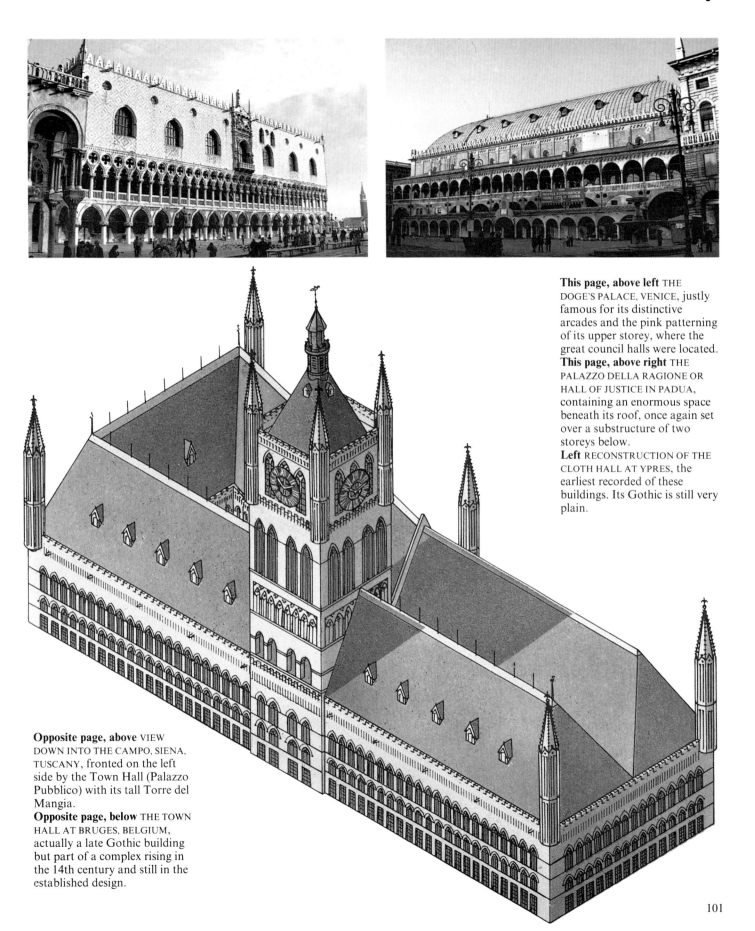

This page, above left THE DOGE'S PALACE, VENICE, justly famous for its distinctive arcades and the pink patterning of its upper storey, where the great council halls were located.
This page, above right THE PALAZZO DELLA RAGIONE OR HALL OF JUSTICE IN PADUA, containing an enormous space beneath its roof, once again set over a substructure of two storeys below.
Left RECONSTRUCTION OF THE CLOTH HALL AT YPRES, the earliest recorded of these buildings. Its Gothic is still very plain.

Opposite page, above VIEW DOWN INTO THE CAMPO, SIENA, TUSCANY, fronted on the left side by the Town Hall (Palazzo Pubblico) with its tall Torre del Mangia.
Opposite page, below THE TOWN HALL AT BRUGES, BELGIUM, actually a late Gothic building but part of a complex rising in the 14th century and still in the established design.

ITALIAN GOTHIC

Milan Cathedral, begun in 1387, is a famous case history. Advisers from France and Germany were called in, who were evidently perturbed at the way the Italian masons had set about it. Meanwhile the Italians consistently rejected the advice given by the northerners. In the 14th century the Italians had become highly experienced in handling Gothic and in building vast structures (for instance, Santa Maria Gloriosa dei Frari in Venice; the Santo (Sant' Antonio) in Padua; San Petronio in Bologna). At Milan they proceeded on their own way, even though Milan Cathedral is by far the most Gothic church in Italy (the prototype is Bourges Cathedral).

During the 13th century there had been a steady absorption of French ideas in Italy, and in the 14th century Gothic tabernacles, Gothic gables, Gothic pinnacles, Gothic lancets and roses abound. However, flying buttresses are not used (except at Milan), windows are inserted singly into the wall and they do not replace the wall (except at Milan), and there is no play with vaulting ribs of the kind universal in late Gothic elsewhere. Gothic decoration is applied like tinsel or ribbons or candles round the solid, foursquare mass of the building, and the rectangular subframe stands out clearly (even at Milan), though the decoration becomes increasingly spindly.

There are further characteristics special to Italian Gothic. Spiral colonnettes and inlaid glass, marble and mosaic, widely used virtually since antiquity, mingle with newer forms. In Tuscany, the pre-Gothic practice of cladding the building in stripes of marble continues unabated, and Pisa Cathedral, begun 1063, set the standard which the Gothic cathedrals of other Tuscan towns emulated. Siena, begun before 1260, Orvieto, begun in 1290, and Florence, begun in 1294, all follow Pisa in general plan and shape, though Orvieto lacks the dome. In the competition, the latest to start fared best. Siena attempted to steal a march by turning the existing church into the transept of a new one, but the project was too ambitious. Pisa made up by adorning the Baptistery, and the façades of the others were designed and fitted out with sculpture well before the building was completed. This habit of starting at the west, and subordinating structure to design, explains the awkward position in which the Florentines found themselves at the beginning of the 15th century.

In an attempt to enlarge their church, the Florentines had expanded the width of their dome beyond the width of the nave which they had already begun. They then found that they needed to vault an octagonal space 42m (140ft) across, which was quite unprecedented, except for the Pantheon in Rome, which is 43m (143ft). Filippo Brunelleschi, one of the architects appointed, probably went to Rome to study it. Certainly he used the same construction procedure, which was to corbel or cantilever inwards a progressively smaller series of rings until he reached the top. However, Florence Cathedral dome does not resemble the Pantheon, partly because it is in every other way Gothic (with ribs), and partly because it was made to resemble the dome of the Baptistery just beside it.

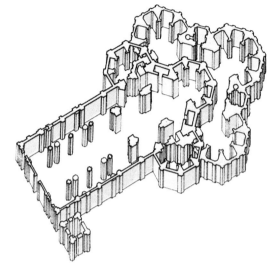

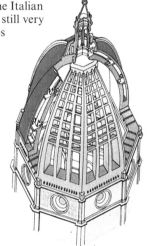

Upper left MILAN CATHEDRAL, the most pinnacly of the Italian Gothic cathedrals, but still very different from examples elsewhere in Europe.

Lower far left SIENA CATHEDRAL. The lower part of the facade was designed by the distinguished sculptor Giovanni

Pisano, but the upper part is of the later 14th century. In between had come the ill-fated attempt to convert this existing building into the transept of a new cathedral.

Lower near left A VIEW OF THE UPPER PART OF SIENA CATHEDRAL'S WEST FRONT, showing its Gothic tabernacles and abundant carving.

Above FLORENCE CATHEDRAL, in plan and seen from the south. The plan shows both the originally intended east end and the much larger east end actually built.

Immediate left ANALYSIS OF THE CONSTRUCTION OF BRUNELLESCHI'S DOME FOR FLORENCE CATHEDRAL. It has two skins; the inner skin is clearly Gothic in its pointed shape and its ribs.

BRUNELLESCHI'S STYLE

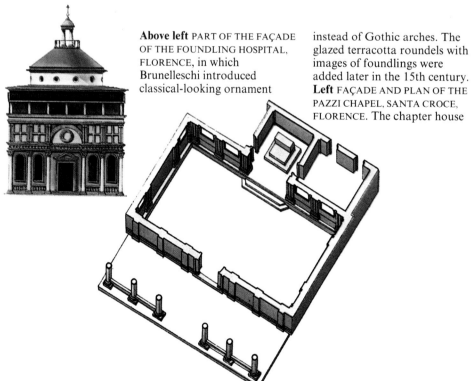

Above left PART OF THE FAÇADE OF THE FOUNDLING HOSPITAL, FLORENCE, in which Brunelleschi introduced classical-looking ornament instead of Gothic arches. The glazed terracotta roundels with images of foundlings were added later in the 15th century.
Left FAÇADE AND PLAN OF THE PAZZI CHAPEL, SANTA CROCE, FLORENCE. The chapter house is fronted by a row of columns like those of a temple and behind them a barrel vault with coffered decoration imitating Roman ceilings. The upper part is more Romanesque than Roman, but may not be Brunelleschi's design. Next, one enters the chapter house itself, in which the decoration serves to demonstrate the underlying geometry.
Opposite page, near right THE CROWNING LANTERN OF FLORENCE CATHEDRAL, distinctly more classical than the dome below it. It has shell-headed arches, a favourite early Renaissance motif.
Opposite page, right VIEW ACROSS THE NAVE OF SAN LORENZO, FLORENCE, showing the system of the Foundling Hospital façade applied to the church; and PLAN OF SAN LORENZO, illustrating its proportional geometry.

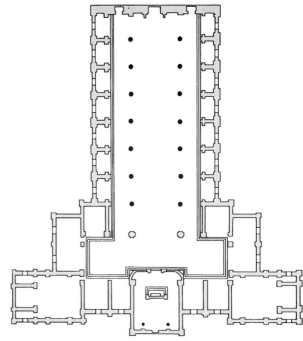

The building of the dome of Florence Cathedral by Filippo Brunelleschi (1377–1446) was regarded as a feat of genius. Brunelleschi's immense reputation took a stage further the emergence of the architect, or architect-artist. Both before and after Brunelleschi Italian architects were usually artists: before him Giovanni Pisano, Arnolfo di Cambio, Giotto; after him Michelozzo, Bramante, Michelangelo, Jacopo Sansovino. Brunelleschi himself was a silversmith. Some sculpture by him survives; he also demonstrated the fertility of his invention in the design of machines and in making the first geometrical perspective paintings.

His experiments with perspective were closely related to certain new methods of surveying, and both were fundamental to the Renaissance style that Brunelleschi initiated in his other Florentine buildings. The first of these was the Ospedale degli Innocenti (Foundling Hospital). For its fronting loggia he freely recomposed elements from the 11th-century façade of the city's Baptistery, though he used a grey stone against white plastered wall instead of classical-looking stripes of marble. These Romanesque elements included classical-looking Corinthian *pilasters*, or flat columns, which he used to frame off the row of arches at the ends of the loggia.

The echo of the Baptistery was significant: it was the building in which children were ritually accredited not only as Christians but as Florentines, and it was believed to be the oldest building in the city, having been converted from a temple of Mars. Brunelleschi, abandoning Gothic ornament, created a distinctively Florentine style.

In his next work, the north sacristy of San Lorenzo, which was the first part of the church to be built, the fundamental geometry of Brunelleschi's new architecture becomes explicit. The building is a central-plan square, except for the altar chamber and two chambers beside it. The altar chamber is also square, and exactly one quarter of the main space. The ground storey, pendentive storey and dome are each the same height. Similar "pure" or integral proportions determine the disposition of the whole building, including the details. Corinthian pilasters and entablature serve to mark the proportions out on the walls. Brackets and, in the later Pazzi Chapel at Santa Croce, "pencil pilasters", pilasters slimmed down to a single fluting (an invention of Brunelleschi's), have the same purpose; marble stripes in the pavement repeat the geometry again.

In San Lorenzo proper and in Santo Spirito, neither of which was completed till after his death, Brunelleschi applied his system to a church. Uniting both plan and elevation in one proportional harmony, based on the square, he went further than the Romanesque logic of the bay or Gothic symmetry of plan. In certain essential elements, such as the double row of columns down the nave, these churches resemble Early Christian basilicas, but in size, shape, ornament and aesthetic they are quite different. It would be better to say that they were late Gothic churches done in a new way.

ALBERTI'S CLASSICISM

Leon Battista Alberti (1404–72) came of noble Florentine family and was educated at the University of Padua. He designed architecture, rather than built: his actual works were directed by master masons, who consulted him at difficult points, frequently by letter. He was a "humanist", a classical scholar, a poet, a mathematician and a writer on many subjects before he turned to architecture; he wrote a famous manual on painting. Almost certainly Renaissance painting would have taken much the same course without him, but his influence on architecture was crucial. Theory, applicable theory, was what the time needed.

Alberti's achievement was to provide a classical vocabulary and some attractive topics for Brunelleschi's new grammar of architecture. Brunelleschi had improvised what he needed out of several sources: a local Romanesque which already contained classical reminiscences; direct observation of classical buildings; existing Gothic forms which he had purified. Alberti's talents were twofold: first of all he had the Latin to read Vitruvius's surviving classical treatise on architecture; and secondly, he had the scholastic training to formulate rules in his own treatise. He defined the classical orders and their use for various kinds of buildings. Still more, he directed both patrons and artists in what was desirable to build, judging by classical example and by "reason": he provided ideals. The vision of a new Rome he conjured up with Pope Nicholas V in the 1440s outlined the terms of the city's spectacular transformation in the following 200 years.

Alberti's own buildings were chiefly churches, which he called "temples". This was a fundamental error, since the western church evolved from the basilica, not the pagan temple. In the event, Alberti had recourse not to temples but to triumphal arches for his new churches. A triumphal arch, consisting of a central arch between columns with or without flanking smaller arches, could be adapted to the nave and aisles of a church: this is the principle of Alberti's façade for the Tempio Malatestiano at Rimini, for Sigismondo Malatesta, tyrant of Rimini, Alberti's first church. Also, Brunelleschi's kind of membering could be translated into the elements of the triumphal arch, and the all-important proportions made compatible with the pre-existing classical system of the Orders. Alberti's last and most important church, Sant' Andrea in Mantua, is entirely "generated" in strict proportion from a triumphal arch unit.

Also in Mantua, Alberti's San Sebastiano is a botched and incomplete attempt to build a central-plan church. Naturally, the Renaissance ethic of proportion cried out for fully symmetrical plans, but usually the demands of liturgy and tradition prevailed against it. The Bishop of Mantua was dismayed by San Sebastiano, and likened it to a synagogue or a mosque.

Opposite page, above THE CHURCH OF SAN MICHELE IN ISOLA, VENICE, built by Mauro Codussi, a follower of Alberti. Its façade is based on the scheme of Alberti's Santa Maria Novella, updated with more obviously classical ornament.

Opposite page, below THE FAÇADE OF ALBERTI'S CHURCH OF SANT' ANDREA, MANTUA. The central arch between four columns and two storeys of smaller arches is a triumphal arch unit. Above it Alberti places a temple-like pediment and rather awkwardly above that an inlet for what in a Gothic church would be a rose window.

This page, left THE COURTYARD OF THE CANCELLERIA (CHANCERY) IN ROME, by Gasparo Romano, also a follower of Alberti. Simple proportions dictate the courtyard façade, and on the outer façade of the building the Golden Section is used.

This page, right DETAIL OF THE FAÇADE OF THE PALAZZO RUCELLAI IN FLORENCE, of the 1440s, designed by Alberti. Alberti here introduced the classical Orders on to a palace front for the first time.

Below ALBERTI'S FAÇADE FOR THE CHURCH OF SANTA MARIA NOVELLA IN FLORENCE. The Gothic arches housing sarcophagi at the lowest part of the façade were previous to Alberti. Alberti did not try to convert the church into a classical-looking building, but to organize its façade on the new principles.

IOHANESORICELLARIVSPAVFANSAL MCCCCLXX

EARLY RENAISSANCE

In all other spheres—law, political theory, philosophy, medicine, literature—the pressure to come to terms with the classical heritage was ineluctable. In the 15th century the pressure extended to art and architecture, and these in turn became an integral part of the rhetoric of the age. Art and architecture served not only the greater glory of God, but the private esteem and public good name of self, family and city.

The rhetoric, though universal, had many different accents and applications. There is, anyway, no single style of classical architecture, despite the codification that continued from Alberti to Palladio and beyond. Further, the aim was to achieve a classical-looking building of harmonious proportions, which was a wide brief. Alberti used triumphal arch forms to adorn his churches; Palladio set temple fronts on his houses.

The architectural rhetoric of Cosimo de' Medici, tacit ruler of Florence from 1434, was low-key, in keeping with his character and policy. He is said to have turned down a proposal by Brunelleschi for the new Medici "palace" on the grounds that it was too ostentatious. The actual Medici palace, though regular and with classical columns in the courtyard, avoided any pretensious reference to ancient Rome; but it had a garden. Discreetly and piously, Cosimo spent on religious architecture, notably the new buildings for the Dominicans at San Marco. Here Michelozzo built a fine cloister with Ionic columns and a serene library in the form of a gallery, lit from both sides.

In contrast, Aeneas Sylvius Piccolomini, a "humanist" elected Pope Pius II in 1458, spent massively on his native village in the Sienese countryside, which he raised to a bishopric. For the new "city" of Pienza he built a cathedral, a bishop's palace, and a Piccolomini family palace. The cathedral is a Germanic hall church of the kind Aeneas Sylvius had seen and admired on his travels, translated into classical language with a charming burr. The palace is of the Florentine type, commanding an idyllic view.

The new palace built by Federigo da Montefeltro at Urbino both commanded and presented a superb view: its twin towers rise imperially over a valley and between them the Duke had his study; he also had a "secret" garden. A second glory of the Urbino palace is its courtyard, the first to be presented with the grandeur appropriate to a façade. It has "perfect" proportions, splendid Corinthian columns, and a frieze in Roman lettering (of the kind that appeared on triumphal arches or on the portico of the Pantheon).

Venetian palaces had none of the fortress air of Florentine and other mainland town houses, but there was a traditional scheme of two towers flanking a single hall which continued to condition their design even in the Renaissance. The old pattern is readily apparent in the most lavish Gothic palace in the city, the early 15th-century Ca' d'Oro (House of Gold), though one of the "towers" is absent. In the course of the 15th century the scheme was un-Gothicked and geometricated: the Ca' Dario is a fine example. Classicization proper, in Alberti's sense, did not take place until the end of the century, in the Palazzo Non Nobis Domine ("Not to us O Lord, but to thy name give glory": Psalm 115).

Opposite page, above left THE CA' D'ORO ON THE GRAND CANAL, VENICE, built in the early 15th century in an extremely rich and individual Venetian Gothic. Beside it a typical 16th-century palace.
Opposite page, below THE PALAZZO CONTARINI DALLE FIGURE, GRAND CANAL, VENICE, dating from the first years of the 16th century. The style is early Renaissance (typical are the strict division of the façade into squares and the thinness

and flatness of the ornament). The awkward pediment was then a novelty.
This page, right VIEW INTO THE COURTYARD OF THE PALACE AT URBINO, by Luciano Laurana, of the 1460s.
This page, below THE TOWN-SIDE FAÇADE OF THE PALACE AT URBINO. The third door on the right leads into the courtyard shown above. The facing of the façade was never completed.

THE ART OF FORTIFICATION

Although the results may seem petty and transient, war was a constant feature of life in medieval and 15th-century Europe, and the architecture of war was a characteristic of the landscape and a conspicuous item of expenditure. In the 16th century some very marked changes in political conditions included far-reaching changes in the conduct of war.

In the 15th century the castle was becoming obsolete militarily, but in northern Europe castles continued to be built or rebuilt, with an apparently ever greater profusion of turrets. There seems to be a delight in the clusters of round, pointed towers in the backgrounds of the illustrations made for the Duc de Berri by the Limbourg brothers, and not much military purpose. These castles were becoming residences or *châteaux* in the modern sense; also in England and Germany defense was giving way to comfort. But castles retained, or exaggerated, their external defences, perhaps as a consequence of the fashion for chivalry and tournaments. Chivalry was not necessarily distinguished from real war: at Agincourt in 1405 the French had regarded the English use of archers against their knights as unfair.

If the strength of the central power, the king, tended to make castles redundant, their fate was sealed by the development of cannon. By the 16th century cannon could have knocked off those turrets in minutes. The use of massive squat towers, then slantwise, arrow-shaped bastions for defence not only against but with cannon began in Italy (the slantwise bastion came in towards the end of the 15th century in central Italy). However, it was not practicable to introduce these massive fortifications to all towns, and besides those that can be seen in 15th-century pictures, the traditional thin "curtain" walls have survived even till today, for instance at Marostica or Montagnana in the Veneto. By contrast, Lucca in Tuscany still has its bastioned mid-16th century walls. During the same period, in Italy, the usual form of country residence became not a castle but a villa, in conscious imitation of Roman precedent.

Fortification fell within the competence of an artist-architect, and most of the famous names of the Italian Renaissance put their hand to it, at least until the second half of the 16th century when there was more specialization. But no-one built more splendid military architecture than Michele Sanmichel (1484–1559). His city gates for his native Verona and his fortress at Sant' Andrea in the Venetian lagoon are two examples.

Cannon, and the greater resources of the monarch, were two of the reasons why Italy could not continue as a hotchpotch of warring city-states into the 16th century. The invasion of Italy and capture of Milan by the French in 1499, the league of all its neighbours that almost took Venice in 1509, and the sack of Rome by the troops of the Emperor Charles V in 1527 altered, if it did not quite choke, the Italian Renaissance profoundly.

Above left VIEW DOWN THE
WALL TO A BASTION AT LUCCA,
TUSCANY.
Above right THE PORTA PALIO
AT VERONA, BY MICHELE
SANMICHELE.
Left VIEW DOWN THE WALLS OF
MONTAGNANA, VENETO.

FINAL FLOURISH OF GOTHIC

Building was intermittent in France and England during the 14th and 15th centuries. The Hundred Years' War drained finances; then in England in the 15th century foreign war was succeeded by the civil Wars of the Roses; in France the French king's relatives, in Burgundy, Berry and Anjou, held more splendid court than he did. However, in both countries the king was able to unite and assert his power towards the end of the century, and to build.

St George's Chapel at Windsor, begun in 1474, was the first of three magnificent royal chapels in *perpendicular* style with *fan* vaulting. It was followed by King's College, Cambridge and by Henry VII's chapel in Westminster Abbey. These are spacious boxes, recalling the hall churches in Germany or even the Sistine Chapel in the Vatican Palace: behind the frescoes by Michelangelo the vaulting technique is remarkably similar, with great half-cones between the windows sustaining a thin shell down the centre. In the English royal chapels ribs "fan" out over the cones and merge into a mesh of liernes in the centre; the window tracery and the stained glass are also essential to the impressive, emphatically over-all effect. The flattened-out pointed arches, composed of arcs drawn from four different centres, are a variation distinctive to this period. Henry VII's chapel is smaller and denser in its ornament compared to its predecessors: in an astonishing feat of virtuosity, the half-cones have spawned on the ceiling further cones that dangle great pendants—a nonsensical license the equal of any contemporary Italian Mannerist trick. The tomb by Torrigiani below them (1512–18) is the first example of Renaissance art in England.

In France, a royal endowment like Saint-Esprit in Rue, begun in 1480, is directly comparable to the English chapels—well-lit, spacious and simple, but with luxurious decoration. Other churches are stark, the freedom of circulation between nave and aisles and the absence of capitals from the piers suggesting German influence.

There is no equivalent of the steady, vernacular Perpendicular of English burghers' churches, except perhaps in the

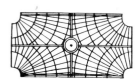

Above STRUCTURE OF THE FAN VAULT AT KING'S COLLEGE, CAMBRIDGE.

Netherlands. Brabant (Brussels region) Gothic is sturdy and coherent: there is a fine example in Burgundy, at Bourg-en-Bresse, built by Margaret of Austria, ruler of the Netherlands. Margaret also employed the painter Jan Gossaert, whose paintings sometimes show a fantastical Gothic decoration that makes an equivalent to the ideal buildings of Italian Renaissance perspective. It is foolish to say that Gothic was exhausted; it is more the case that the north was entranced by the novelty of Italian design. Italian influence spread rapidly after the invasions of Italy by the French, and was established by François I's invitation of Italian artists to his court.

Below KING'S COLLEGE, CAMBRIDGE FROM THE WEST. KING HENRY VII'S CHAPEL, WESTMINSTER ABBEY is one of the most densely decorated chambers in the world. It was designed as a precious box in which Henry VIII's master masons could demonstrate their well known skills.

HIGH RENAISSANCE

Above THE WEST FRONT OF NEW ST PETER'S, completed nearly a century after Bramante began work.

Below BRAMANTE'S TEMPIETTO, San Pietro in Montorio, Rome.

Donato Bramante (1444–1514) trained as a painter in Urbino, moving to Milan by 1481. In Urbino he could have learnt perspective from the painter Piero della Francesca; in Milan he associated with Leonardo da Vinci. In 1499, when the French invaded Italy and took over Milan, he went to Rome, where he supported his close relative Raphael and made an enemy of Michelangelo.

He shared with Leonardo and Michelangelo and several others, though not Raphael, the habit of starting projects "in order not to finish them", as was said of Leonardo. The habit is perhaps a consequence of the incredible perfection of detail that these artists could achieve, and on their superbly grandiose vision. Already Pius II, as he proudly relates in his memoirs, had rewarded the architect at Pienza for grossly exceeding his budget, because thereby he had made a finer and more glorious building. With this attitude, it is not surprising that so many Renaissance buildings were unfinished.

Bramante's buildings in Milan generally have the slightly bizarre character of much early Renaissance architecture, and it is accounted his achievement to have ironed out this trait and to have produced in Rome a kind of "classic" classicism. His first work there was the cloister at Santa Maria della Pace. It owes much to the courtyard of the Ducal Palace in Urbino, but the co-ordination of "correct" classical order and "perfect" integral proportions is more thoroughgoing. The classical orders had not been designed to express Renaissance integral proportions, and there were plentiful technical problems involved in making them do so. Basically, Bramante solved them by "floating" the orders over a substructure of piers and arches—adapting the solution evolved by the Romans themselves when they had used the orders in buildings to which they were not appropriate, for instance on the Colosseum. In the cloister the pilasters, like the columns on the Colosseum, instead of being lengthened disproportionately, are set on bases. Instead of being thickened they stand forward in relief to their correct thickness against a wider pier: this seems to be a new, Renaissance device.

Bramante next built the Tempietto, a tiny central-plan shrine meant to form the centrepiece of a cloister, never built, at San Pietro in Montorio. It has no use: but it is a brilliant, "perfect" example in stone of the kind of ideal building that closes off the perspective in so many Renaissance pictures.

Bramante's greatest, and by far his most unfinished, work was the design of New St Peter's. Old St Peter's, built by Constantine the Great, was falling down, and rather than restore it Pope Julius II decided to transform it into the largest and of course the most "perfect" church in Christendom. This meant certainly that it had to have a dome, exceeding that of Florence Cathedral, and quite possibly also that it should be central plan. It would exceed the Pantheon, and also the greatest vaulted Roman baths and basilicas; probably it was to surpass Hagia Sophia in Constantinople, too. However, although he could make a convincing imitation of the appearance of imperial Roman buildings, Bramante probably did not know how he was going to construct the dome. As he is reported to have said on another occasion, he would see about that when it came to it.

THE NAVE AND CROSSING OF NEW ST PETER'S, ROME. The absolute grandeur of the building was certainly part of Bramante's conception, though it required Michelangelo's final intervention to achieve it.

RENAISSANCE CIVIC BUILDING

VIEW OF THE SENATOR'S PALACE
ON THE CAMPIDOGLIO, ROME,
with the Roman statue of
Marcus Aurelius, moved to this
position in the 16th century, in
front of it. The Campidoglio
was a Renaissance creation on
what had been the unimpressive
back side of the Capitol Hill in
Roman times. Its laying out
was motivated by shame that
the old centre of the city had
fallen into unsightly ruin and
disrepair.

The major symbol of the Renaissance popes' new Rome was
Bramante's New St Peter's, a modern church that would be
superior to the old, classical one. However, it was only one
element in a programme that included the fortification of the
Vatican palace and city, the Borgo; the laying-out of the
Borgo and linking it with smart new roads through the old
city; the expansion and embellishment of the Vatican palace;
and the refurbishment of the old city itself. It must be said
that this was the last item on the list, and the old centre of the
city, the Capitol, did not receive its modern form, as the
Campidoglio, until the end of the 16th century, to a design by
Michelangelo Buonarrati (1475–1564). The area around the
Pantheon had to wait till the 17th century. Nonetheless the
papal programme was the prototype for all subsequent
campaigns of urban renewal, just as Rome itself was the
great model for any aspiring city.

No city in Italy was more improved and embellished
during the Renaissance than Venice. In this period the Grand
Canal became grand, and the Piazza in front of St Mark's
and the adjoining Piazzetta beside the Doge's Palace were
rationalized and complemented with the public Library of St
Mark's by Jacopo Sansovino (1486–1570). St Mark's housed
and expressed the religious identity of the city, the Doge's
Palace its political identity; the Library housed and expressed
its cultural claims. In the courtyard of the Doge's Palace,
with its ceremonial stair, the Gothic style of the rest had
given way to a lavish classicism. Now Sansovino's Library
surpassed the antique, not only in its numerous perfections,
but also because it incorporated a solution to a notorious
technical problem raised by Vitruvius in his discussion of the
Doric order. Sansovino managed to solve it by adapting
from Bramante the device of laying the classical pilaster
against a wider pier.

Sansovino's Library was the major source for the Basilica
in Vicenza by Andrea Palladio (1508–80), actually a repair to
the old justice hall. Palladio managed to make the rebuilding
appear much more perfect than its medieval core permitted,
with great technical skill; and the building could claim to be
the first true basilica in the old Roman sense.

In Florence conflict between republicanism and the pursuit
of power by the Medici, who eventually prevailed, inhibited
civic projects. However, a new library for the Medici church
of San Lorenzo was for public use. The vestibule of the
library, by Michelangelo, is a foremost example of so called
Mannerist architecture, and demonstrates that there is no
better way of showing knowledge of the art than by breaking
all the rules expertly. It possesses of course the vital quality
for the Renaissance, that the Romans would have admired it
had they seen it.

Brunelleschi's pattern of coloured stone membering
against white plaster is retained, as is his proportionateness.
But the stair in particular asserts the higher priority of the
artist's own genius. The form of the stair is not, however,
pointless: Michelangelo intended the middle steps for the
master, the side ones for his servants.

Above ST MARK'S LIBRARY, VENICE, by Jacopo Sansovino.
Left VIEW DOWN ONE SIDE OF THE UFFIZI, FLORENCE, towards the Palazzo Vecchio. These buildings were state offices, with the gallery that is still there on their uppermost floor. They were constructed for dynastic rather than civic reasons. Nevertheless Giorgio Vasari designed them in full consciousness of their scenic effect—extending the public space in front of the Palazzo Vecchio out towards the river Arno.
Right LOGGIA DEI CAPITANI, VICENZA, by Palladio. Loggias served as meeting-points and were standard elements in the main squares of Italian cities by the 15th century. This loggia was converted into a celebration of the Venetian and European victory over the Turks at the Battle of Lepanto in 1570, by the addition of stucco reliefs at its sides.

THE RENAISSANCE TOWN HOUSE

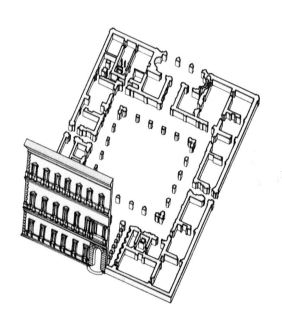

The prototype of all 16th-century Italian town houses, or "palaces", was the "House of Raphael", or the Palazzo Caprini in Rome, built by Bramante for himself, inherited by Raphael, and destroyed in the 17th-century rebuilding of the Borgo, or Vatican city. On the ground floor, the roughened or *rusticated* stonework characteristic of early Renaissance Florentine palaces is retained; on the first floor, following a precedent first set by Alberti, there is the grand parade of a classical order. Bramante produced a memorable combination: the use of columns, not "pilasters", doubled, not single, higher than the ground floor, not the same size, rendered the first floor a true *piano nobile*. The order in fact rises up to incorporate the third storey, of which the windows peep through the frieze. Above all, the ornament is rich and robust, making early Renaissance architecture look spindly

and flat by comparison. This quality is brought out by Palladio's drawing of the palace and is a leading characteristic of Palladio's own architecture.

Successors were created first by Raphael and by others in Rome, then by Giulio Romano in Mantua, Michele Sanmicheli in Venice and Verona and Jacopo Sansovino in Venice. The Palazzo Farnese in Rome by Antonio Sangallo (1483–1546), is the largest, grandest and most harmonious, despite the enlivening dissonances added after his death by Michelangelo; its courtyard is built like the Colosseum. In Venice the largest, grandest and most distinguished palace is Sansovino's Palazzo Corner nicknamed Ca' Grande, which also takes account of the first specifically Venetian classical palace, Codussi's Non Nobis Domine.

Palladio's palaces draw on all these sources. They are all in Vicenza, commissioned by the men who awarded him the design of the Basilica. The most ambitious of them was the Palazzo Chiericati, facing an open square in an undeveloped part of the city. By introducing a loggia into the façade, Palladio rather fondly imagined he could re-create the effect of an ancient "stoa" beside an "agora" or "palaestra". The effect is certainly grand, airy, balanced and wonderfully classical-looking. In other palaces Palladio took greater liberties, or was more inventive or more "Mannerist". The fragmentary Palazzo Porto Breganza runs one single order up the whole façade: the ground-floor windows peep out between the bases of the columns, and the piano nobile windows hang strangely between them. There is nothing so dramatic even in Baroque architecture.

Far left PLAN AND VIEW OF THE FAÇADE OF THE PALAZZO FARNESE IN ROME, begun in 1534 by Antonio da Sangallo the Younger, and completed by Michelangelo shortly after 1546. It is famed for its size, its magnificent vaulted entrance way, its remarkable ornament added by Michelangelo, and for establishing such norms of palace design as the alternating round and triangular heads to the windows.

Near left THE PALAZZO NON NOBIS DOMINE, GRAND CANAL, VENICE, built by Mauro Codussi from about 1502. Its windows compromise between the old Venetian Gothic form and the new classical style, but the almost free-standing columns and the massive friezes are up-to-date with the High Renaissance.

THE RENAISSANCE VILLA

The Renaissance villa was rather more than a house in the country. A *villa suburbana* was hardly in the country at all, but a pleasure chalet just outside the town which one would visit for the day for a party—these usually have no bedrooms. Otherwise villas were usually residential farmhouses, though seldom the owner's only residence, but they had classical overtones as well. In the classical sense, sometimes consciously evoked, they were places of leisure or study, where one could escape children, clients, wives, or the heat—or, after 1347, recurrent outbreaks of the Black Death. Many farmhouses had once been fortified, which may be why vestigial towers may remain in the design; some villas might better be called châteaux. Many villas had outer enclosing walls either because of the plague, or to restrain livestock, or to protect their gardens.

One recurrent villa design is much like the Venetian palace: two towers or blocks flank a central loggia. In the Medici villa at Poggio a Caiano it was decided in the late 15th century to impose a "temple front"—a row of columns under a pediment—across the loggia. The practice by no means became obligatory—even for Palladio—but it provided elegance and grandeur, and largely due to Palladio's variations on the theme spread eventually throughout Europe. Palladio justified the "temple front" on the grounds that the temple had evolved from the house in the first place, which, though possibly true, underlines the fact that no surviving Roman villas were then known.

However, descriptions of Roman villas were well known, and in the suburbana Villa Madama just outside Rome, Raphael (1483–1520) set out to reproduce some of the amenities Pliny had described in his villa at Tusculanum; also some of the features of newly discovered Golden House of Nero (and of the baths partly built over them). It was also fashionable in Rome at this time to create evocatively classical gardens, offering for delectation excavated or modern sculpture, fountains and a cool grotto, or *nymphaeum*. The Palazzo del Tè, a "suburbana" built by Raphael's pupil Giulio Romano (1499–1546) for the Duke of Mantua, makes self-conscious Mannerist play in this spirit in its architecture and art. In much the same taste, the extensive Boboli gardens behind the Pitti palace in Florence, a town house converted into a "suburbana" for the Medici Duke, were laid out in the late 16th century; so were the famous gardens of the Villa d'Este at Tivoli outside Rome (partly on the site of the Emperor Hadrian's villa).

The contrast to Palladio's villas is dramatic: they are stripped, spare, pure, delicate and serious-minded. Partly the serious mind was his patron's; the "suburbana" Villa Rotonda outside Vicenza was built for the decorous bees of an elderly prelate, and the working farmhouses were mostly part of a campaign of agricultural improvement and reclamation. But Palladio himself was equally, if not more, serious-minded, insisting that money be spent not only on function but also on beauty, and that a house without "perfect" proportions was not worth the building. There is much that is ideal in his realized projects.

Opposite page, above THE VILLA AT POGGIO A CAIANO OUTSIDE FLORENCE, built by Antonio da Sangallo for the Medici in the later 15th century.

Opposite page, below A DETAIL OF THE PALAZZO DEL TE OUTSIDE MANTUA, built by Giulio Romano for the Gonzaga Dukes. It shows the palace's famous dropped triglyph—the stone is suspended at mid point between the two columns partly to create the accent traditional at this point, partly to show spirit and wit.

This page, above left THE VILLA BARBARO AT MASER, VENETO, by Palladio. The classical front is flanked by two unpretentious dovecots: the effect is serene and civilized, not imposing.

This page, above right REAR VIEW OF THE VILLA MALCONTENTA, DOLO, VENETO. The organization is comparatively complex, having to match the temple front on the other side of the villa. Note the semicircular window with two mullions in the centre —such "thermal" windows had been seen by Palladio in Roman bath complexes.

Below THE VILLA ROTONDA, VICENZA, VENETO, perhaps the most famous of Palladio's villas and certainly the most "perfect" in its symmetry.

THE RENAISSANCE CHURCH

Brunelleschi's principle, that buildings should have integral proportions, was applied particularly to churches. Under the influence of 15th century Neo-Platonic mysticism, "perfect" proportions were believed to be divine in themselves. However, the adoption of the most fully "perfect", or entirely symmetrical, central plan was limited almost invariably to shrines. Shrines were either tomb chapels, as Alberti's San Sebastiano in Mantua was probably intended to be or as St Peter's in Rome, housing the body of St Peter, certainly was, or they housed a miracle-working image, most commonly a Madonna. For the latter type Brunelleschi's Old Sacristy of San Lorenzo (itself actually a tomb chapel) provided the model—for Santa Maria delle Carceri outside Prato, for S. Biagio outside Montepulciano, and even for S. Maria dei Miracoli in Venice, though that has a long nave.

It was tacitly accepted that for an ordinary church a central plan was impractical, though "perfect" proportions should otherwise prevail. This is clear in the case of San Francesco della Vigna in Venice, designed by Sansovino with a façade by Palladio. One of the friars attached to the church produced a learned memorandum in which he out-

lined the advantages and significances of building the church to a unit of nine foot; he also mentioned both preaching and choir music, for which both a long nave and an extension behind the altar were required. This provision for the choir was a specifically Venetian innovation, to aid acoustics, or even to dramatize them: both sound and light would have welled out from behind the altar in Palladio's San Giorgio Maggiore.

The brief for the church of Il Gesù in Rome by Giacomo Vignola (1507–73) was essentially similar. The concerns were preaching and proportion, though the details of this were left to the architect; and also of course the budget. The Gesù, the first Jesuit church, which was widely influential, was itself an expertly simplified version of Alberti's Sant' Andrea at Mantua. There is no radical change in church plan after Brunelleschi and Alberti, except perhaps for Vignola's experiments with an oval plan, which potentially at least offered a novel combination of central plan and longitudinal nave.

However, the task of applying the classical orders to the standard elevation encouraged an enormous variety of solutions. Even these derived originally from two prototypes by

Alberti: in Santa Maria Novella he had laid one order on top of another; in Sant' Andrea he had threaded a lower order through an upper one. The Romans had done it on triumphal arches: flanking, major columns carry the entablature over the arch, the arch has its own order. But in the second half of the 16th century a third variation appeared: a so-called *giant* order, which seems to be described by Vitruvius, encloses two minor orders on top of one another.

Vignola's Gesù, and subsequent churches built by the Counter-Reformation orders, have the first option, two orders. Though less influential, Palladio's solutions for his three Venetian façades (San Francesco, San Giorgio and the Redentore) were more brilliant, interweaving not merely two orders but two temple fronts.

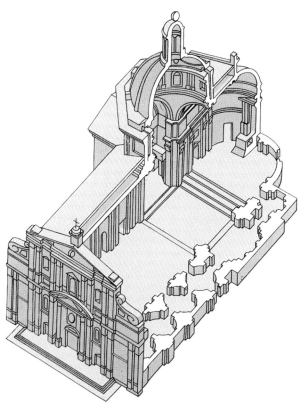

Left TWO VIEWS OF SANTA MARIA DEI MIRACOLI, VENICE, by Tullio Lombardo. It was built to house a miracle-working Madonna, and the flood of pious donations made possible its extremely rich decoration inside and out. The geometric patterns on the marble are typical of the Venetian 15th century.
Right CUTAWAY VIEW OF THE CHURCH OF THE GESÙ, ROME, by Giacomo Vignola. It was at first an extremely bare church, but in the 17th century was adorned with an unprecedented richness of marble, not to mention its enormous ceiling paintings.
Below SAN GIORGIO MAGGIORE, VENICE, by Palladio, perhaps the most successful church of the Renaissance. It is light, clear, grand, harmonious and uplifting.

FRENCH RENAISSANCE

French Renaissance architecture is dictated from a single centre, the French king. Court architects determine the country's style. After piecemeal beginnings, Italian Renaissance artists invited by François I (reigned 1515–47) adapted their native vocabulary to the French needs, and at Fontainebleau created a palace ensemble the equal of anything in Italy in novelty or quality. From the middle of the 16th century, French architects confidently affirmed a national style superseding Italian authority. The architecture books of Philibert de l'Orme and Jacques Androuet du Cerceau make this very clear.

The three French kings who invaded Italy, Charles VIII, Louis XII and François I, were most impressed by the glittering surface of Italian life and art, and set out to acquire not its principles but its ornament. The earliest of François's Loire valley châteaux, Blois, does not even have regularly spaced windows. Its most conspicuous feature, its outside spiral staircase, is not an Italian idea (there is a clear precedent in the 15th-century Gothic palace of chancellor Jacques Coeur at Bourges), and has Gothic vaulting behind its Italianate ornament. Chambord has another such staircase and is still very much a castle like 14th-century castles before it, though it may incorporate one or two traits of Italian villas, and is firmly symmetrical. Its roof would be a forest of Gothic pinnacles, except that so many details are classical.

Gradually the Italian cosmetic becomes part of the French physique. An Italianate or classical repertoire is developed for the tiered portals, mullioned (divided) windows, dormer (roof) windows and gables of French tradition. This repertoire is disposed in a regular way round a customary plan, consisting of a central block (*corps de logis*) with wings extending forward either side of a courtyard fronted by a wall with a central gate. The Italian architect Serlio attempted to introduce an Italian-style loggia into the courtyard, but the idea was quashed. Perhaps instead, a long gallery was introduced at Fontainebleau, to which another fine stair gave access (the present one is the third on the site). The gallery, with its paintings, sculpture and architectural ornament by Primaticcio and Rosso, survives, though much else is lost; also the Château de Madrid is lost, with its even more exuberant, colourful ornament, emulated by Henry VIII at his palace of Nonesuch, also lost, and by Joachim II, Elector of Brandenburg, in a lost palace in Berlin.

The subsequent phase, which may be marked by the starting of the oldest element in the present Louvre, the Cour Carré, in 1546, shows instead a balanced or massive coherence, even though there is still much Mannerist detail. The Cour Carré has balance; the surviving gateway of the Château d' Anet is massive; the Château d' Ecouen has the first use of the "giant" order in France.

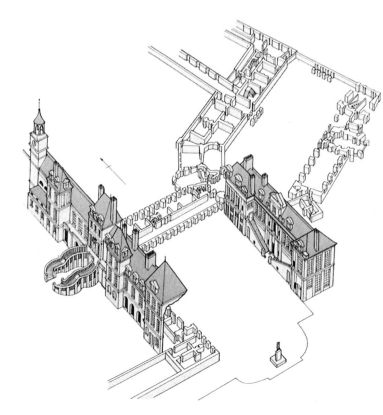

This page, above THE CHÂTEAU AT CHAMBORD, begun in 1519. Its completion belongs to the later part of François I's reign, to the 1530s.
Opposite page, above THE STAIRCASE AT BLOIS, IN THE LOIRE VALLEY, dating from the years 1515 to 1524.
Opposite page, below A PLAN OF THE CHÂTEAU AT FONTAINEBLEAU. The curved staircase (not the original 16th-century one) leads into the Long Gallery, almost all that remains of the work of Rosso and Primaticcio in the palace.

This page, above A VIEW ACROSS THE GARDENS TO THE FONTAINEBLEAU PALACE.
This page, left THE PORTE DORÉE (GOLDEN GATE) AT FONTAINEBLEAU, built by Gilles Le Breton between 1528 and 1540. The ornament is classical, but peculiarly French is its arrangement into vertical strips—Gothic taste living on in the new forms.

GERMAN RENAISSANCE

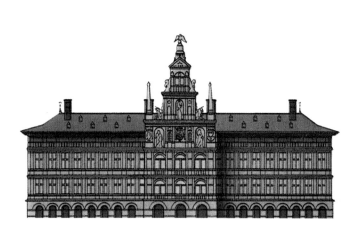

In the Holy Roman Empire the diffusion of Italian Renaissance ornament was much more sporadic and quirky than in France, and though it began at much the same time it never matured in the same way. In the last years of the 15th century, however, the architect Benedikt Ried in Prague achieved instantly a brilliant fusion of Gothic and classical and demonstrated a mastery superior to Bramante's in Milan, if not perhaps to his work in Rome. He treats the orders with cavalier freedom, but they are solid and elegant; in the Vladislav Hall they harmonize with the Gothic ribs. In St Barbara at Kutná Hora the geometry of the ribs is as divine as any Italian church.

At first, before the appearance of textbooks, immigrant Italian artists carried various elements of the Italian Renaissance to all parts of Europe, to England, Poland, Hungary and Russia as rapidly as to the German-speaking lands. Nowhere do they affect the elements of building, only its ornament. Since the Italians offered no interesting ornament for ceilings, Gothic ribs continue to be used right into the 17th century. Much the same elements as in France are subjected to ornament, though the plan of Schlösser ("castles") is less constant than of châteaux: the stair at Schloss Hartenfels, Torgau, is one like the stair at Blois; there are dormers, gables, pitched roofs, and elaborate piled-on portals. Equivalent to Fontainebleau are imitations of Giulio Romano's Palazzo del Té, at Trent on the border between Germany and Italy, and at Landshut in Bavaria.

In the Netherlands and in France the new ornament eventually ceases to be something on the surface and becomes part of the fabric. By the middle of the century the classical style has been assimilated. In Germany, though flat and single forms give way to thicker and compound ones, there is no settled vision. But it is important to remember here the German resistance even to Romanesque. It is not a failure to adapt; there simply never was a comparable tradition or innate sense of proportion to which Italian ornament could have been adapted.

There was no lack of interest in theory or direct contact with Italy and the antique. Ottheinrich van der Pfalz, builder of the Ottheinrichsbau at Schloss Heidelberg, had studied the works of Vitruvius. The Antiquarium of Duke Albrecht V of Bavaria in his Residenz at Munich was not only a long gallery; it also was meant to be what Vitruvius had called a "cryptoporticus", a vaulted gallery. Yet the broad arches on stubby piers are neither classical nor Italianate.

These are the years of the Reformation in Germany, but there is no difference yet between Protestant and Catholic church architecture. The Jesuit church of St Michael in Munich has better Protestant precedents than Catholic ones. It resembles a design developed in the chapels of Schlösser and soon taken up widely: a hall church, but the aisles have a gallery like the circle in a theatre; the east end is modest, with the emphasis on the congregation.

Far left THE TOWN HALL, ANTWERP, of the mid-16th century, attributed to Cornelius Floris. The Renaissance ornament is applied with considerable sophistication to the central "frontispiece".
Next left, opposite page THE BAKOCZ CHAPEL, ESZTERGOM CATHEDRAL, HUNGARY. Thanks to the policies and culture of King Matthias Corvinus, Hungary had been open to Italian influence since the mid-15th century: this accomplished Renaissance work is late 15th-century.
This page, left THE CHURCH OF SAINT BARBARA, KUTNÁ HORA, CZECHOSLOVAKIA, by Benedikt Ried. Its dazzling vaults have ribs that spiral in a complex virtuoso geometry.
This page, below THE TOWN HALL, AUGSBURG. This dates altogether from the early 17th century, and is by Elias Holl.

IBERIAN RENAISSANCE

Influences both from Italy and from the Netherlands had percolated through to Spain and Portugal throughout the 15th century: there is no sudden outbreak of Italian ornament comparable to the rash that infected the rest of Europe in the 1490s. Instead, classically derived forms fuse and merge with the native vocabulary, which already mingled Gothic and Islamic motifs, to produce distinct styles known as *Plateresque* in Spain and *Manueline* in Portugal. Both of these styles prevailed from the beginning to the middle of the 16th century, and extended beyond the Iberian peninsula to Sicily, which had been in Aragonese hands since the late 13th century.

By the middle of the 16th century Spain had emerged as the major European power, enriched by the wealth its ships brought back from the New World, following its discovery by Columbus in 1492. In the same year Granada fell, the culmination of a long campaign to expel the medieval Arab conquerors; and the whole country was soon united under the Most Catholic King. Portugal was briefly annexed to Spain in 1581.

Although "Plateresque" derives from *platería*, meaning silverware, it is a purely architectural style, developed by masons and not adopted by them from elsewhere. It is comparable to English Perpendicular, although its forms are different, because it is a surface incrustation, and yet it is quite highly organized: the basic shape of the building is uncompromised. Although they may be carved in a rich texture, there are clear framing elements. The preponderance of Islamic, Gothic and Italianate in the mixture varies: the portal of the University of Salamanca recalls first of all Gothic portals, partly because it incorporates heraldic devices as Gothic por-

tals often do; the convents at Belém and Tomar in Portugal have an Islamic flavour thanks to the lobes on the inside of their arches. The Cathedral built at Granada after the conquest is predominantly classical, though its proportions are Gothic and its vaulting ribs recall French Flamboyant ones.

Just after the middle of the century there is a reaction against these highly decorative styles and a stricter classicism comes in, which often seems by contrast excessively plain. The monumental, austere, gloomy Escorial, a church plus monastery plus palace built for King Philip II just outside Madrid from 1562, marks the turning point. Though the architects were Spanish, there is a close dependence on Italian examples: for instance the centrepiece of the main front is a church front in the pattern of the Gesù in Rome; one of the courtyards derives directly from the Palazzo Farnese in Rome. Also, the church at the centre of the complex and indeed the plan of the complex as a whole were designed to embody a "perfect" geometry.

There is much about the Escorial that can be associated with the new strictness of the Catholic Counter-Reformation, but the academic restraint and the calling to order of all this ornament also has parallels with the changing mood of architecture in Europe as a whole in the mid 16th century.

THE CLOISTER OF THE CONVENT OF CHRIST, TOMAR, showing its typically "Manueline" arches. The detail is from a window of the chapter house in the cloister.

Above THE ESCORIAL, OUTSIDE MADRID, SPAIN, begun by Juan Bautista de Toledo and completed by Juan de Herrera. The ideal geometry of the building was further perfected by the incorporation of features of the Temple of Solomon as described in the Bible. It was originally intended also as a memorial to Philip II's father, the Emperor Charles V.
Below THE FAÇADE OF THE PORTAL OF THE UNIVERSITY OF SALAMANCA is a rich example of the Spanish Plateresque style. It dates from after 1513.

MAYAN, TOLTEC AND AZTEC

Until the Spaniards arrived in the early 16th century, the cultures of Middle and South America (Mayan, Aztec, Tolmec and Inca, to name the most important), evolved without any contact whatsoever with the outside world. This astonishing fact is balanced by another: the inconsistencies within these cultures themselves. Despite extremely advanced knowledge and achievements in such abstruse subjects as astronomy and the measurement of time, the people of the Americas had no wheel, no systematic use of beasts of burden, and no system of weights and measures. They did not use iron tools, nor did they have the true arch, that hallmark, in Western eyes, of a sophisticated architectural skill. Yet despite these deficiences, they produced some of the most awe-inspiring buildings the world has seen.

The earliest great example in Mesoamerica is Teotihuacan, the City of the Gods, about 30 miles from present-day Mexico City. Originally the capital of the Mayas (who flourished from the 2nd century BC to the 15th century AD), this city of 8 square miles was at its height from 200BC to AD750. A major centre for religious rituals, it was dominated by two vast temple-pyramids, the Pyramid of the Sun and the smaller Pyramid of the Moon, both dating from the time of Christ. These monoliths are the largest and oldest in the Americas, and served as models for all the pyramids that followed them. The top of the structure was truncated to provide a flat area for the temple proper, while its sides were stepped in several ascending terraces. Monumental stairways linking each terrace were designed to appear continuous when viewed from below. Another important temple at Teotihuacan was dedicated to Quetzalcoatl, the Plumed Serpent, one of the most powerful and pervasive gods of Mesoamerica. Teotihuacan was destroyed by fire in the 8th century, but the worship of Quetzalcoatl was adopted by the Tolmecs when they settled in Central Mexico in the 10th century, and later by their successors, the Aztecs.

The Yucatan is particularly rich in Mayan and Tolmec remains. Perhaps the most beautiful Mayan city of all is Uxmal, in northwest Yucatan, built towards the end of the 10th century. Here the highlight is the Governor's Palace; a

Pre-Columbian

Top left TEOTIHUACAN, CITY OF THE GODS, MEXICO (*c.* 200BC–AD750) was a major city for Mayan religious ritual. The sheer scale of its buildings, given the comparatively simple knowledge of architectural techniques, is extraordinary.

Bottom left Detail of the carving on the terraces of the Pyramid Temple of Quetzalcoatl, the Plumed Serpent. Mayan artists excelled in low-relief carvings, which often took grotesque or hybrid forms, themselves skilfully abstracted into geometric motifs and patterns.

Top right CHICHEN ITZA, YUCATAN (main buildings 12th century AD): THE *CARACOL* OR OBSERVATORY. The name derives from the Spanish for snail, and refers to the fine circular staircase inside the building which was built in five stages over a number of years. Agricultural, religious and astronomical data were calculated from sitings of the stars taken through apertures in the domed upper structure.

Bottom right UXMAL, YUCATAN (late 10th century AD) built at the height of the Mayan renaissance and perhaps the most beautiful of their cities.

superbly proportioned structure composed of a central building flanked by two identical wings, the vaults of which were the highest in the Mayan world. The play of light and shade is cleverly accentuated by the low relief carving (in which the Mayas excelled) that adorns the upper half of the exterior with over 20,000 geometric and symbolic motifs. This assured product of the Mayan renaissance has been called "the single most magnificent building ever constructed in the Americas".

Similarly skilful balancing of mass with ornament is to be seen at El Castillo, the Quetzalcoatl temple and most impressive part of the Tolmec-Maya city of Chichen Itza, also in the Yucatan. Here the stepped pyramid, the stairs and the temple itself are all adorned with rich carving—principally serpent

motifs, jaguars, eagles and warriors. Tenochtitlan, the capital of the mighty and bloodthirsty Aztecs, was begun in AD1325, in the middle of Lake Texoco on the site of present-day Mexico City. At 2,400m (8,000ft) above sea level, it was divided and irrigated by a grid-system of canals, and joined to the mainland by three great causeways raised on dykes. The sacred centre, the Great Plaza, probably contained temples to the gods of the Rain, Winds and Sun, while the highest pyramid supported the temple of the Aztec tribal deity, Huitzilopochtli. The Conquistadors were reputedly amazed by the sophisticated planning of Tenochtitlan when they took the city in AD1521. Unfortunately their appreciation of Aztec workmanship did not prevent their burning the city to the ground and slaughtering its inhabitants.

THE INCAS OF PERU

At first sight, the Inca civilization of the Peruvian Andes may appear architecturally inferior to the Mayan culture of Mexico and Guatamala. Much more recent, shorter lasting and leaving far less to posterity, the Incas created an architecture that lagged behind the Mayan achievement in design, proportion and embellishment. But in their sheer scale, their grandeur of conception and their basic architectural craftsmanship, the Incas are unparallelled.

In fact, the Incas were arguably the most accomplished stonemasons ever. Their stone was quarried in enormous blocks without explosives; finely shaped and finished without iron chisels, it was transported without the wheel or draught animals for anything up to 20 miles over the most difficult mountain terrain. And when assembled, these blocks were finally placed into exact position with the benefit of only the most unsophisticated system of leverage, so accurately, indeed, that a knife blade could not be inserted between them.

A varied technique was needed for construction. At Cuzco, the capital, more or less regular rectangular blocks were used, while at Sacsahuaman, the mountain fortress defending Cuzco, the stones were irregular polygons. Everywhere it is the scale that amazes. At Sacsahuaman, for example, these blocks were sometimes as much as 8m (27ft)

high, and the north wall of the city-fortress stretches unbroken for 360m (1,200ft). Just how the Incas managed to assemble their mighty buildings is one of the fascinating but unsolved mysteries of architectural history, like the construction of the Egyptian pyramids, or the true meaning of Stonehenge.

Moreover, the Inca achievement was spread over a vast area. Their Empire began as a small kingdom at Cuzco around AD1200, and by AD1530 it had expanded to include much of Ecuador, and stretched south through Peru and Bolivia, reaching into parts of the Argentine and Chile. Running through this territory was the Royal Road of the Andes, no less than 3,250 miles through the most demanding conditions. This highway remained the longest arterial road in the world up until the 19th century. The Incas also boasted a coastal road, only a little shorter. Both roads used bridges extensively: rivers were spanned by cantilevered or pontoon constructions, while deep gorges were crossed by suspended rope walkways.

Cities were strung along these roads. Most of these were designed around a central plaza, adjacent to which stood the principal temple, dedicated to the Sun, and the palace dwellings of the aristocracy. Design and buildings were quite uniform, testifying to a well-organized and centralized system of government within the Empire. This organization is best seen at Machu Picchu, whose austere granite remains unfailingly impress all who see them.

We find virtually no traces of ornamentation on Inca buildings. Many surfaces were left plain; those deemed worthy of embellishment were granted the most lavish treatment—being plated in sheets of beaten gold. We can only imagine the splendour of such cities. An early visitor to Cuzco reported seeing ". . . a quadrangular building . . . measuring 350 paces from corner to corner, entirely plated with gold; of these gold plates they took down 700, which together weighed 500 *pesos* of gold . . .". And ironically it was just this

Top left MACHU PICCHU, PERU (13th century AD), a fortress city dramatically situated above the Urubamba gorge. It consists of an elaborate cluster of sacred plazas, temples and houses that cling to the terraced mountainside.
Bottom left MACHU PICCHU, SOLAR OBSERVATORY.

Top SACSAHUAMAN, PERU (AD1438–1500), was a mountain fortress defending the Inca capital Cuzco. This huge structure was built by 30,000 Indians using only the most primitive of tools. The north wall is 1,500 ft long.
Above GENERAL VIEW OF CUZCO AND SACSAHUAMAN.

splendour that spelled the end of the Incas. The Spaniards, never the gentlest of colonizers, could not resist such fabulous riches. Just 12 years after Cortes had destroyed Montezuma's capital Tenochtitlan, Pizarro, the scourge of Peru, destroyed Cuzco. The Inca leader Atahualpa and 6,000 of his followers, who had surrendered under a flag of truce, were ruthlessly massacred in 1532. With its central authority defeated, the Empire collapsed. The loss was incalculable and incomparable.

OTTOMAN AND SAFAVID

Above THE SULTAN AHMED, OR "BLUE" MOSQUE, ISTANBUL (1609–17) was built by the imperial architect Mehmed. It is the only Istanbul mosque with six minarets.

Right THE GREAT MOSQUE OF SELIM II, EDIRNE (1569–75) was considered by its 80-year-old architect, the brilliant Sinan, to be his masterpiece.

Bottom right VIEW OVER THE TOPKAPI PALACE COMPLEX, ISTANBUL (1462–72). Its completion marked Istanbul's establishment as the seat of the imperial government of the Ottomans.

In some parts of the world of Islam we find buildings that are impressive but not essentially creative. But such a charge could never be levelled at the Ottoman Turks, whose architecture was profuse and inventive. The experiences of Byzantine, Seljuk and Armenian forerunners were refined and subjected to constant experiment by a group of architects whose most brilliant member was the celebrated Sinan (1490–1580). There are more than 350 buildings ascribed to this native of Anatolia: the influence he exerted on his successors was considerable. Developing the Byzantine domed cross plan, Sinan and his followers addressed themselves to setting a perfect circle on a perfect square. Their most successful structures are austere and geometrical, with decoration playing a secondary role.

In the domed central-plan Seyzade Mosque (1544–48) in Istanbul, Sinan revived classical method by setting the drum of the dome on four arches opening into four apses with semi-domes. The massive exterior is offset not only by the apparent lightness of the dome but by two needle-like minarets typical of Ottoman structures. The Suleiman Mosque (1550–57) was inspired by Justinian's Hagia Sophia. Placed atop Istanbul's highest hill, it has the same ground plan as Hagia Sophia, and continues its theme of clustered domes and arches ascending monumentally, yet gracefully upwards. The Great Mosque of Selim II at Edirne (1569–75) was the architect's own favourite. Again dominating a city from a hilltop, its harmonious outline is accentuated by four slender minarets. The internal space, under a dome raised on eight arches spreading the weight onto as many columns, has

an extraordinary feeling of lightness and graceful proportion.

As we have already seen, the Persian architectural tradition was a venerable and highly accomplished one. The last important phase of building in Persia belongs to the Safavids (1501–1736), a wealthy and essentially aristocratic dynasty. To the ancient heritage were added traits derived from the predecessors of the Safavids, the Timurids—bold experiment in the creation of space and lavish tiled decoration in blue, turquoise, yellow and green. A superb Timurid mosque is the Blue Mosque at Tabriz (1462–65).

The most sumptuous display of Safavid style is at Isfahan, their capital under Shah Abbas the Great. Nowhere else in Islam was brickwork so relentlessly patterned and embellished; nowhere else does purity of line run such a risk of disappearing under profuse decoration. Such virtuosity has often met with a harsh response from Western critics, who hate to see structure compromised by "a decorative crust" of excessive colour. But such criticisms not only undervalue the luxuriously refined world of the Safavids, but fail to appreciate the desire of the Muslim artist to create effects of transcendence in the viewer. The balance of geometric (male) and vegetal (female) elements, the use of stylized calligraphy, and the suggestion of a whirling dance of energy within all appearance are the results not just of a overly sensuous court but of a mystical philosophy that is found in the best of Islamic culture. Such Isfahan monuments as the Mosque of Shaykh Lutf Allah or the Masjid-i-Jami illustrate, in Persian terms at least, that most popular saying of the Prophet: "God is beauty, and He loves what is beautiful".

Below TOPKAPI PALACE, INTERIOR OF THE HAREM QUARTERS.
Right MASJID-I- JAMI, OR "FRIDAY" MOSQUE, ISFAHAN, IRAN. Its domed chambers date from the 11th century.

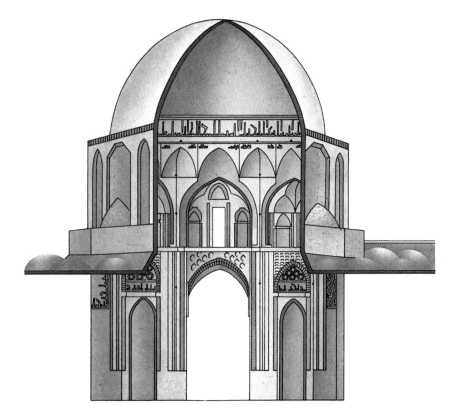

ISLAM IN INDIA

It would be hard to imagine two world views more different than Islam and Hinduism. Doctrinally, socially and aesthetically they were diametrically opposed, yet they met head on in India and have existed there together for almost 1,000 years. The conflict between the two was not only religious. The Mongols (Mughals), Afghans, Turks and Persians who entered in waves from the northwest were above all freebooters, seeking fortune from India's fabled wealth. Ruthless iconoclasts though they were, they could also build, and the hybrid Indo-Islamic school is one of the most interesting chapters in the history of architecture.

The invaders brought a mature system of building, using true arch and dome. They met an indigenous post-and-beam tradition and one of decorative sculptural embellishment. The first mosque in India, the Might of Islam (1192) in Delhi, shows the style emerging. Here the Muslims flattened scores of temples and built over the remains, using some bits of the earlier structures in their own. Thus pillars carved in a very un-Islamic style (for instance the vase-and-foliage fertility motif) adorn the cloisters of the prayer hall. The Persian victory tower inspired the minaret here, the ornately carved Qutb Minar (1199). The main iwan is an ogee arch utilizing both Hindu corbelling and Islamic voussoirs.

Mosques and tombs displaying Turkish, Afghan and Timurid influence were built by various sultanates over the next 300 years. But it is in 1526, with the arrival of the Mughals, that the Indo-Islamic style comes of age. The second Mughal emperor, Humayun, spent many years in exile in Persia. When he did return, in 1555, he brought with him ideas and craftsmen from the Safavid court. From now on, Persian influence was to quicken the new style. Humayun's tomb in Delhi (1556–72) was built by an Iranian architect. It boasts an airy Persian dome atop a façade lightened by many niches and false windows, and is set in the middle of an ornamental Persian garden (*chahar bagh*).

Humayun's son, Akbar the Great, was a wise and tolerant ruler, keen to reconcile the various factions within his empire. Architecturally, this allowed an eclecticism most successfully realized at Fatehpur Sikri (1558–82) near Agra. This red sandstone citadel is essentially Iranian in concept, but the pillars, corbels, architraves, heavy sloping eaves, balconies and pillared domes (*chatris*) are unashamedly Hindu. The somewhat monumental heaviness of the place is relieved by the yellow sandstone and white marble of the royal Friday Mosque (1571–72). The combination of sandstone and marble, with the latter gradually predominating, is a feature of Mughal buildings, especially in Lahore, Delhi and Agra.

The garden tomb was brought to perfection in India's most celebrated building, the Taj Mahal (1632–43) in Agra. Shah Jehan's mausoleum for his favourite wife is one of the truly great buildings of the world. Constructed of white marble, inlaid with black marble outside and exquisite precious and semi-precious stones inside, part of its extraordinary effect derives from its judicious setting in an ornamental garden on the banks of the Jumna river. Architecturally, it is a brilliant synthesis of two traditions; symbolically, it is a representation of the pearl of Paradise, the eternal feminine nature from which all creation arises at the will of Allah.

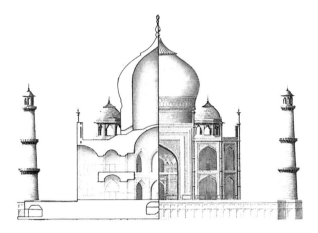

Top TAJ MAHAL, AGRA (1632–43). The Persian double dome is 230 ft high. The sarcophagi of Shah Jehan and his wife lie in the crypt.
Middle GOLCONDA, near Hyderabad. Royal tomb of the Shahi dynasty (1507–1687).

Bottom left FATEHPUR SIKRI, NEAR AGRA (1569–84). View over the Musician's Tank to the Five Storied Palace.
Bottom right FATEHPUR SIKRI, detail of carving from the Turkish Wife's Palace.

Above THE QUTB MINAR, DELHI (1199). This Indian version of the Persian victory tower served as the minaret of the first mosque in India, the Might of Islam, built by Qutbuddin Aibak. It stands 238 ft high and rises in five storeys, built of red and buff sandstone sometimes faced with marble. The three original storeys are heavily indented with varied styles of fluting: alternately round and angular for the first storey, round on the second and angular on the third. The tower was damaged twice by lightning—in 1326 and 1368—and its crowning cupola fell down during an earthquake in 1803. **Left** THE BALCONY OF ITS FIRST STOREY, showing *muqarna* stalactite bracketing and rusticated decoration. The calligraphic bands are in Persian ornamental kufic script, and proclaim the glory of the builder.

JAPANESE SENSIBILITY

One of the most striking religious structures in Japan is the celebrated Phoenix Hall of the Byodoin Temple (1053) in rural Uji-machi. This is a fine example of the Heian and Fujiwara periods (784–1185) when architecture developed independently of the decorative trends occurring in China. Byodoin preserves a classical clarity of line typical of the T'ang period, in its central pavilion, transverse galleries and corner pavilions.

At this time, too, capital cities were being laid out on Chinese lines: rectangular blocks divided by broad avenues and arranged around a central palace. The civil war years prior to the establishment of the Tokugawa shogunate in 1616 gave rise to another form of secular architecture: massive fortified residences in stone, of which Himeji Castle (begun late 16th century) is the most assured. Its many stories superimposed on each other, though each retains the Chinese curved eaves and hipped gable, are a Japanese innovation.

In Japan, no less than in China, the creative tension between life at court and the more peaceful life in the country was of great cultural importance. One tangible result was the creation of the *besso*, a rambling country residence where the aristocracy could enjoy family time away from the pressures and intrigues of their work. The besso generally displays a less rigid adherence to Chinese norms, and so in both form and function expresses something characteristically Japanese. The supreme example of the besso is the Katsura Palace (early 17th century) in Kyoto. It is set in wooded sur-roundings, in accordance with a trend, observable in the cultivated nobility since the 14th century, to return to the simplicity of nature. The architect, Kobori Enshu, was a master of the Zen tea ceremony, and his work incorporates both the farmer's cottage and the ceremonial tea hut in its conscious re-creation of a rustic idyll, albeit on a grand scale. The buildings are framed in light timbers, closed by unadorned walls, and employ a triangular truss in the roof, rather than the pillars and bracketing of the Chinese convention. The basic unit of measurement was the *tatami* (rice straw mat) and the wood was left plain, sometimes still with the bark.

The three main buildings show a refined balance between the formal *shoin* style and the domestic *sukiya* style. The form governs the entrance block (*ko-shoin*) with its guest apartments and public refreshment rooms. The latter is displayed in the middle (*chu-soin*) and rear (*shin-goten*) blocks, each having small intimate rooms for the family to relax in, including an area for the storing of musical instruments. A sense of ease of movement is encouraged by sliding screens covered with translucent paper as doors and partitions, and by the unobtrusive verandahs to bridge the gap between house and garden. Indeed, both elements were designed very much as complementary parts of a whole. Great attention is paid to framed, formal views from various angles, and the meticulously designed garden, said to be the most perfect of its kind, is laid out with interconnecting stone pathways.

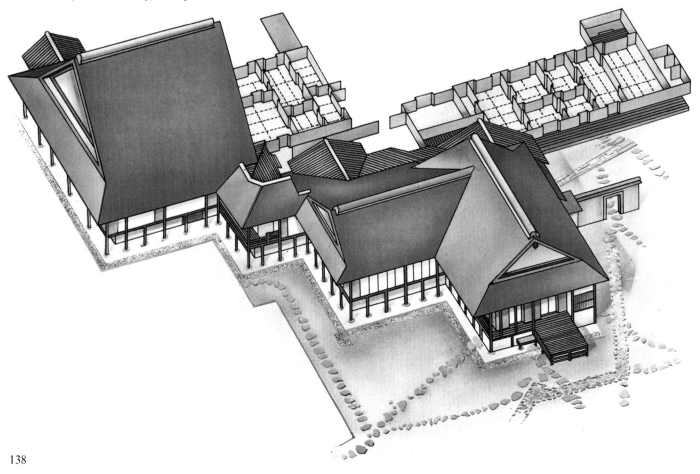

Later Oriental

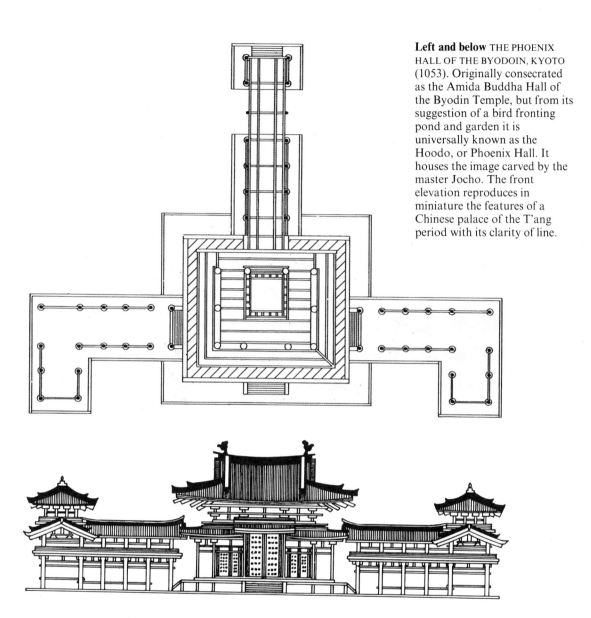

Left and below THE PHOENIX HALL OF THE BYODOIN, KYOTO (1053). Originally consecrated as the Amida Buddha Hall of the Byodin Temple, but from its suggestion of a bird fronting pond and garden it is universally known as the Hoodo, or Phoenix Hall. It houses the image carved by the master Jocho. The front elevation reproduces in miniature the features of a Chinese palace of the T'ang period with its clarity of line.

Left KATSURA PALACE, KYOTO (early 17th century), built by Kobori Enshu to express his ideals of rustic simplicity and picturesque nature. The complex is divided into three components, Ko-shoin, Chu-shoin and Shin-goten, which are designed to be of a piece with the beautiful ornamental garden. There is an atmosphere of austerity and balance throughout, and the palace was strongly influenced by traditional tea ceremony architecture.

CHINA: HOUSE AND CITY

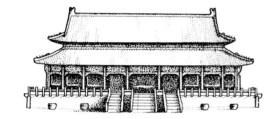

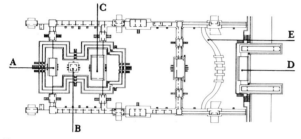

Above THE FORBIDDEN CITY, PEKING (15th century, with substantial 17th century reworking). A) Hall of Protective Harmony (*Baohedian*); B) Hall of Middle Harmony (*Zhongedian*); C) Hall of Supreme Harmony (*Taihedian*); D) Meridian Gate (*Wumen*); E) Golden River. **Top** Hall of Supreme Harmony. **Below** Entrance to the Hall of Supreme Harmony. The monumental bronze lions are from the Ching dynasty (1644–1911).

The most impressive example of the Chinese ideal of a ruler's fortified city is the Forbidden City in Peking. Planned and begun by the mighty Kublai Khan in the middle of the 13th century, it dates properly from 1404, and is the only surviving imperial palace in China. The lay-out of the complex follows a pattern in keeping with the general practice of Chinese town planning. The rectangular plan, the north-south axis with entrance from the south, and the central palace and command post are all inherited from pre-Han times.

At the centre of the complex lies the Purple Forbidden City (so called from the colour of its walls), the residence of the Emperor and Son of Heaven. Around this imperial and symbolic hub a second walled rectangle, the Imperial City, formed the seat of the government, with residences of court functionaries and departments of administration. The walls of this compound no longer exist; its southern and main gate, the famous Gate of Heavenly Peace, now opens onto Tian an Men Square, the burial place of Mao Tse Tung and centre of modern Peking. The third area was the Inner, or Tartar City, where the alien Manchu (or Tartar) rulers lived. (It was during their reign that the Chinese were made to wear pig-tails as a sign of submission). The fourth precinct was the Outer City, where the native Chinese lived. An interesting light is shed on traditional Chinese values by the fact that only three categories of citizen had to live beyond these outer

walls: merchants, prostitutes and foreigners.

The grandiose plan (measuring 5.3 miles north-south by 5 miles east-west) has not been affected by the many later additions and alterations, particularly attributable to the Manchu Ching period (AD1644–1911). The enormous open courtyards, the sweeping roof lines and judicious blocks of sombre colour are highlighted by two features typical of the Ming period (AD1368–1644). One is the combination of brick and marble with wooden pillars, and the gentle waves of bridges, eaves and roofs that these produce. The other is carved ornament: flowers, clouds, imperial dragons (male) and phoenixes (female) entwine themselves sinuously around stairs, balustrades and eaves. In addition, clusters of extravagant polychrome brackets support the beautifully tiled roofs, while ceramic designs enliven the walls dividing the various courtyards.

The interior of a Chinese building, of whatever scale, followed precise rules of symmetry derived from the precepts of Confucianism, the system of social ethics that governed all aspects of traditional Chinese life. Each room had its function in the family rites that ordered daily life. In contrast to this formality, the garden was an expression of the spontaneous and mysterious in life, and of man's inescapable relationship with nature. The philosophy that shaped the garden was Taoism, a contemplative outlook emphasizing harmony with all life. Both house and garden were sited according to the principles of orientation laid down by *feng shui*. This was an ancient magic dealing with the correct relationship of objects with each other and the cosmic energy-lines so as to ensure the maximum harmony. Such abstract considerations, quite mystical to the Western mind, should not be forgotten as the hidden, but underlying, premises on which the practical architectural achievements of the Chinese rest.

Left THE TEMPLE OF HEAVEN, PEKING (1420, rebuilt 18th century). This circular building stands on a triple marble platform and has brilliant blue roof tiles as befits its function. Here the Emperor gave offerings to his ancestors at the New Year, before giving offerings to the nature deities at the nearby Altar of Heaven, a mound of three concentric marble terraces. The three roofs represent the heaven and earth, with the Emperor as intermediary between them.

Below GARDEN OF HARMONY, SOUZHOU (18th century).

TEXTBOOK ARCHITECTURE

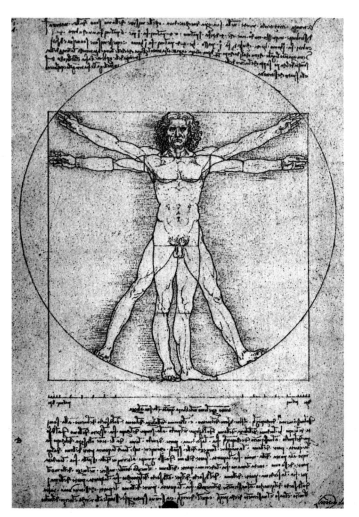

Both in art and in architecture preparatory diagrams, drawings and sketches had long preceded commencement of the work itself. The use of these tools now multiplied and became more comprehensive. Leonardo is credited as the first man to have "thought on paper" both in art and in architecture—to have tried out in free sketches variations on a chosen theme, to have composed, for instance, centrally planned churches even though nobody had asked him to build one. Indeed, although Leonardo built nothing himself, he may have influenced Bramante, who enjoyed considerable architectural patronage.

In the 15th century the invention of woodcutting, engraving and printing followed in rapid succession. The works of both Alberti and Vitruvius on architecture had been printed before the century was out, and in 1521 the first translation of Vitruvius appeared, with diagrams. Vitruvius's difficult text was gradually elucidated and correlated with the details of surviving classical buildings, which began at this time to be surveyed accurately and committed to paper. In 1550 a memorable edition was produced by Daniele Barbaro, with illustrations by Palladio.

Much more influential than either Alberti or Vitruvius, however, were the books on architecture by Sebastiano Serlio (1475–1554). These books were the basis of the spread and shape of the style of architecture called Mannerism throughout Europe, granting of course that not all the designs in it were Serlio's own; also, many architects made use of them without reproducing them (including Palladio). Serlio published the first volume in Venice in 1537, and when

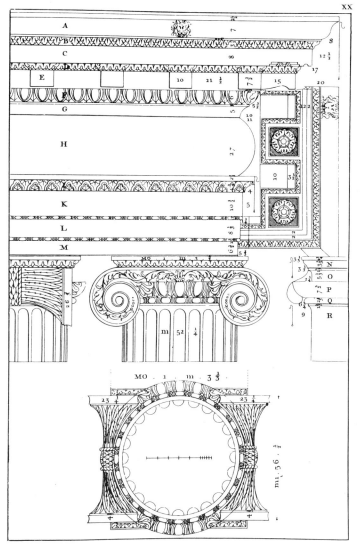

the second was published in 1540, dedicated to the French king, he was invited to France, where he published four further volumes. The books were picture books of architecture, showing various types of building, the details of the orders, and various ideas for designs. The sixth volume, a collection of portal designs, is particularly interesting; it provides exactly what northern architects were looking for, ideas for features on a building. They are indeed *frontispieces*, the French term both for the decorative design at the beginning of a book and for the portal of the forecourt of a mansion. Northern Mannerist architecture consists, broadly speaking, of arrangements of frontispieces. Serlio was soon translated into many languages, and others published their own designs in a similar pattern, notably Netherlandish designers, the last and greatest of them Wendel Dietterlin (1550–99).

Palladio's *Four Books of Architecture*, published in 1570, stand in much the same way to 17th-century architecture in northern Europe as Serlio's did to 16th-century building. His work appealed to changed times partly for the same reasons as Serlio's: it was lucid, practical and well illustrated; and partly because what was wanted was not frontispieces but order, grandeur and propriety. It was an ideal tool for what has been called the "academic" reaction to Mannerism at the end of the 16th century. If Palladio's influence was limited in France, that may be because in France this "academic" trend was already established.

Above left LEONARDO DA VINCI'S FAMOUS DRAWING OF "VITRUVIAN MAN". According to Vitruvius, the proportions of the human body dictated those used in building. The Vitruvian doctrine was a great fillip to the Renaissance, since it meant for them that the classical orders, like man, were in the image and likeness of God.

Below left Modern drawings of the capitals of the orders. From left to right, Doric, Ionic, Corinthian, Composite. (Composite combines Corinthian and Ionic.) The orders were also ranked: Doric is the most primitive and massive, the Composite the most ornate and refined: different orders were appropriate to buildings of different functions.

Above and right DRAWINGS FROM PALLADIO'S FOUR BOOKS OF ARCHITECTURE, first published in Venice in 1570. One shows the capital of the Ionic order; the other Palladio's design for the Villa Sarego.

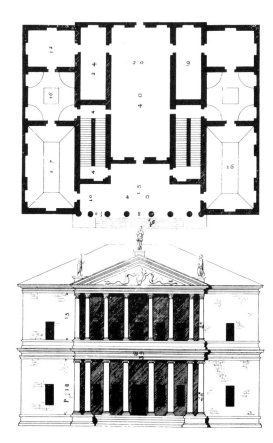

ENGLAND AND INIGO JONES

The reign of King Henry VIII (1509–47) in England coincided with the reign of King Francois I in France (1515–47): there was a parallel development in architecture. For all the rivalry of the two kings, François clearly set the lead, even if Henry employed his own Italian craftsmen: actually at least one of his Italians had previously worked at Fontainebleau, and the English version of the Italian taste tended very much to be French-influenced.

After the death of Henry VIII, Lord Protector Somerset acquired a role comparable to that of Constable Montmorency under the French successor to François I, Henri II. It is interesting to note that Protector Somerset's new house on the Thames (now known as Old Somerset House) had features in common with Montmorency's Ecouen, outside Paris. Its land front had a central portal and two flanking window units composed with the orders in the latest and balanced French fashion. However, it also had subtle differences that mark the emergence of an English style that develops away from French "classicism". One of these was the cut-stone facing; another was the setting of the window elements not at the corner but just in off the corner, heralding the way Elizabethan "prodigy" houses consist of spare, jutting window blocks arranged around a square in elegant symmetry. There are direct connections between Old Somerset House, now lost, and Longleat, the earliest Elizabethan great house built deliberately for show and to please the Queen, as a "prodigy". Part of the show was the obvious, though complex symmetry, into which the functions of the house had to be fitted rather haphazardly. On a smaller scale this symmetry could take on metaphysical significance, as was the case in the triangular building at Rushton representing the Trinity, for instance.

Old Somerset House was also an important influence on the building of Inigo Jones (1573–1652). Jones is the most conspicuous example of the "academic" trend that emerges from 16th-century Mannerism. He not only used Palladio as a grammar, starting off from a Palladian example for each of his own designs, but had been round Italy checking the buildings and the classical ruins against Palladio's book, as the annotations of his surviving copy prove. Another conspicuous "academician" is Jones's contemporary, the painter Rubens, who also studied in Italy, where he versed himself in Titian and in classical literature in order to paint. King Charles I delighted in both, and having had Jones build the Banqueting House at his Whitehall Palace, and having had Rubens decorate it, he ceased to use it for the receptions it was built for, to avoid the risk of fire or damage to so perfect a pleasure-hall. However, such devoted patronage came to a crude end with the English Revolution.

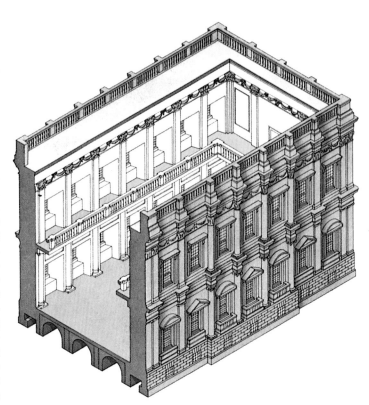

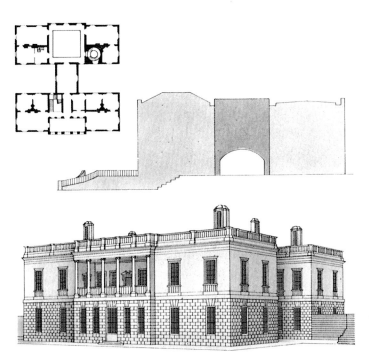

Above right CUTAWAY VIEW OF THE BANQUETING HOUSE, WHITEHALL, LONDON, built 1619 to 1622 by Inigo Jones for King Charles I. It was intended as part of a much larger palace complex, that was never built.

Above PLAN, SECTION VIEW AND GENERAL ASPECT OF THE QUEEN'S HOUSE, GREENWICH, NEAR LONDON, built by Inigo Jones between 1616 and 1635. The two halves of the house are joined by a bridge, which crossed a public road. House and bridge linked the royal palace at Greenwich, on one side of the road, and the park of the palace, on the other. Note the cube room in the middle of one half.

ENGLISH COUNTRY HOUSES OF THE 16TH AND 17TH CENTURIES.
Top left BLICKLING HALL, NORFOLK, built about 1620. Jacobean.
Top right AUDLEY END, ESSEX, begun about 1603, now missing its large entrance court, at least in its original form. Jacobean.
Above left BURGHLEY, NORTHAMPTONSHIRE, built from 1572 by the Elizabethan courtier William Cecil.
Above right WILTON HOUSE, WILTSHIRE, 1630s and 1640s. Built by a nominee of Inigo Jones, Isaac de Caus. Note the twin towers. It is famous for its double-cube room, hung with splendid Van Dyck portraits.
Left LITTLE MORETON HALL, CHESHIRE, of the mid-16th century. Tudor.

BURGHERS' BUILDINGS

The beautiful city of Bruges preserves as no other place does the appearance of a northern European town at the beginning of the 16th century; its uncrowded streets of houses in light-coloured brick with simple stepped gables can be compared against the views in paintings of the time. Architecture of this kind changed very gradually—not at all in fundamentals. But from about the middle of the 16th century the portals, windows and gables of the more well-to-do begin to borrow some phraseology from Italian Mannerism, though with scant interest in its correct pronunciation.

Churches continued to be Gothic until into the 17th century. Town halls and other public buildings went Italianate after the mid 16th century: the Town Hall of Antwerp, 1561–65, with a piled-up "frontispiece" taking the place of the traditional tower, set the trend, not only for other town halls, but also for the style of architecture that began now to be perpetrated in engravings made in the Netherlands. However, there was little important building in the troubled second half of the 16th century in the Netherlands.

At the beginning of the 17th century the upsurge of building everywhere except in Germany, ravaged by the Thirty Years' War, brings the consolidation of this adapted Mannerist repertoire. It has national and regional variants, but the use of stone *quoins* to pattern the corners or other parts of a building, plus the use of scrolls to decorate gables, and various forms of pediment over doors and windows are almost universal. Most importantly, this upsurge is often accompanied by a new kind of town planning, first seen in the squares laid out in Paris by Henri IV. The identical, unostentatious but comfortable houses of the Places des Vosges in Paris are just about the earliest terrace houses anywhere; the square they line is the first town square conceived as a place to "promenade". The Places des Vosges was begun in 1607; a new plan for Amsterdam was made in 1613; Inigo Jones's Covent Garden complex in London and the via Roma in Turin followed in the 1630s.

French influence is predominant in the major 17th century buildings of the now divided Netherlands. Although the works of Jacob van Campen (1595–1657), notably the Mauritshuis for the Stadtholder (Prince) Maurits of Nessau and Amsterdam Town Hall (now the Royal Palace) are often compared to the works of Inigo Jones in England, they have little to do with Palladio and much to do with François Mansart, his contemporary in France. However, Protestant craftsmen emigrating from the southern Netherlands influenced bourgeois architecture across the Channel; also, Lutheran churches built in Holland by van Campen and others, experimenting with central plans, offered some important precedents for the churches built by Wren in London in the late 17th century.

The change from Gothic in churches in the first half of the 17th century was influenced by churches in Rome (not necessarily the latest ones), in the Catholic southern Netherlands and probably by German examples in the Protestant north. Protestant churches have broad arches, well-lit space, limited decoration and theatre-circle-like galleries. The Tuscan order is preferred, being the lowest, simplest and plainest of the five.

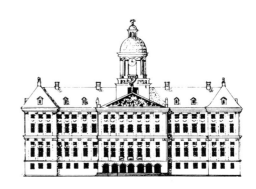

Above THE TOWN HALL (NOW THE ROYAL PALACE), AMSTERDAM, by Jacob van Campen, built between 1648 and 1665.
Below THE WESTERKERK, AMSTERDAM, by Hendrick de Keyser, begun in 1620. It has no side-chapels and is a plain, airy box, suitable for Calvinist worship and preaching.

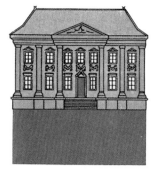
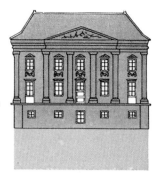

Above, top THREE FRONTS OF THE MAURITSHUIS, THE HAGUE, built by Jan van Campen for Prince Maurits of Nassau from about 1633. This work of "academic" classicism has both charm and grandeur.
Above, middle left THE TOWN HALL, BRUSSELS. The conception is still Gothic, but the detailing is Baroque.
Above, middle right THE ZUIDERKERK, AMSTERDAM, with a traditional spire organized into classical orders.
Left THE GRAND PALACE, BRUSSELS, rebuilt after 1695 following a seige, but very typical of 17th-century squares and their architecture.

THE BAROQUE IN ITALY

There is a persistent current in Baroque architecture that already existed before Gianlorenzo Bernini (1598–1680) and Francesco Borromini (1599–1667), the two great architects of the early Baroque in Rome, made their entrances. It can be seen in the Cappella Paolina, Pope Paul V's tomb chapel in Santa Maria Maggiore in Rome, which was completed in 1615. Though the chapel has traditional Renaissance form, it is heavily loaded. The piers are invariably compound, that is, incorporating at least two, often more, relief pilasters—a device that had been fundamental to the High Renaissance, but had not been used to make a continuously modelled, undulating wall. It had not slurred the pulse of the divisions.

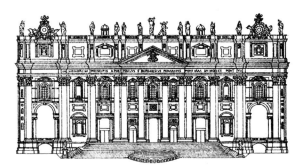

The effect of coating is increased by a large consignment of sculpture and coloured marble.

This rich mix, the latest product of Italian Mannerism, excessive rather as Wendel Dietterlin's engravings are excessive, is endlessly regurgitated in Italian, Spanish and South American churches of the 17th and 18th centuries. It is a polar opposite to stark Protestant meeting-halls, and it is difficult to like both—which may indicate the strength of feeling separating the two religious camps of Europe.

In the Catholic headquarters, Rome, the severity and scrutiny which the first shock of the Reformation had induced gave way to a new kind of conscience, keen but also worldly. There must be more prayer and charity, but art and enjoyment were permitted. The transformation of Rome was taken up again, enriched now by a feeling for vistas—the obelisks set at the end of new link roads—and the provision of fountains. This was part of the state of things before the arrival of Bernini, but it culminated in Bernini's Piazza before the newly completed façade of St Peter's and in his fountains in the Piazza Navona. The great colonnades that extend out from St Peter's impart some of the sanctity within to the pilgrim, like a blessing. It became common to create long walkways along which the devout would be drawn up towards their goal, the shrine at the top of a virtuous hill.

The façade of St Peter's shows, by contrast with earlier

façades, first a tendency to stagger and recess the elements, creating a more marked undulation, and secondly subordination of the sides to the centre, giving it some thrust. But even St Peter's façade looks flat and static, with one bit added to the next bit, beside the curvacious counterplay of Borromini's San Carlo alle Quattro Fontane façade, which ripples turbulently. Other architects in Rome sculpted their façades still more vigorously, using free-standing column groups. But this *dynamic* quality, as it is usually called, is not found outside Rome, not even in a church like Santa Maria della Salute in Venice, which is otherwise Baroque, and is notably scenic.

Opposite page A VIEW DOWN INTO BERNINI'S PIAZZA IN FRONT OF ST PETER'S, ROME. The broad avenue that now leads all the way down to Ponte Sant' Angelo was cut through the old Borgo, or Vatican suburb, in the 20th century. The inset shows the front of St Peter's itself, newly completed when Bernini was working on the great colonnades.
This page CUTAWAY VIEW OF SANTA MARIA DELLA SALUTE IN VENICE, built by Baldassare Lognhena from 1631.

SPACE, LIGHT AND GEOMETRY

Baroque architects in Rome produced vistas and dramatized façades on the outside; their churches were sometimes very theatrical on the inside, too. Advancing beyond the intergral proportions and simple geometry of Renaissance design, Bernini, Borromini and others introduced complex, even irrational figures (such as the oval or the hexagon) into plans and elevations. At the same time they designed buildings for the sake of the effect of their lighting and space, creating an environment from which the ordinary and tangible are excluded.

In Bernini's work architecture, sculpture and painting create the effect together: the *Ecstasy of St Theresa* in the Cornaro Chapel in Santa Maria della Vittoria, the *Apotheosis of St Andrew* in Sant' Andrea al Quirinale are just two examples. In Borromini's great works, San Carlo alle Quattro Fontane and Sant' Ivo della Sapienza, the effect is all in

Above CUTAWAY VIEW OF FRANCESCO BORROMINI'S SAN CARLO ALLE QUATTRO FONTANE, ROME. The church proper and its dome dates from 1638–41, the façade was added in 1665–67.
Right THE FAÇADE OF SANTA MARIA DELLA PACE, ROME, by Pietro da Cortona, was added to the existing church in 1656–57.

the light, the space and the geometry. Both these are central-plan churches, possessing therefore an ultimate divine unity, into which the extremely complex geometrical elements interlock (San Carlo is basically oval, Sant' Ivo hexagonal). In both the diffused light penetrates undifferentiated from the dome (through completely invisible windows in San Carlo); in both the walls are continuous, like an enclosing tent or skirt (lacking any colour in Sant' Ivo), so that despite the multiplicity the church is one indivisible space.

One receives from Borromini, as from Michelangelo earlier and from an architect like Soane later, a sense of form that transcends its components, as if an abstract shape inhabited the recognizable parts. Santa Maria della Salute in Venice, for all its scenic effects both inside and out, its calculated fluxes of light, and its original geometry (it is basically octagonal), does not have such a quality. It is clearly divisible

into its true Palladian parts. The churches built by Guarino Guarini (1624–83) in Turin, San Lorenzo and Santissima Sindone (Chapel of the Holy Shroud), are not quite in the same class either, for all their extraordinary domes and curved-plan arches.

Guarini had visited Rome and is a true successor to Borromini. But he also with little doubt drew on the late Gothic tradition of patterned vaulting ribs, a tradition still very much alive in the new Counter-Reformation churches of southern Germany. He united and combined the geometrical fascinations of both north and south, and he drew on Italian experiment with light effects. Shortly after his death, Roman Baroque influence would spread still further north, producing the aerial delights of Catholic churches in 18th-century Bavaria.

CUTAWAY VIEW OF BERNINI'S
SANT' ANDREA AL QUIRINALE,
ROME, a Jesuit church built
between 1658 and 1665.

FRENCH ORDER AND PLANNING

The later 16th century, during which Spain was the dominant European power, and France was embroiled internally in the Wars of Religion, constitutes an interlude in French architecture. After Henri IV, acceding in 1594, had re-united the country, there is a consistent and continuous development.

There are no outstanding architects and no shift of style in the reign of Henri IV, but the new squares the King laid out in Paris announce the ambitious, highly measured planning of the new age. The rational use-function of his projects contrasts with the visual, scenic redevelopment of Baroque Rome.

There were also, for the numerous *nouveaux riches* of 17th-century Paris, many new *hôtels* or mansions built, at first very much in the same style and according to the standard plan evolved in the 16th century. The Palais de Luxembourg for Marie de Médici by Salomon de Brosse (1571–1626), though conceived as a villa suburbana very much on the lines of the Palazzo Pitti in Florence, has the usual *corps de logis* or main block, projecting wings, and a front wall with a frontispiece portal to close off the courtyard. However, de Brosse has purified out decorative complications and produced powerful conjunctions of massive blocks.

Subsequent architects develop this direction further: François Mansart (1598–1666) then strips out de Brosse's chunkiness and builds severe, precise buildings in which there is actually abundant ornament, but it is so highly structured

Left COURTYARD FRONT OF THE HÔTEL LAMBERT, PARIS, begun in 1640 by Louis Le Vau.
Above INTERIOR OF THE GALLERY IN THE HÔTEL LAMBERT, terminating in an apse window.

that it seems plain, not decorative at all. Mansart and others also provide numerous new conveniences, such as a garden behind the house, an orangery, a long gallery, *porte-cochères* or coach porches, and spectacular staircases. Sometimes having to fit all this into an irregular plot and yet still achieve the appearance of symmetry, architects were required to show brilliance not simply in the handling of classical detail, but in the disposition of suites of rooms, in lighting, in novel shapes of rooms and staircases. The great master of such elegant ensembles was Louis Le Vau (1612–70).

The masterpiece of the age is Mansart's château de Maisons (1642–46). The following lines by Voltaire, believed to refer to Maisons, contain all the clichés of "classicism", then newly minted:

Simple was the noble architecture of it; every decorative feature, set in its place, seemed to have been put there by necessity: the art was hidden under the appearance of naturalness. The eye could take in its form with satisfaction, always enchanted and never surprised.

All this shares certain features or interests with Italian Baroque, but has few points of direct contact. When Bernini was invited to Paris in 1665 to consult on the first great architectural enterprise of the reign of Louis XIV, the rebuilding of the Louvre, there was nothing he could offer that the French needed or took.

Right THE CHURCH OF ST GERVAIS, PARIS, showing the façade designed by Salomon de Brosse in 1616 for the Gothic core. The three tiers of orders recall the gateways to hôtels and châteaux.

THE LOUVRE AND VERSAILLES

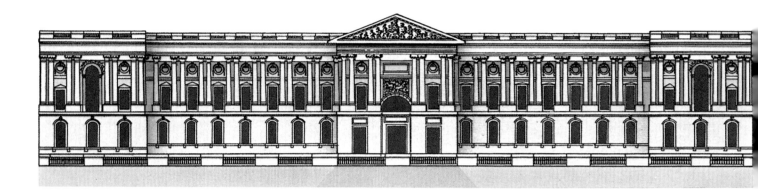

Immediately before Louis XIV came to the throne French royal building had been limited: certainly nothing on the scale of the new Louvre had been undertaken, which explains the initial uncertainty during which Bernini was called in. Eventually a committee of three, Louis Le Vau, Claude Perrault and Charles Lebrun, designed the new east front, a turning-point (1667–70). The new Louvre became the model for large palace fronts throughout northern Europe, displacing Italian examples, and outperforming all rivals, from the Spanish Escorial to Charles I's Whitehall Palace project, revived in exactly these years at Greenwich Palace.

However, Louis XIV had always been disinclined to live in Paris, and in 1669 he began to rebuild a château at Versailles to the soutwest of the city for a new palace. For this there was a very good precedent, the château at Vaux le Vicomte which Le Vau had just designed and Lebrun had just decorated for the chancellor, Nicolas Fouquet. A particular beauty of the château was its park, laid out by André Le Nôtre. No sooner had Fouquet invited the King to see it,

than he was disgraced, his goods confiscated, and the same team of artists called into the service of the King.

At Versailles Le Vau encased the core of the previous château in resplendently sharp, pristine blocks, given feature and variety by paired Ionic columns, which stand full forward like those of the Louvre though not a giant order. Had Le Vau known that his central blocks were soon to be extended left and right he would no doubt have made them larger. Inside, the rooms were much broader, higher and plusher than anything ever seen before, though decorated in a combination of stucco and painting ultimately deriving from Fontainebleau; but there was much more glass, both windows and mirrors (the Galerie des Glâces was a great novelty), and much of the original furniture was of silver, producing the kind of vast, opulent glitter that ballrooms would reproduce endlessly. Versailles was indeed intended as one perpetual state occasion: there was always a fête on or in preparation, the building itself was constantly being modified, and was only complete when it was deserted.

Above THE EAST FRONT OF THE LOUVRE, added from 1667, by Louis Le Vau, Charles Lebrun and Claude Perrault. The formula of a high basement, double columns and a crowning central pediment became standard, though the Louvre itself derives from Bramante's House of Raphael in Rome (see p. 118).
Right TOWN SIDE OF THE CENTRAL COURT OF THE CHÂTEAU OF VERSAILLES, the nucleus of the vast edifice.

It may seem odd to introduce beside these two archetypal Baroque palaces Neoclassicism, the beginnings of which are usually dated about 1750. But the new Louvre, with its range of round columns standing free beneath a straight architrave, and its precision of detail, is a prototype Neoclassical building. And the chapel at Versailles, added at the beginning of the 18th century, sets arches over piers on the lower floor and straight entablature over columns on the upper floor, thus divorcing the marriage made by the Romans and the High Renaissance between the column and the arch. The French Neoclassical theorist Laugier was soon to insist on this, that columns should not be "applied" and should not bear arches.

Above left VIEW TO VERSAILLES ACROSS LE NÔTRE'S GARDENS.
Above right TWO MORE VIEWS OF THE CHÂTEAU IN ITS SETTING. The central blocks, by Louis Le Vau, were laid out in 1669, and additions continued into the 18th century: the building was expanded further and further outwards. Also, the adornment of the garden continued over a long period.

THE IDEAL OF A GREAT CHURCH

St Peter's in Rome was succeeded by just two colossal domed churches answering to the ideal formulated by Bramante in the High Renaissance—St Paul's in London and Sainte Geneviève, now the Panthéon, in Paris. Both, like St Peter's, were originally designed as central-plan churches, embodying an intellectual perfection, but both were modified into longitudinal churches to meet the demands of tradition and practice—the Panthéon to a lesser degree. However, while St Peter's had been built to be the cathedral of Christendom, both St Paul's and the Panthéon were explicitly national monuments. Other similarly motivated central-plan domed churches were built in other capitals, for instance the Marble Church in Copenhagen, and the full story of the ideal would involve countless more, but architecturally only these two, Wren's St Paul's and Soufflot's Panthéon, rival St Peter's.

Sir Christopher Wren (1632–1723) had proposed a domed church in place of the crumbling medieval cathedral of the city of London six days before the Great Fire of London in 1666. The actual church, begun in 1675, is the fruit of continuous evolution in those nine years and further modification to the detail afterwards. The detail, the giant order, and so on, are up to date with French Baroque before the Louvre and Versailles: Wren had visited Paris in 1665 and declared that he had studied the work of the best masters, both French and Italian. He may indeed have met Bernini, who also visited Paris in 1665. For the dome, Wren drew particularly on the Val de Grâce in Paris, begun by Mansart, and on a design by Mansart for a central-plan tomb church for the French Bourbon dynasty (which eventually materialized in Soufflot's church). The dome of the Val de Grâce was itself a variation on Michelangelo's dome for St Peter's, having two skins, the lower to harmonize with the inside, the outer to create an imposing silhouette; its exterior was also a variation on Michelangelo's. Mansard's Bourbon design incorporated a typically Baroque light effect: the inner dome was open at the centre to let in light from invisible windows in the level above. Wren's dome actually has three skins, a lower open at the centre, an inner cone to support the crowning

lantern, and the outer shell. Wren's exterior again reflects Michelangelo's, but also, better still, has the shape of Bramante's Tempietto.

Unlike St Peter's, Wren's crossing is an octagon, and the dome is the full width of nave and aisles together. His inspiration might have been Florence Cathedral, but more probably it was the octagon of the crossing at Ely. For this building of Gothic size Wren employed flying buttresses, but these are hidden by screen walls so that the aisles appear on the outside to be the same height as the nave, making the building incomparably grand, coherent and compact.

The Panthéon, by Germain Soufflot (1709–80), is almost no more than a purist revision of St Paul's. It has again the outside walls rising to the height of the nave. The design of the dome and the crossing is just like St Paul's, but it has columns, not piers, and at the corners of the crossing, where one would expect massive buttressing, it has spindly galleries that light and lighten the interior wonderfully. Such finesse was made possible by the use of iron within the stone: Soufflot's Neoclassicism depends upon the Industrial Revolution.

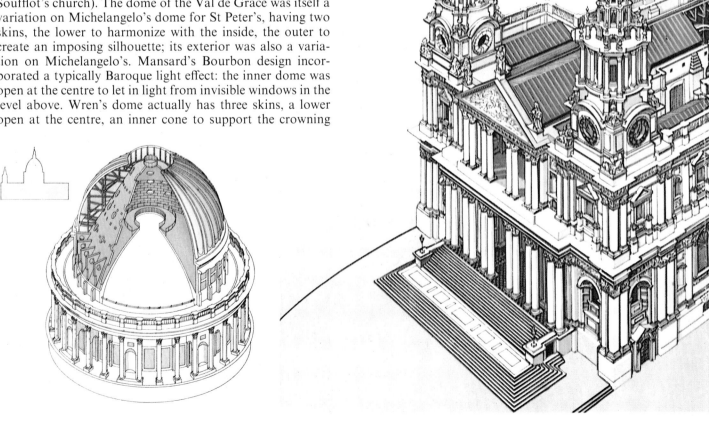

156

Left ST PAUL'S CATHEDRAL, LONDON, built between 1666 and 1718 by Sir Christopher Wren. With an additional detail showing the interior of the dome.
Right THE VAL DE GRÂCE, PARIS, built by François Mansart and then Jacques Lemercier from 1645.
Below right VIEW INTO THE DOME OF THE PANTHÉON, PARIS, built by Jacques-Germain Soufflot from 1757.

THE LONDON CITY CHURCHES

Above THE SPIRE OF ST BRIDE'S, FLEET STREET, LONDON, added to the church in 1702–03; church and spire by Sir Christopher Wren.
Right THE CHURCH OF ST MARTIN'S IN THE FIELDS, TRAFALGAR SQUARE, LONDON, by James Gibbs, 1721–26.
Opposite page, top CUTAWAY VIEW OF ST STEPHEN'S, WALBROOK, LONDON, by Sir Christopher Wren, 1672–87, showing the complex central plan.
Opposite page, bottom THE CHURCH OF ST JOHN'S, SMITH SQUARE, by Thomas Archer, 1714–28.

The Great Fire of London in 1666 was not felt as an unmitigated disaster: the destruction of the medieval city made possible its rebuilding and replanning on rational principles. New schemes were presented within days of the fire ceasing. This new London was subsequently in its turn engulfed by later rebuilding and finished off by the bombing in World War II, but the same rational principles—broad streets, regular plans and fronts, building-trade controls—lie behind the restful streets and squares of London's later western expansion, which is better preserved.

But London's new Baroque parish churches mostly survive. They fall into two groups—those built by Wren in pursuance of the Act for Rebuilding London of 1670, and those built by a variety of architects in pursuance of the 1711 Act for Building Fifty New Churches. Wren, replacing Gothic churches built for the old liturgy with modern churches for Protestant services, had to start virtually from scratch—except for Inigo Jones, some precedents in Holland, and his trusty Serlio and Vitruvius. He evolved what he regarded as his most satisfactory design in St James's, Piccadilly, of 1683. It was "beautiful and convenient", and one could "hear distinctly, and see the preacher". The more experimental churches may now seem more interesting, such as the central-plan St Stephen's, Walbrook, based on van Campen's Nieuwe Kerk in Haarlem but also a trial-sketch for the problems of St Paul's. Wren had even less precedent for his task of finding a classical equivalent for Gothic towers and spires, but that favourite Baroque rediscovery, the obelisk, came in useful.

The architects of the 1711 Act had Wren's precedents to follow. Nicholas Hawksmoor (1661–1736), Wren's chief draughtsman, built the largest share and the most remarkable of these churches, but St John's, Smith Square by Thomas Archer and St Martin's in the Fields by James Gibbs (1682–1754) offer two further distinct styles. Both these architects had visited Italy; Gibbs had actually been trained in Rome. His St Martin's, of the type of Wren's St James's, combined a temple front with a central steeple behind in a design of enormous influence in Protestant New England.

Hawksmoor's style may seem blunt and rugged by comparison. His buildings are compositions in the classical orders to a much lesser degree. In 1699 he had gone into partnership with Sir John Vanbrugh (1664–1726), who believed "'tis certainly the Figure and Proportion that make the most pleasing Fabrick and not the delicacy of the Ornaments". In their joint and individual works columns are handled as cylinders, arches are shaped voids, walls are masonry blocks. It is paradoxical that so much of this very "masculine" architecture is fake: on the outside, columns merely front, arches bridge nothing, the masonry is pure ornament. On the inside, it is very often plaster and wood painted like stone.

THE ENGLISH COUNTRY HOUSE

Above AERIAL VIEW OF CASTLE HOWARD, YORKSHIRE, by Sir John Vanbrugh, built between 1699 and 1712.
Right THE HALL OF HOLKHAM HALL, NORFOLK, by William Kent and Richard, Lord Burlington, begun in 1734. The room is based on an "Egyptian" hall described by Palladio.

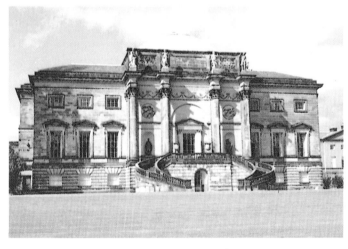

In the early 18th century the English Revolution and the government of the country by an oligarchy of landowners under a constitutional monarch bring clear architectural consequences. There is no great royal palace like Versailles or the imitations of Versailles throughout Europe. Instead, there are plentiful *country houses* with palatial pretensions, miniature capitals of miniature kingdoms.

The first of the great English country houses is Castle Howard, built by Vanbrugh and Hawksmoor from 1699. Its immediate precedent was the palace project, first for Whitehall then for Greenwich, that had evolved intermittently since Inigo Jones's time. In 1704 the same two began Blenheim for the Duke of Marlborough, whose victories over the French on the continent began Britain's 18th- and 19th-century ascendancy. Vanbrugh's houses always possess a fortress air, and consist of an architecturally self-contained centre block flanked by additional elements rather like outposts. The swagger of these houses is quite individual, but many of the motifs are culled from the 1684 Vitruvius edited by Perrault (one of the designers of the Louvre).

It is a mistake to suppose that country houses built in the so called Palladian movement were fundamentally different from the Vanbrugh and Hawksmoor type. The Palladians were not so much against Baroque as against foreigners. They purged the obvious French and Italian elements from their buildings, reverting instead to Inigo Jones and his anglicization of Palladio and Vitruvius. The model house was now Wilton House (actually Jonesian rather than by Jones), but this was easily compatible with the Vanbrugh type, which continued to influence scale, plan and the ideal of the country house as a "pile". Houghton Hall, built for Prime Minister Walpole by Colen Campbell, editor of *Vitruvius Britannicus*, published in 1715 as the manifesto of the Palladian apologists, is proof of it.

There is some change, however, between Houghton and Holkham, its neighbour in Norfolk, begun in 1734 (12 years later) by William Kent and Richard, Lord Burlington. The surfaces are flatter, the detail is fussier, and the house, though perhaps the most beautiful country house in all Britain, has something of a scale model about it. From Holkham it seems a comparatively short step to the style of Robert Adam (1728–92), whose numerous country commissions begin in 1758. For all Adam's greater knowledge both of antiquity and of continental ideas, he remains entirely within the tradition marked out by Holkham. He preserves certain strictly English-Palladian motifs, and his finesse, his chilly subtleties, and his immaculate grandeurs have a leaven from Burlington.

Top SEATON DELAVAL, NORTHUMBERLAND built by Sir John Vanbrugh between 1720 and 1729, one of his last.
Middle KEDLESTON HALL, DERBYSHIRE, by Robert Adam, dating from about 1761.
Lowest HOUGHTON HALL, NORFOLK, built by Colen Campbell and then by James Gibbs from 1722 to about 1730 for the Prime Minister, Sir Robert Walpole.

FRENCH ROCOCO

It is helpful to start a style at the beginning of a century, and the Salon de l'Oeil de Boeuf in Versailles, dated 1701, has been designated the first manifestation of Rococo. The grand style of Louis XIV's early years now becomes attenuated, lightened, even playful. Then Rococo develops into the style of Louis XV's reign, much less glorious, less pompous, even frivolous, reaching its highest point about 1735 in the decorations of the Hôtel Soubise, by Germain Boffrand (1667–1754). After that there is a Neoclassical reaction; straight line and first principles dismiss scornfully curvacious filigree and grotesque ormolu.

There are other ways of reading it. It is reported that Bernini, visiting Paris in 1665, agreed with French connoisseurs that Borromini's architecture betrayed the spirit of "Vitruvian Man"—the rational basis of architecture. Rococo is partly the triumph of a license like Borromini's towards tradition, partly an openness, which is also in Borromini, towards the exotic. Gilles Oppenordt, who had been to Rome, was a designer who drew upon Borromini directly. French Rococo, a style predominantly of pleasure buildings, also drew naturally on "villa" forms, those of the grotto or "nymphaeum" (known as *rocaille*), those deriving from Nero's garden palace or Golden House (*grotesque*), those of Mandarin gardens (*chinoiserie*), and those of an idealized primitive or pastoral condition (*singerie* or ape-work and *bergerie* or shepherdess-work). In England, these forms are rarer, but there is an analogous taste for Gothic, for ruins and for wildernesses. This is also Rococo, because it is an indulgence in the un-classical and the irrational.

Both in England and in France grand buildings and public façades are largely unaffected by such inappropriate caprices. Between the Louvre of Le Vau, Perrault and Lebrun and Neoclassical public building there is little change—no interruption, and no progress. What change there is is English-influenced: the façade of Sainte Sulpice in Paris echoes St Paul's in London, like Soufflot's Panthéon after it. A Borrominesque design by the Rococo decorator Juste Aurèle Meissonier was rejected: buildings were not to look like pieces of china.

Elsewhere it is more difficult to distinguish Rococo from Baroque because elsewhere the Baroque is already integrally Borrominesque. It is Rococo, arguably, when it is French or French-influenced. The work in Munich of François de Cuvilliés (who was appropriately enough a dwarf) reflects his training in Paris. On the other hand Pöppelmann's Zwinger at Dresden is remarkably similar in plan (a rectangle with curved angles) to the Place de l' Hémicycle at Nancy in Lorraine, by a pupil of Boffrand. Boffrand also worked for the Duke of Lorraine, designing an X-plan pavilion never built, but recalling the X-plan of the Palazzo Stupinigi by Filippo Juvarra outside Turin. Juvarra and Pöppelmann have nothing to do with Paris, but exploit the heritage of Borromini independently.

Right THE AMALIENBURG PAVILION, NYMPHENBURG PARK, MUNICH, by François Cuvilliés, 1734–39. In the pattern of 17th-century Vaux-le-Vicomte by Louis Le Vau, the pavilion has a central curved room bulging through the façade. But the scale is much smaller and the detail more exquisite.
Below TWO FRONTS OF THE PETIT TRIANON, IN THE GROUNDS OF VERSAILLES, built by Jacques-Ange Gabriel for Madame du Barry in 1763 and later used by Marie Antoinette. Though rather severe and compact, it was a building for recreation, and its finesse and charm are Rococo.

GREAT BAROQUE PALACES

Versailles set the standard for a royal country residence in the 18th century, the Louvre for a town palace. However, the rulers all over Europe who attempted to imitate or emulate the one or the other usually employed architects trained in the current Italian Baroque style.

The most weighty of these figures was Johann Fischer von Erlach (1656–1723), who built in Vienna for the Emperor Charles VI. Charles VI's Versailles was Schonbrunn, intended by Fischer to outdo not only Versailles but also the Golden House of Nero. Fischer's extraordinary blend of evolved Baroque and literal quotation from antiquity recurs in his Karlskirche: the result is at least scenic. His book on architecture, published in 1721, is traditional in form but Rococo in its range, extending to China and to the primitive in the shape of Stonehenge. His younger contemporary, Lukas von Hildebrandt, was responsible for the Upper and Lower Belvederes in Vienna, mere villas by comparison, though the Upper has a fine staircase hall in which Michelangelesque giants bear up the vault while the visitor enters. Though there is no such feature at Versailles, the spectacular staircase is often the greatest glory of these German and Italian palaces.

Generally the free-standing colonnades and the sternness of the stone of the Louvre are avoided: paint and pilasters are preferred. The Palazzo Madama in Turin by Filippo Juvarra (1678–1736) directly recalls Versailles and the Louvre, but has much more texture. Juvarra worked all over Italy, in Portugal and Spain (he died in Madrid) and consulted to Germany, Austria and France. In Russia, French and Italian influence mingle in the French-trained figure of Bartolomeo Rastrelli, architect at the Peterhof, Tsarskoe Selo and the Winter Palace in Leningrad. In Stockholm, the royal palace is Italian Baroque with French Rococo interior decoration.

Schonbrunn, Charlottenburg in Berlin, or Caserta for the Bourbon kings of Naples, about the largest and last Baorque palace to be built, can be dull; but certain German Residenzes can be exhilarating. Würzburg, for instance, with its ceiling frescoes by Tiepolo, also has a magnificent staircase and most felicitous decoration inside and out. The Zwinger at Dresden, by Matthaeus Pöppelmann (1662–1736) is undoubtedly the most pleasurable space ever created in the pleasure-loving 18th century. Its shaped architecture curvets

and hoops in an indescribably enchanting way.

The most diverse of these palaces is Potsdam, built mostly by Frederick the Great, King of Prussia. It is a series of essays at first in Rococo (in the villa called Sans Souci), later in Versailles mode and with strong influence from the English country house, with all that that implies in the garden—a full Picturesque repertoire.

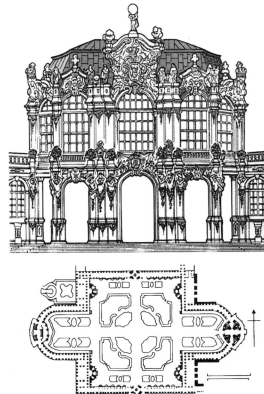

Left THE KARLSKIRCHE, VIENNA, begun 1716 by Johann Bernhard Fischer von Erlach. Its loaded and dramatic Baroque style carries off its classical references, notably to the Column of Trajan and the Pantheon.
Above THE UPPER BELVEDERE, VIENNA, built 1720–23 by Johann Lukas von Hildebrandt for Prince Eugene.
Right ONE OF THE PAVILIONS AND PLAN OF THE ZWINGER, DRESDEN, built by Daniel Pöpelmann between 1718 and 1728 for Augustus the Strong of Saxony.

CENTRAL EUROPEAN BAROQUE

During the 18th century northern Italy, southern Germany, Austria and Bohemia (now Czechoslovakia) constitute almost a single artistic region. They are all Catholic, and the religion is well rooted in a devout peasantry and rich abbeys. The northern architects are as well trained in the Italian Baroque tradition as the Italians themselves; the Italians, moreover, are hardly less receptive to residual northern traditions. Guarini had used Gothic rib vaulting; in Santa Maria del Carmine in Turin Juvarra laid a loaded, light-filled Baroque over a galleried hall church of the northern type (specifically, St Michael at Munich). Bernardo Vittone in Piedmont and Giovanni Santini in Prague continue the use of ribs on ceilings.

Despite Juvarra, and despite Fischer von Erlach and his Karlskirche in Vienna, the architects involved were trained rather than taught: though touched also by French Rococo, particularly in Munich, where Cuvilliés trained the Zimmermann brothers, they had not been to an Academy. They were guided not by reason but by faith. But they were not latter-day Gothic masons, either: they were more equivalent to the medieval carpenter. Their churches have an extraordinarily sophisticated design on paper—combinations of ovals in plan, unquantifiable curves in elevation—but the design is achieved not in cut masonry but in moulded plaster and paint.

The Asam brothers (Cosmas Damian and Egid Quirian) in Munich are the most famous practitioners. The chapel of St John Nepomuk, which is house-sized, is so "dynamic" despite its scale that one has to call it explosive. On the façade, the "live" rock beside the splayed door at once recalls

Bernini's fountains but here, far from being decorative like French rocaille, it underlines the message of the whole façade, that this is a mystic cave where the supernatural is present. And so it is, inside: over the altar the three figures of the Trinity are presented in vivid silhouette against an aura of unearthly light.

One finds this style, and these effects, propogated in parish churches throughout the region. In and around Prague, Christoph Dientzenhofer was practising it as early as the first decade of the century. Care was lavished particularly on pilgrimage churches, such as Die Wies by the Zimmermann brothers. Vierzehnheiligen (Fourteen Saints), by Balthasar Neumann, author of the Würzburg Residenz, has fascinatingly interpenetrating spaces, and a superb site. Too often the rebuilt monasteries squander their hill-top sites on long, dull façades in Versailles mode, as at Melk, though the view on to the west front of the church is splendid.

Below THE PILGRIMAGE CHURCH OF DIE WIES, SOUTH OF MUNICH, was built and decorated by Domenikus and Johann Baptist Zimmermann from 1745 to 1754.

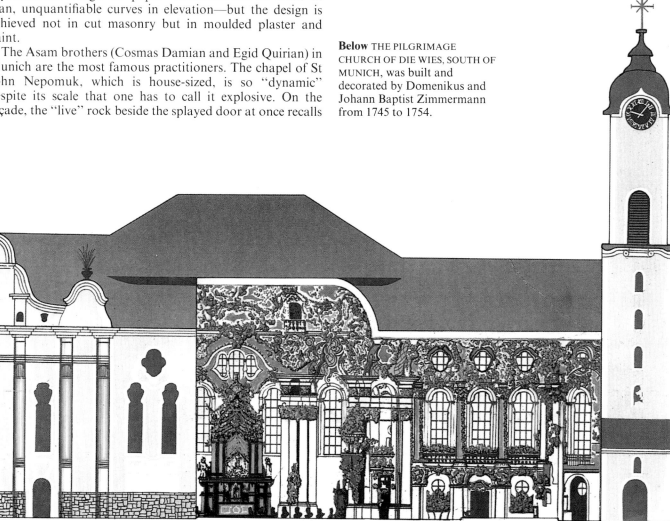

Left ST NICHOLAS, PRAGUE, was
built by Kilian Ignaz
Dietzenhofer between 1703 and
1711.
Above THE MONASTERY AT
MELK, AUSTRIA, was rebuilt in
the first half of the 18th century
by Jakob Prandtauer. The
church is fronted by an open
courtyard and a curved screen
overlooking a precipitous drop
to the river below.

LATIN BAROQUE CHURCHES

Since the influence of Bernini and Borromini was felt so far north, one might expect that it should also spread south, and from Rome, its centre, affect the whole of Catholic Christendom. But this is not so. Instead, the Italian late Renaissance style of the very end of the 16th century occupies the ground first, and refuses to mature into a "dynamic" Baroque, though it may be extremely richly decorated and has to be called Baroque anyway. One version of this style, already mentioned, is the Cappella Paolina in Santa Maria Maggiore in Rome; another is the Cappella dei Principi beside San Lorenzo in Florence, intended as a successor to Brunelleschi's Old Sacristy and Michelangelo's New, but in fact marking the end of fine architecture in that illustrious city.

Both these versions affect Naples, the capital of the Two Sicilies. Hence the standard elements of Baroque in southern Italy, loaded white plasterwork and heavy coloured marbles or other inlays on a simple, big frame. However, though the architecture is worth little comment, the decoration is very often splendid. The city of Lecce, for instance, is outstanding for its superb stonework, which is as versatile as stucco. Individual towns are marvellously gay, such as Ragusa or Noto in Sicily.

In Spain the situation is similar. Plateresque gave way to the severe Mannerism of the Escorial in the later 16th century. In the 17th and 18th centuries nothing moved architecturally, though interiors were often highly decorated in a style named after a family of its perpetrators, Churrigueresque. Sometimes exteriors, too, are decorated, though more commonly they are vast and blank, and very unfriendly. Like Plateresque before it, Churrigueresque encrusts its framework but neither obscures nor lightens it.

This style was then transferred to Spanish colonial America. Any direct Pre-Columbian influence was conscientiously eradicated by the Spanish missionaries. Nevertheless the Latin American quality often called "exuberance" persisted or resulted. A local feature was the so-called "retable" church façade, in which two towers frame a colossal composition, more sculpture than architecture. Interiors are usually darkened, to enhance the gilt displays in the chapels.

In Portugal, once again independent from Spain, foreign architects were more frequently invited in, fostering a more cosmopolitan style effervescent enough to be called Rococo. This in turn was transmitted to Brazil, and Antonio Lisboa also known as Aleijadinho became there an architect worthy of the name, practising an individual variation.

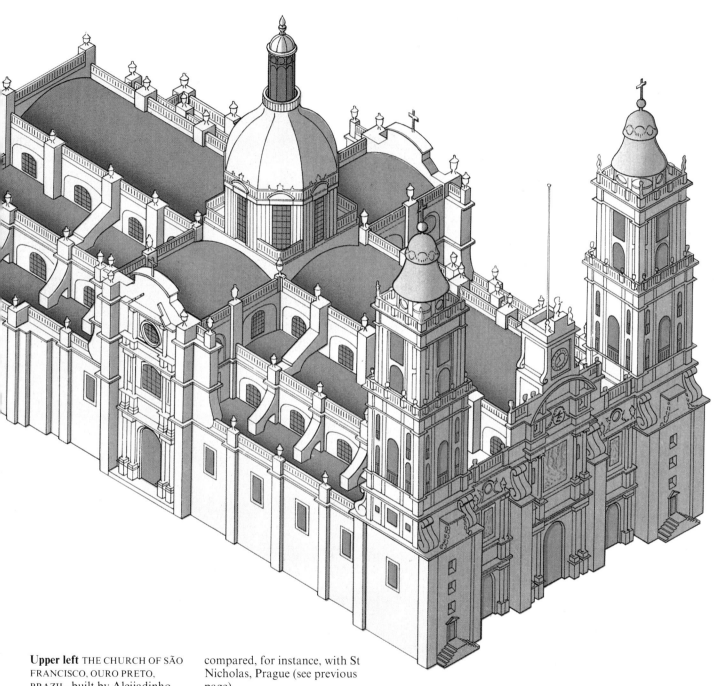

Upper left THE CHURCH OF SÃO FRANCISCO, OURO PRETO, BRAZIL, built by Aleijadinho between 1766 and 1794.
Lower left THE CATHEDRAL OF SANTIAGO DE COMPOSTELA, SPAIN, in its Baroque reworking. The Romanesque church was transformed intermittently between the later 1660s and the later 1730s. In its final state it might be compared, for instance, with St Nicholas, Prague (see previous page).
Above THE CATHEDRAL, MEXICO CITY. This massive double-aisled church possesses chapels and altarpieces of highly elaborate decoration. It is essentially an early 17th-century building, in which Gothic (including rib-vaults) are still employed.

PICTURESQUE ARCHITECTURE

Above right VIEW TOWARDS THE PALLADIAN BRIDGE IN THE GARDENS OF STOURHEAD, WILTSHIRE, laid out by the banker Prince Hoare in the 1740s. His house was by Colen Campbell, and strictly Palladian.
Right ROYAL CRESCENT, BATH, 1767–75, by John Wood the Younger.
Far right PETWORTH HOUSE, SUSSEX, with its lake and lawns laid out by Capability Brown in the later 18th century.
Below ROYAL PAVILION, BRIGHTON, created for the Prince Regent by John Nash, from 1815. It is remarkable not only for its rather inaccurate Mughal style, but also for its use of iron—including iron railings painted to look like wickerwork, and iron columns looking like palms.

"Picturesque" once meant a quality related to the modern term "painterly", and not, as it now means, something nostalgic and pretty like a thatched cottage. In 1794 it was defined as a third type of aesthetic experience beside the "sublime" and the "beautiful". Later again it was the "unexpected". Through all its shifts of meaning the picturesque is *not* grand, classical or rational, but *is* appealing, romantic or even humorous. Very much like Rococo, it is pleasurable, open to the exotic, and has to do with the "villa".

Picturesque architecture starts with Vanbrugh. Vanbrugh Castle at Greenwich, built as a joke "Bastille" (where the architect had once been imprisoned), is in no particular style,

though it has turrets: it is a pure fancy. However, Horace Walpole at Strawberry Hill, once again a private villa beside the Thames, had genealogical and antiquarian interests and therefore made the house deliberately Gothic. Its great fame spread the idea: the architect James Wyatt became a professional Gothic builder. For the millionaire dilettante William Beckford, Wyatt built the most colossal of all such follies, Fonthill Abbey, after Beckford had knocked down his father's new Palladian mansion on the site.

Thus by 1800, the date of Fonthill Abbey, the picturesque had supplanted the beautiful and the classical, and the country house, once a district palace, was now a garden ornament. This change of values began with the Palladians: they reduced the country house to a villa, and they dissolved the formal garden, which, Versailles-fashion, had radiated out from the palace, and imposed its symmetry on the landscape. Instead they made the garden into an informal, Rococo exotica. Stowe, where Vanbrugh, the Palladian William Kent and the professional landscapist "Capability" Brown worked successively, epitomizes the evolution of the "English" garden, as it became known internationally. Stourhead has the complete picturesque garden, a landscape of associations, with Gothic ruins, classical temples, a grotto and a thatched cottage. Finally the mansion itself was treated as part of the garden, and there appeared, for living in, mock castles, mock Taj Mahals, mock Tudor and, not least, mock Greek temples. The picturesque embraces the prototype of the modern English suburban house; the Prince Regent's Brighton Pavilion in magnificent pseudo-Indian; and some aspects of the Greek Revival or Neoclassicism.

John Wood I, the father, began developing Bath as a classical re-creation, a Vitruvian city; John Wood II, the son, the inventor of the terrace *crescent*, transformed it into a picturesque "garden city". A still greater masterpiece of picturesque planning is John Nash's layout in London of Regent's Park, Regent's Street and Buckingham Palace. It is very clear in Nash's work that variety and effect count for much more than correctness or classicism, or dull old beauty.

Above left CARLTON HOUSE TERRACE, FRONTING THE MALL, LONDON, a mansion of apartments, by John Nash, from 1827.
Above right ALL SOULS, LANGHAM PLACE, LONDON, by John Nash, 1822–24. Both buildings belong to Nash's redevelopment of the west end of London between Regent's Park and the Mall.

NEOCLASSICISM IN EUROPE

Neoclassicism, which in the early 19th century became an international style, was fundamentally a French style, originating in the Royal Academy in Paris and its offshoot in Rome. It is therefore from the beginning a highly theoretical style; it is conspicuous for its superb draughtsmanship, wonderfully well taught at the Academy, and for its great precision of detail; and it frequently becomes a prize-winning exercise rather than a natural response to need or function.

It is a style above all of public buildings, indeed the public building as such is virtually a Neoclassical concept. In Paris it first appears in Soufflot's Panthéon, already mentioned as a purified version of Wren's St Paul's. It is pure in its flat walls,

its round dome, its straight colonnades, and in its spare trim. In London the first public Neoclassical building is William Chamber's new Somerset House, in which the sharp detail betrays Chambers's Parisian training and the organization of the long façades the influence of the Louvre and its most recent French successors.

Neoclassicism in private buildings is not quite the same animal. Often it has much more in common with Rococo: though not curvacious, it is distinctly pretty and sometimes bizarre. This is true of the town houses of Claude-Nicolas Ledoux (1736–1806) in Paris and of Robert Adam's town and country houses in England. Adam, too, was partly French trained, and his detail is exquisite; though he has some grand interiors, he himself preferred to "take off the glare" of marble and gilt, and his "Pompeian" and "Etruscan" styles were more congenial. These, for all their archaeological novelty, have the same delicacy as chinoiserie.

Archaeology, or the 18th-century beginnings of a scientific investigation of the artefacts of the past, provided architects with much new information about classical buildings, in

particular Greek buildings, about which virtually nothing hitherto had been known. This information is often incorporated into Neoclassical buildings, hence the name. However, archaeology was more a means than an end. By exploiting the discoveries of archaeology architects could substitute their own ideas for the Renaissance tradition. In this sense Neoclassicism continued the undermining of old principles by Rococo, and opened the way for modern architecture. Indeed some so-called Neoclassical architects were already modern and not classical at all, Ledoux for instance. His toll posts at the gates of Paris are free inventions, indeed much too free, and Ledoux was dismissed for exceeding his budget. His estate for a salt-mine at Arc-et-Sénans has nothing classical about it at all: instead, the buildings were to "express" their function like giant symbols. In England John Soane (1753–1837) is a comparable figure, though the weird and wonderful spaces inside his Bank of England have been destroyed; fortunately the equally weird and wonderful spaces of his own house in Lincoln's Inn Fields, though on a much smaller scale, survive.

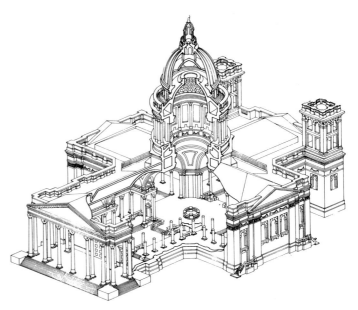

Far left, above KEDLESTON HALL, DERBYSHIRE, by Robert Adam, built in about 1761.
Below SOMERSET HOUSE, LONDON, by Sir William Chambers, 1776–80, built on the site of Old Somerset House. The outer wings were added in the 19th century.
Above THE PANTHÉON, PARIS, by Jacques-Germain Soufflot, from 1757.

NEOCLASSICISM IN AMERICA

Right A NEW ENGLAND CHURCH, one of many based on Gibb's design; early 19th-century.
Opposite page, left THE GOVERNOR'S HOUSE, WILLIAMSBURG, VIRGINIA, finished 1722.
Opposite page, right THE VILLA OF MONTICELLO, NEAR CHARLOTTESVILLE, VIRGINIA, designed for himself by Thomas Jefferson in 1772 and modified at the turn of the century. Though the ornament is Palladian, the interior planning is much inspired by French hôtels.

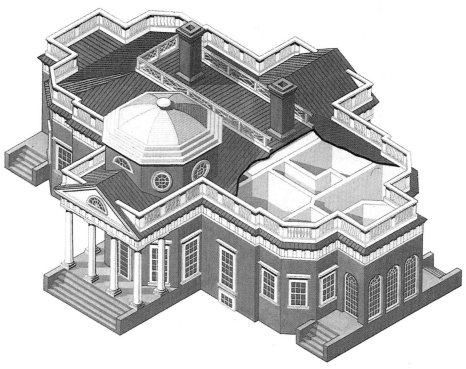

As soon as they could, the first settlers in North America naturally set about reproducing the kind of homes they had left. The most ambitious kind of architecture was the settlement meeting-house or church, and construction was almost invariably in wood. During the 18th century there was an increasing use of architectural books published in England, the most popular being James Gibbs's, of 1728: his St Martin's in the Fields was widely reproduced, and houses were taken faithfully from his plates—even the patterns for stone quoins at the corners, which hardly make sense in wood.

After Independence it became desirable to construct more imposing government buildings and to plan for a new nation. One would expect a certain amount of idealism. The idealism was strongly coloured by current "Enlightenment" thought, in which early was best: republican Rome was a virtuous model for the new society, and ancient Greece stood for "noble simplicity", civilization at its springtime, and the kind of closeness to nature that Europe had since lost. All this is clearest in the buildings of Thomas Jefferson, particularly his Virginia State Capitol. Here he enclosed all the government functions in a box made to look like the Roman temple known as the Maison Carrée in Nîmes—an emblematic

figurehead of reason, which Jefferson would not have been pleased to learn was in fact built by the aide to an emperor.

One disadvantage of this approach is that it tended to neglect the city. The early American leaders did not really like cities: their vision was of village life. Therefore town-planning was on the whole unsubtle: the commissioners laid out New York in the grid it still has "since right-angled houses are the most cheap to build, and the most convenient to live in". This was to shut away the Rococo and Picturesque, and to ignore considerable European advances in town-planning. Manhattan, which meant "Island of Hills", was flattened out.

The first professional architect to practice in America was Benjamin Latrobe, trained in London with a style close to John Soane's. Best known for his work on the Capitol in Washington, though he did not plan it, Latrobe trained the leading architects of the next generation in an educated Neoclassicism. Nevertheless America remained well in the wake of European thinking until the second half of the 19th century—except for certain innovations in prison design which excited European interest, and for hotels, which had become famous for their comfort by mid-century.

THE STYLELESS CENTURY

Claude-Nicolas Ledoux built his revolutionary buildings before the French Revolution, by which time he was exiled, lucky to have his head. Ledoux's and Soufflot's kind of Neoclassicism was continued not in Paris but in London by Soane and in Berlin by Schinkel. In Paris Napoleon, once established in power, fostered a heavy, conservative kind of Neoclassicism that recalled Louis XIV, not the Parthenon, despite the rows and rows of peristyle columns. Typical is the Madeleine in Paris, a monumental feature closing off the Rue Royale. Napoleon's ambitious urban projects included the Rue de Rivoli, still the smartest street in Paris, but they

were actually completed by Louis Philippe and Napoleon III in their "Second Empire" style, not in Napoleon's own "Empire".

In this kind of dynastic building there was no break with the past. But under Napoleon a certain Jean-Nicholas-Louis Durand (1760–1834) published two books that mark the beginning not just of the modern style of architecture but of a quite new kind of architecture. It can be called bourgeois, capitalist or rationalist. It was a response to the vast numbers of new buildings, and new kinds of buildings, commercial and institutional, that the 18th and then the 19th century required. These were hospitals and prisons; libraries, museums, galleries and college buildings; theatres; banks, exchanges; tenement, apartment and terrace housing; offices of all kinds. All of this was now architecture—but none of it architecture as it had been.

Durand was a professor not of an academy but of a polytechnic, which is another sign of the change. In his books, he set out a utilitarian way of building, in modules, in this style, in that style, in no particular style—classical, Gothic or "Romanesquoid". His modules or units are a sorry heritage of the religious and aesthetic faith in "perfect" proportions: the harmony of proportions is now ready for machine reproduction. Durand himself makes no judgement about the different styles he parades: he is clearly indifferent. Particularly telling is his attitude towards Soufflot's Panthéon, which he illustrates with the caption: "the Panthéon as it is— this cramped building cost 18 million". Beneath he puts his own design, a very simple, large round dome: "The Panthéon

176

as it should have been done, costing only nine and vast and magnificent". Durand might have been thinking of the dome of the Pantheon in Rome; more likely, he had in mind the timber dome of the new Paris Corn Exchange. In 1809 this dome was replaced by another in iron and glass. Durand was a prophet.

It is generally accepted that the greatest French building of this period using iron and glass is Henri Labrouste's elegant Library of Sainte Geneviève (1843–50). The greatest traditional-looking building is Charles Garnier's Opéra (1861–75), an element in Baron Haussmann's layout of Paris. Garnier was asked what style his Opéra was meant to be in: "style Napoléon III", he replied, which is its merit.

Opposite page CUTAWAY VIEW AND FAÇADE OF THE OPÉRA, PARIS, by Charles Garnier, the most resplendent 19th-century building in Paris.
This page, right CUTAWAY VIEW OF THE LIBRARY OF SAINTE GENEVIÈVE, PARIS, by Henri Labrouste. Its round arches are typical "Rundbogenstil".
This page, below THE PLACE VENDÔME, PARIS, with its Empire column imitating Trajan's Column in Rome, raised after 1807.

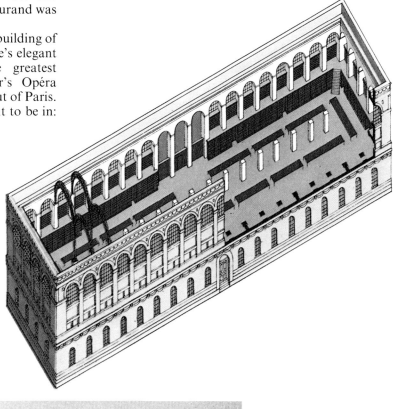

SCHINKEL AND SEMPER

The influence of Durand's books was greater still in Germany than in France, and Durand's "Romanesquoid" style or non-style there received a name, *Rundbogenstil* (round-arch style). Besides this there flourished the styles of the past that Durand had noted, and some new old ones: from the dominant Neoclassicism of the opening years of the 19th century there is a shift to a predominant neo-early-Renaissance style, often associated with the use of terracotta facing. Fortunately amidst all this there was an architect of genius, Karl Friedrich Schinkel (1781–1841), enabled to practice old-fashioned architecture by the patronage of Kings Friedrich Wilhelm III and Friedrich Wilhelm IV of Prussia with their capital in Berlin.

Schinkel, who became court architect in 1815, was preceded by Carl Gotthard Langhans, who built the severe, pure Brandenburg Gate, and by Friedrich Gilly, whose design for a monument to Frederick the Great was a most influential

Above THE NIKOLAIKIRCHE, POTSDAM, by Karl Friedrich Schinkel, begun in 1829. Its dome is a pure hemisphere; its body is a pure cube.
Below THE ALTES MUSEUM, (EAST) BERLIN, by Schinkel, 1824–28.

Romantic vision. He set a Parthenon on a mountainous podium, but the podium and subsidiary monuments round it had plain, flat, sharp, "cubic" shapes and surfaces, producing a kind of bitterness then regarded as "sublime". Schinkel was very much heir to this, as well as to Durand. In the original design for an early work, the Neue Wache (New Guardhouse), he reduced the columns to plain slabs; as it was built they were made, more conventionally, Doric. His Theatre (Schauspielhaus) and Museum (Altes Museum) in Berlin reveal his extraordinary balance, clarity and control: though it is a very straight-lined sort of architecture, it has a zing quite lacking in other 19th-century work.

At Potsdam, for Friedrich Wilhelm IV as he would be, Schinkel built some beautiful garden villas, obviously indebted to the things English he had seen on a visit to Britain in 1826. These are compositions in a non-specific Neoclassicism, anticipating the new kind of house design of a Le Corbusier or Frank Lloyd Wright in the 20th century. Schinkel in architecture is like Brahms in music: still working in the classical tradition, very much of his own time, and strikingly advanced—all three together.

Gottfried Semper (1803–79) is a typical figure of the mid 19th century in Germany, indeed in Europe, which he travelled. He used a great number of styles, except on the whole the classical, and attempted to draw up some principles by which to govern it all. He began with the function and materials of buildings: the building should "express" its function, that is, the exterior should make plain, or at least correspond with, the interior; and he argued that certain kinds of material were suitable for certain kinds of ornament. The original principle behind reviving a style, to recall certain qualities of the past in the modern building, was steadily eroded.

THE SCHAUSPIELHAUS (THEATRE) IN (EAST) BERLIN, by Schinkel, 1819–21, is both highly rational and strictly Neoclassical.

GREEKS AND GOTHICS

In Britain, choice of style was sometimes a matter of passionate commitment. The amateur and enthusiast Thomas Hope in 1804 published a pamphlet proving the moral imperative to build the proposed new buildings of Downing College, Cambridge in a true Greek style: his reasons were found convincing and his protégé, the architect William Wilkins, was launched. Another professional practitioner of Greek was Robert Smirke, whose most famous work is the British Museum, with its front of 48 enormous Ionic columns. Wilkins got the National Gallery, London, but this was adjudged bitty and muddled, and scuppered his career.

By far the most exciting neo-Greek building in Britain took place in Edinburgh. Edinburgh New Town was being laid out in the second half of the 18th century, and in the 19th received monuments appropriate to its claim to be, in philosophy, "the Athens of the North". A replica of the Parthenon was undertaken, but abandoned, and now serves very well as a picturesque ruin; the Royal Scottish Academy and the National Gallery of Scotland look very fine and pure, isolated on a kind of promontory; the High School is as good as anything French or German. At the same time Gothic was used, for instance for the monument to Walter Scott—appropriately enough, since he wrote medieval romances. Nor was Smirke averse to Gothic on occasion. But the attitude of Augustus Welby Pugin was different again.

Pugin's father was already a Gothic specialist, but a draughtsman, not an architect or a moralist. Pugin the son grew up with the idea that Gothic, not Greek, was the virtuous style, because it was the style of "the Age of Faith" and because it was British, not imported. He published his *Contrasts*, stating this case, in 1836, just when people were beginning to question whether long colonnades and flat, severe walls were what they really wanted, and just before the religious revival of the Victorian period. Architecturally, it was unfortunate that he won the day. Pugin disliked the beauties or the picturesqueness of buildings, and part of the moral superiority of Gothic was actually founded in its ugliness. So the tendency was to build not just dull buildings but eyesores. Pugin so far carried the day that he was appointed beside Charles Barry as architect to the new Houses of Parliament. Barry hitherto had sought some well-judged alternatives to the prevailing Greek style, using, for instance, for his Travellers' and Reform Club buildings in London, an Italian Renaissance style, or in the country a style sometimes called "Jacobethan".

Far left THE HOUSES OF PARLIAMENT, LONDON, by Sir Charles Barry and Augustus Welby Pugin, 1840–65.
Left DETAIL OF THE IONIC FAÇADE OF THE BRITISH MUSEUM, LONDON, finished by Sir Robert Smirke in 1847.

IRON, GLASS AND STEEL

Above THE IRON BRIDGE AT COALBROOKDALE, by Thomas Farnolls Pritchard, 1777–79. The novelty was not the use of iron for a bridge, but its use for the arch.
Right VIEW UP INTO THE EIFFEL TOWER, PARIS.

The use of iron in buildings goes back at least to the 14th century, when Italian masons introduced iron tie-beams and chains across arches and through masonry. Most architects were happy to use iron wherever it was useful and appropriate both before and after the advent of the iron girder in the late 18th century. Inevitably, and on the whole without fuss, iron replaced timber in many parts of buildings: the Houses of Parliament have an iron roof, even though Pugin, who pronounced against the use of iron in churches, was involved in them; the cathedral of Chartres was given a new roof of iron in 1837–39.

The obvious and major use of iron and, later, steel in the 19th century was to vault a huge span. It was also thought at first to be fireproof, but it was discovered it would burn at just about the same time as it was discovered it could float. Iron was very soon used for bridges, then for mills and factories, and for roofing; then for buildings which could be called pure roof. The most famous of these is the Crystal Palace built by Joseph Paxton for the Great Exhibition in London of 1851, since burnt: it was in fact an enormous greenhouse, of the kind built by Paxton, who was a gardener, previously on a smaller scale. The similar Palm House at Kew Gardens, erected from 1845, still survives.

Other such buildings went up in later exhibitions of this kind, and the Eiffel Tower as well in the Paris exhibition of 1889. About this date non-technical considerations come clearly to influence such iron structures: Gustave Eiffel added arches that were not needed between the "feet" of his tower, and Baker and Fowler certainly intended to make their steel Firth of Forth bridge, begun in 1883, beautiful as well as long. At first, however, there was no thought that an iron building might be beautiful in itself, or any idea how it might be, except be imitating a style (almost always Gothic). The University Museum at Oxford, 1854–60, is a good example of a literal imitation of Gothic in iron. With the Eiffel Tower and the Forth Bridge there is an approach towards Art Nou-

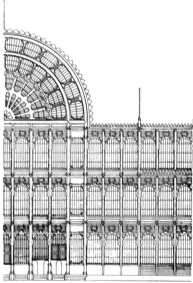

Far left THE EIFFEL TOWER, PARIS. The Eiffel Tower was originally only one element of the Great Exhibition in Paris in 1889, but the other iron buildings, including the vast exhibition hall, were afterwards dismantled. **Near left** Detail of the frame of the "Crystal Palace" created by Joseph Paxton for the Great Exhibition in London in 1851. The exhibition was the first of its kind.

veau, in which new materials at last came to the fore.

Two further kinds of structure were particularly suitable for iron, being products of the Industrial Revolution—the railway station and the department store. Railway stations were invariably fronted in masonry in a "style": the iron roofs over the platforms, though they might be interesting technical achievements, were just sheds. The early department stores have not survived, but shopping arcades of the 19th century are often still with us: the largest ever built was the Galleria Vittorio Emmanuele in Milan (1865–77).

FINAL FLOURISH OF CLASSICISM

Above left THE VITTORIO EMMANUELE MONUMENT, ROME, by Count Giuseppe Sacconi, 1884–1922.
Lower left COUNTY HALL, LONDON, by Ralph Knott, 1908–22.

Above THE OPERA HOUSE, VIENNA, by Van der Nüll and Siccardsburg, 1861–69.
Right GOVERNMENT BUILDINGS, NEW DELHI, by Sir Edwin Lutyens, 1914–31.

The Gothic style introduced by Pugin fortunately did not prevail everywhere, despite the powerful advocacy of two successors, John Ruskin the critic and George Gilbert Scott the architect. Though enthusiastic for true Gothic, and involved in the iron Gothic University Museum in Oxford, Ruskin rapidly grew bitterly disillusioned with modern Gothic. And George Gilbert Scott was thwarted by the sense of the Prime Minister, Palmerston, who insisted on a classical style for the new government offices in Whitehall, decided on in 1857. These were finally built by Scott in a style deriving from the French "Second Empire", of which Garnier's Opéra in Paris is the leading example. The Second Empire style, loosely classicistic, but always richly ornamented, was widely followed in Europe and America.

The Second Empire style then evolves into what is usefully called the Beaux-Arts style, because it was propagated by the architectural school of the Beaux-Arts in Paris. The Beaux-Arts, rationalist in the tradition of Durand, but less philistine, taught professionalism, flexibility and good sense in architecture, and despite thinking always in terms of an applied "style", laid the ground for the modern principle that function dictates the form. This principle emerged particularly in Chicago, but many "Chicago School" architects were trained in Paris. However, their principle was also a modification of Gottfried Semper's rationale, shown in the work of

Semper and others in Vienna in the energetic building programme initiated by the Emperor Franz Josef after his accession in 1848. The government buildings situated round the new Ringstrasse were in a deliberate variety of styles, Neoclassical, Gothic, Renaissance and, in the Burgtheater and the Neue Burg wing of the Palace, Baroque.

There are several very large, very impressive public buildings dating from the second half of the 19th and even the first half of the 20th century that deserve to be called Baroque and deserve perhaps to be appreciated more than they are. Because they are of masonry, in·a classicist style, and are broadly speaking imperialist, they are regarded as antiquated rather than modern. An early one, begun in 1866, is the Palais de Justice in Brussels, enormous, marvellously sited and both magnificent and severe. A later one is Milan Central Station, designed in 1906 and completed in 1931, in a sort of Egyptian, and Ramassean in scale. Later still, designed in 1914 but not built until after World War I, is the government palace at New Delhi by Edwin Lutyens. Lutyens is a good example of an architect who could use a repertoire deriving fundamentally from the past but in his own way, blending satisfactorily and sensitively but not slavishly, indeed with marked originality. These are the best qualities of the Beaux-Arts tradition, and they tip very easily into Art Nouveau.

AMERICA: HOME AND OFFICE

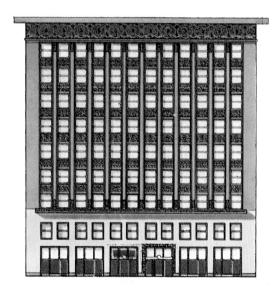

EARLY SKYSCRAPERS BY LOUIS SULLIVAN. **Above** THE WAINWRIGHT BUILDING, St Louis, 1890–91. **Middle** THE GUARANTY BUILDING, BUFFALO, NEW YORK, 1894–95. **Bottom** AUDITORIUM BUILDING, CHICAGO (now part of Roosevelt University), 1887–89.

The Industrial Revolution not only turned peasants into workers, it turned merchants into businessmen. Both factories and offices proliferated in the second half of the 19th century, especially in America, where capitalism was particularly uninhibited. Commercial and industrial buildings developed according to their own logic: not for nothing was the principle, form follows function, applied by a builder of offices, Louis Sullivan (1856–1924).

James Bogardus had created Laing Stores in New York out of prefabricated cast iron in 1849, and the use of iron rapidly became standard, even if it was used together with masonry. Then the Haughwout Building in New York in 1857 had a lift. The technology with which to build skyscrapers now existed, and under the pressure of increasing downtown rents, it was soon exploited. Early upward-pushing buildings were still hampered by the supposed need for masonry, but the first steel-frame skyscraper, the Home Insurance Building in Chicago, emerged from the office of William Le Baron Jenney in 1883. Sheathed in brick, terracotta and glass, it was conceived as a self-reproducing Renaissance *palazzo*. The firm of Burnham and Root then led the way towards a satisfactory form for the new monster. They conceived the Monadnock Building in Chicago, 1884–92, as a colossal column, with the base at the street, the shaft as the main section, and some kind of capping at the top. This was the principle taken over by Sullivan, and made explicit in his article, *The Tall Office Building Artistically Considered*, explaining his Wainwright Building in St Louis, 1890–91. It came to be adopted universally, even though in New York the conception of the skyscraper as a tower remained popular.

Sullivan's firm was also commissioned to design houses, but these, after 1888, tended to be passed to Frank Lloyd Wright (1867–1959). If Sullivan decided the pattern of the 20th-century American's office, Wright decided the pattern of his home. At first Wright worked in the so called "Shingle" style, named after the cladding of 18th-century American building, which was now of course revived. But the catalyzing influence was the sight he had at the 1893 Chicago World's Fair of a Japanese house. He now conceived of a house not as a box divided into rooms but as a central heat-source, the "chimney core", round which the rooms of the house clustered. This in turn would change as central heating came in. More important, these rooms were of various shapes and interconnected, to constitute one living space, and this is still characteristic of suburban housing. Wright also tried out new materials in these "prairie" houses, including concrete (which an eccentric called Orson Squire Fowler had advocated as the material of the future for houses as early as 1853), and throughout his career was interested in the kinds of surface patterning the new materials could bear. This was an interest also of European Art Nouveau at the time, and of European "Brutalism" later.

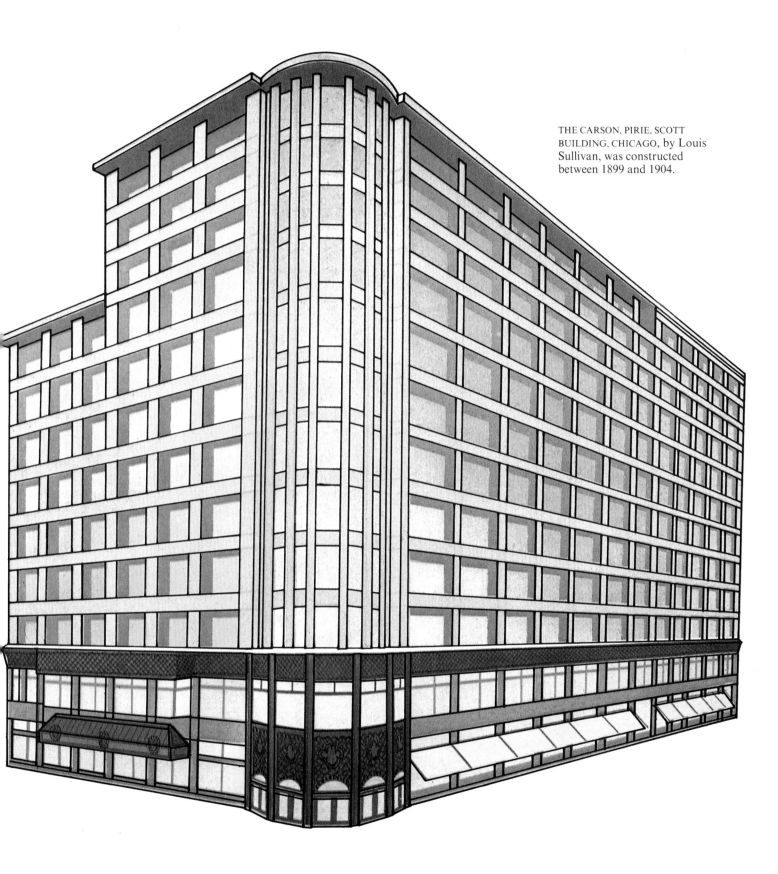

THE CARSON, PIRIE, SCOTT
BUILDING, CHICAGO, by Louis
Sullivan, was constructed
between 1899 and 1904.

ART NOUVEAU

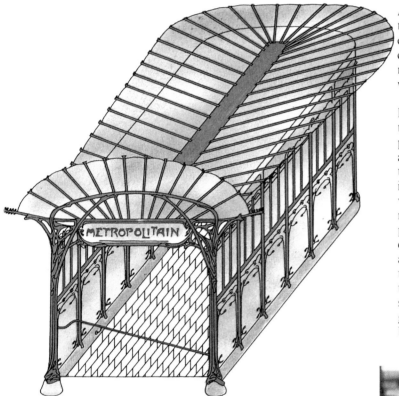

Art Nouveau flourished before World War I. Though it contained many seeds for the future, it was innocent of 20th-century shock and devastation. It packaged an affluent, comfortable society in which art was still a matter of taste, not of ideals. Though it opened the way to Modernism, it was never radical.

It was rooted in various ways in the Gothic revival. Possibly the tendril patterns of Art Nouveau grew from the tracery of windows in revived Gothic churches. But its precursors were not Pugin or Ruskin, but William Morris and Eugène Viollet-le-Duc. William Morris, father-figure of the Arts and Crafts movement, advocated a care and interest in individual craftsmanship like that which had once prevailed in the Middle Ages: Art Nouveau is characteristically made beautifully, it is personal and "one-off". So not surprisingly Art Nouveau is extremely diverse. Viollet-le-Duc's contribution was to strip Gothic bare—no longer to see it as an image of religious faith, or as a kind of ornament, but as the medieval mason's equivalent of iron and steel—a structural method. His new insight greatly assisted the new understanding of style, or form—style was what you built in. This general outlook was reinforced by contemporary sculptors' belief in "truth to materials".

Interest in materials unites all the practitioners of Art

Above ONE OF THE PARIS MÉTRO ENTRANCES by Hector Guimard, in sinuous ironwork, executed between 1898 and 1901. Guimard was the leading architect of Art Nouveau in Paris.
Right DETAIL OF THE IRONWORK OF A MÉTRO ENTRANCE.

Nouveau, from Frank Lloyd Wright, concrete and the "prairie" style in America to Charles Rennie Mackintosh in Glasgow; from Victor Horta and Paul Hankar in Brussels to Antonio Gaudí in Barcelona to Peter Behrens in Darmstadt. Victor Horta, the earliest of these to practise an explicit Art Nouveau, typifies the widespread inspiration from plant forms, but there is a lot more to it. His outstanding quality is the careful, elegant design of his Brussels terrace houses, in which every article is re-thought, specially created and lovingly installed. There is great delight in modernity—not merely in the use of iron for a staircase, for instance, but the incorporation of a radiator into the design of a room, and a design provided for the radiator cover, different in every room. Charles Rennie Mackintosh, by contrast, liked straight verticals (which may also derive from Gothic), both in furniture and in buildings (his interest typically extended to both). Antonio Gaudí's debt to Gothic is also clear, for all that he was the most extreme and uninhibited of the Art Nouveau designers, creating phantasmagoric shapes, colours and textures.

Art Nouveau finally broke down an old habit of seeing, in all the arts. As representation gave way to abstraction in painting and sculpture, the use of ornament or a "style" gave way to pure form in architecture, the building as nothing else than its own bulk.

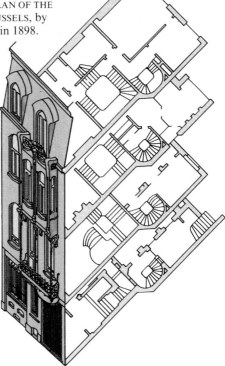

Lower left CUTAWAY VIEW OF THE CASA MILÁ, BARCELONA, by Antonio Gaudí, dating from 1910. It was an apartment block—the typical kind of building on which Art Nouveau architects were employed—round two courtyards.
Above THE SCHOOL OF ART, GLASGOW, by Charles Mackintosh, 1896–1909. The need to provide light was a crucial factor.
Right TWO DETAILS OF ART NOUVEAU IRONWORK FROM THE HORTA HOUSE, RUE AMERICAINE, BRUSSELS.
Below right FLOOR PLAN OF THE HORTA HOUSE IN BRUSSELS, by Victor Horta, begun in 1898.

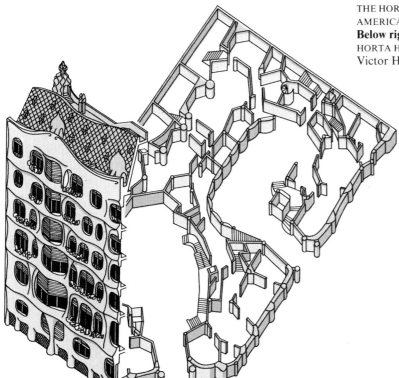

CORBUSIER AND HIS BACKGROUND

The idea of ferro-concrete is as old as the use of iron in building, but it was not until the 1890s that its engineering was perfected and its potential made practical. The technology was French. In 1904 Auguste Perret built an apartment block in reinforced concrete at Rue Franklin 25bis, Paris. Though the building has since been much praised, its essential lines were dictated by building regulations. It was a technical, not a stylistic, advance.

Also in 1904, Perret's one-time fellow student Tony Garnier produced his first plans for an "Industrial City", published in 1917. Garnier's advance was not so much stylistic as conceptual. Though once again theorizing about what a city should be was not a new idea, Garnier started with the ecology and thought the city through from there (his presumed site was like that of his native Lyons). He initiated the 20th-century debate in which architecture was no longer an individual art but a feature of the total environment, economic and political. This is essentially what is "modernist" about modern architecture: it has to find premises, a theory, before it can act. It is as much political as aesthetic.

Charles Edouard Jeanneret, called Le Corbusier (1887–1966), moved from Art Nouveau first to the idealism of Garnier, whom he met in 1907, and then to the modern techniques of Perret, for whom he worked in 1908. In 1910 he worked for Behrens in Berlin—then building the most important architecture in Europe. However, though he built a few houses, Corbusier was more active in theory than in practice, and was also a painter, in those heady days for the avantgarde. His first influential concept was his Maison Dom-Ino (punning on domino and *domus*, a house), of 1914–15. The idea was an indefinitely repeatable and variable unit, the domino—a slab of concrete dotted with the pillars that sustained it. His *Towards Architecture* of 1923 consolidated his ideas for "living-space" houses, in which the consequences of building in concrete were exploited in free plans, flat roofs, flat walls, and ribbon windows. The look and shape of these houses for the middle classes were conditioned by Corbusier's current "Purist" abstract painting, and by mathematical harmonies—for which he has been compared to Palladio. But they were important ultimately because they were practical and marketable, like cars.

Corbusier then nearly won the most prestigious architectural competition of the inter-War period, the design for the League of Nations building in Geneva. He received as much credit for it as if he had won. His purist but bold shaping on the one hand, his multiple-unit construction and design on the other, were adopted all over Europe. However, Corbusier himself almost immediately turned to other paths, of which the most important for the future was the exploration of texture in modern materials. In direct opposition to the definition of the "international style" just then being made, its outcome was post-War European "brutalism".

Left APARTMENT BLOCK AT RUE
FRANKLIN 25BIS, PARIS, by
Auguste Perret, dating from
1904. The use of reinforced
concrete was a novelty. Perret
employed a concrete shell which
he set back at the front to allow
as much light as possible
through the large, square,
metal-frame windows.
Above PART OF THE
WEISSENHOF HOUSING ESTATE
AT STUTTGART, which had
buildings by Gropius, Mies van
de Rohe and Le Corbusier, 1927.

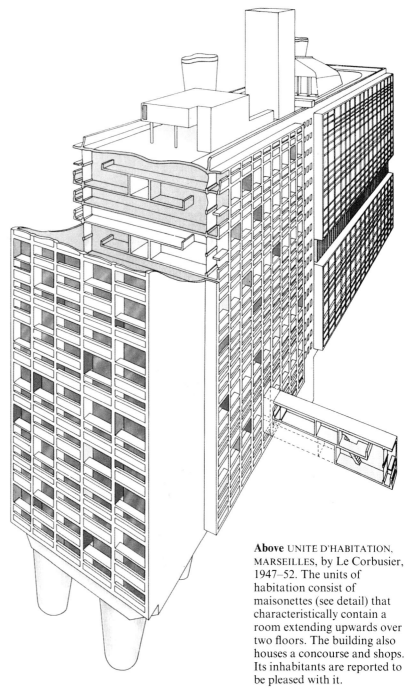

Above UNITE D'HABITATION,
MARSEILLES, by Le Corbusier,
1947–52. The units of
habitation consist of
maisonettes (see detail) that
characteristically contain a
room extending upwards over
two floors. The building also
houses a concourse and shops.
Its inhabitants are reported to
be pleased with it.

FROM WERKBUND TO BAUHAUS

In Germany the floating forms of Art Nouveau crystallized round the Deutsche Werkbund (German Industrial League), formed in 1907. The aim of the Werkbund was to promote German industry, which was now ready to challenge the rest of the world in sound, smart, modern design. These qualities are pre-eminent in the work of Peter Behrens (1868–1940) for the A.E.G. (General Electric Company). His brief was to create a "house style", pervading all aspects of the company: his architecture was to be an advertisement much like his posters. His famous turbine factory built for A.E.G. in Berlin in 1909 was certainly efficient and purpose-built, but it was never utilitarian or functionalist. It was a "designer" factory, which is chiefly evident in its sleek, not straight lines: subtle curves and tensions, and perfect finish, transform his train-shed shape into something much more impressive and friendly.

Significantly, Behrens was shortly afterwards commissioned to design the new German Embassy in St Petersburg: his industrial style immediately became the official style. This is partly because, as Behrens himself made clear, he had looked back to Schinkel for a sense of order. He had used, of course, quite different materials, in particular expanses of glass almost flush with its frame. His handling of glass had lasting influence, for instance on Walter Gropius's Bauhaus building in Dessau, but also, in the second decade of the 20th century, glass became something of a religious symbol for the German avantgarde.

Behrens trained both Walter Gropius (1883–1969) and Ludwig Mies van der Rohe (1886–1969), first and third directors of the Bauhaus. Both were gripped by the fervour and ferment in Germany during and after World War I, but both remained sound, practical and brilliant professionals, attuned to the necessities of industry. The "Expressionist" avantgarde contributed much to the vision that formed the Bauhaus, founded in 1919, including the fundamental principle, "no boundaries between the crafts". But it was the direct applicability of what was designed that "made" the Bauhaus, or made it make the 20th century. By contrast, De Stijl in Holland became marooned in its own theory in the late 1920s; the Bauhaus became increasingly pragmatic.

This unusual degree of cooperation between German industry and the avantgarde can easily be obscured by the political debate which convulsed not just the avantgarde but the whole country after World War I. Or perhaps the unusual receptivity to avantgarde ideas was a symptom of Germany's social instability. Ideas for housing that remained experimental or on paper elsewhere were put into effect on a larger scale in Germany, until the Nazi regime identified the avantgarde with socialism and attempted to revert to tradition.

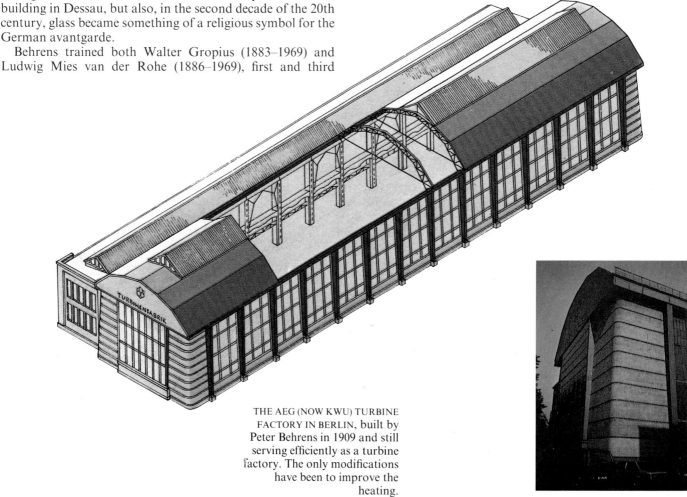

THE AEG (NOW KWU) TURBINE FACTORY IN BERLIN, built by Peter Behrens in 1909 and still serving efficiently as a turbine factory. The only modifications have been to improve the heating.

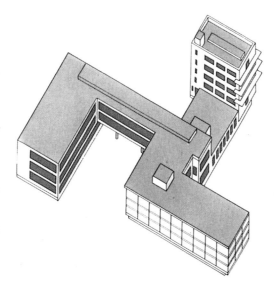

Above THE GLASS PAVILION ERECTED AT THE 1914 WERKBUND EXHIBITION IN COLOGNE, designed by Bruno Taut. The mystique of iron and glass would also soon infect Mies van der Rohe and Walter Gropius.

Right THE BAUHAUS AT DESSAU, by Walter Gropius, 1925. The building has a clean grace, due in part to its excellent finish. Between the two main blocks were administration offices; the tower contained accommodation.

Far right BUILDING BY GROPIUS AND MEYER FOR THE WERKBUND EXHIBITION OF 1914 AT COLOGNE.

OTHER MODERNISMS

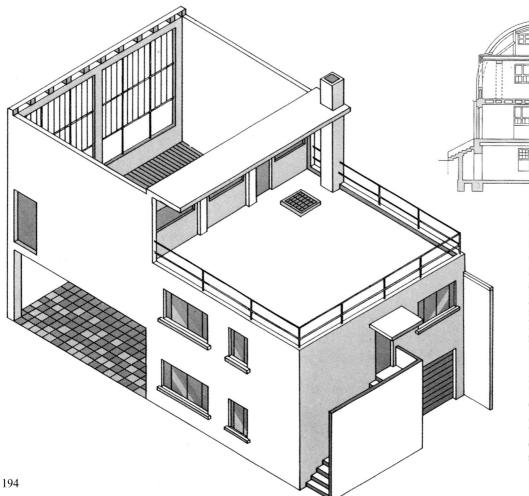

Upper left THE STOCLET
PALACE, BRUSSELS, by Josef
Hoffmann, 1904–11. The house
was built for the industrialist
Stoclet and can well be classed
as Art Nouveau, though its
geometric lines anticipate
modernist ideals.
Lower left THE
SCHRÖDER-SCHRÄDER HOUSE,
UTRECHT, by Gerrit Rietveld,
1924. The geometric lines were
now dictated by De Stijl theory,
though the commission was
once again private.
Above THE STEINER HOUSE,
VIENNA, by Adolf Loos, 1910,
once again with geometric
shapes and ingenious planning.

Although the lion's share of modernism belongs to France and Germany, to Corbusier and the Bauhaus, the lesser contribution of Holland was nonetheless vital. It can be traced back to Petrus Cuijpers, who was in close touch with Viollet-le-Duc, and who had established a Dutch national revival style in his Rijksmuseum in Amsterdam, 1877–85. His pupil Hendrik Berlage became admired internationally for his Exchange in Amsterdam, 1897–1909. Here there is no style (except "Romanesquoid"), and the ornament is all strictly rational and explicable in terms of structure or function: it "expresses" rather than adorns, and it is not fixed or stuck on.

After World War I, the artists of the Dutch group De Stijl had considerable influence not only in art but also in architecture. Their particular point of view was not only purist—the basis of De Stijl ("The Style") was an elementary geometry and colour code—but also anti-individualist. This desire to reduce all mankind to an identical way of life was inspired not so much by socialism as by World War I: according to De Stijl, individualism had caused the war. Though its motivation was rather unusual, the universal claim of De Stijl had great appeal, for instance at the Bauhaus, where Theo van Doesburg lectured in 1921. Gerrit Rietveld also anticipated and influenced Bauhaus designers in the simplicity and practicality of his furniture, and his Schröder-Schräder house in Utrecht was an important experiment in flexible "living space", though its construction method was traditional. Rietveld's later chair made from a single sheet of bent laminated plywood shows him abreast of the Bauhaus, though he had left behind De Stijl geometry and colour theory. Jacobus Oud, who had left it behind almost immediately to become city architect to Rotterdam, built some of the earliest and most elegant housing estates in plain white concrete, iron and glass.

In Vienna an isolated figure, Adolf Loos, worked once again on lines that led to the "International" style. He was one of the first to criticize the taste and ornament of Art Nouveau and to pose architecture as a political problem. From as early as 1910 he built a few odd, cubic, ornamentless houses: their interiors were more tasteful and less radical, though Loos favoured free space and from the 1920s built "split-level". By then his ideas had been republished and assimilated by Le Corbusier.

If ideas and theories made architecture, then the importance of Soviet Russia would be overwhelming. As it is, a direct influence can be traced from the Moscow Vkhutemas (Artistic and Technical Studio) on the Bauhaus via the Hungarian Lazlo Moholy-Nagy, who joined the staff in 1923—but nothing more enduring. The problem was not so much the fertility or extravagance or inability of the Russian intellectuals to agree, as the fact that the country actually had very few factory workers: and modernist architecture was not suitable for peasants. Now that Russia has industrialized, its architecture is by contrast unimaginative "International Modern".

PLAN OF THE KIEFHOEK
HOUSING ESTATE, ROTTERDAM,
by Jacobus Oud, 1925. The
inset shows a house façade.

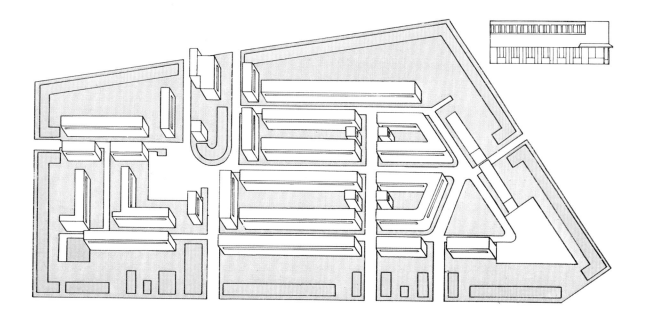

THE INTERNATIONAL STYLE

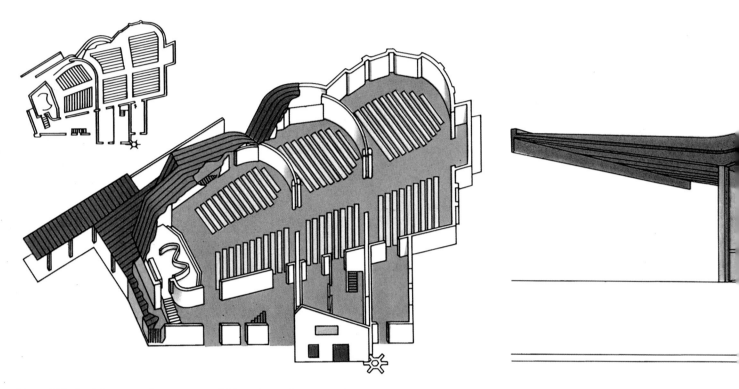

Even if it had been a victory not of ideas but of economic
expediency, a specifically 20th-century architecture had been
created—the "international" style, as the Bauhaus director
Walter Gropius had called it in 1928. A more descriptive
term might be "abstract", since it was a strictly non-figura-
tive, or non-ornamental architecture, involving instead the
play of shape, volume, material, silhouette, etc, like a contemporary painting or sculpture.

This was the common ground from which different people
and different countries could move differently. Early "international" shapes and materials tend to be simple—work of
the 1920s and early 1930s, with its now usually dirty and
chipped concrete, its metal windows, its iron rails, and
particularly its rounded corners, is as recognizable and as
datable as Art Deco. Some persisted in this kind of simplicity, particularly Mies van der Rohe, who had been
particularly caught by the German avantgarde enthusiasm
for glass. He designed, and after World War II, built very
ideal, very strict all-glass and steel buildings the beauty of
which made mockery of his label, "functionalist".

One of the first to extend the variety of "international-
style" architecture was Alvar Aalto in Finland. He did not
desert the "functionalist" ethic, in other words he did not
borrow recognizably from the past, but he made his buildings internally quite intricate and externally had them blend
with their setting in a way that could be called "organic".
(The term had been appropriated for similar qualities in his
own buildings by Frank Lloyd Wright.) It has also been
called "traditional". This is certainly untrue. But Aalto

cannot be called a "modernist", either, because he has not
written about his architecture and also because he and his
work failed, immediately after World War II, to transplant
to America.

In Italy, not so much an individual as a national version of
the "international" style emerged under Mussolini. An outstanding example is the Casa del Popolo in Como by Giuseppe Terragni, which is very pure, and also very slick. Its
marble fronting makes a difference, but this does not mean it
is traditional, or even "neoclassical". There is no reference to
classicism—no more than in Mies, anyway. Another superb
modern Italian work is Rome Central Station. After World
War II Pier Luigi Nervi became widely renowned for his brilliant shaping and handling of concrete, with a sprightly elegance all Italian.

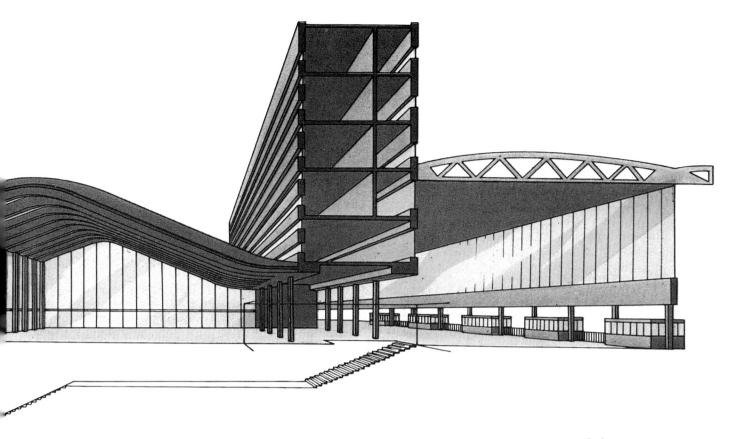

Left THE EXHIBITION HALL,
TURIN, by Pier Luigi Nervi,
1947. Like the Rome station,
the use of concrete is
spectacular and stylish.

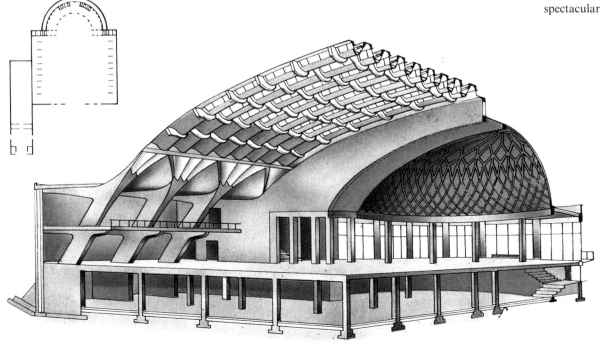

EARLY MODERN AMERICA

By running off to Europe with a client's wife in 1911, Frank Lloyd Wright injected the influence of his "prairie" style into European architecture on the one hand, and on the other became the equivalent of an avantgarde, since he was cold-shouldered by his colleagues. In this period he himself absorbed much from Europe, which he put to good use when he re-emerged as a leading "modernist" in the mid-1930s.

Meanwhile, across America, social and architectural response to the new age was more romantic than futurist. Houses, offices and public buildings tended to reflect a dream inspired by the past. This is most apparent in the "movie palaces" of the 1920s, or in the comment of an architect of one of them, "watch the bright light in the eyes of the tired shopgirl who hurries noiselessly over carpets and sighs with satisfaction as she walks amid furnishings that once delighted the hearts of queens". Indeed their extreme Aztec, Egyptian or Versailles creations would have choked any European socialist architect. But the *lobby* now emerges from its origin in the Baroque staircase hall to take on a vital role in American architecture.

The American attitude is shown again in the 1922 international competition for the Chicago Tribune Tower, to be "the world's most beautiful skyscraper". European "functionalist" entries lost to a home design basing the form on a Gothic spire and a Finnish runner-up basing it on a ziggurat. The latter, by Eliel Saarinen, was the more influential—for instance on the Empire State Building in Chicago. The American attitude is shown again in the work of Albert Kahn, who built "international-style" factories but whose other buildings invariably have ornament.

In the later 1930s Frank Lloyd Wright was again given an important commission, the Johnson Wax offices in Racine, Wisconsin. This famous building, incorporating some stunning effects—the mushroom-like internal columns, the tube lighting that made the building glow in a way to gladden the heart of an Italian Futurist or a German Expressionist—opened out the way from the "international" style to an indulgent sensuality that was fully "modernist". (Wright had much to say about the building, notably that it was "organic".)

Also at this time Wright built his Fallingwater house, which may be said to combine the "prairie" style with Le Corbusier. The Austrian immigrants Rudolph Schindler and Richard Neutra, who had worked with him for a time, explored even further the creative possibilities of new materials in California, now becoming one great El Dorado. Now one could dream as well in the style of the future as in the style of the past.

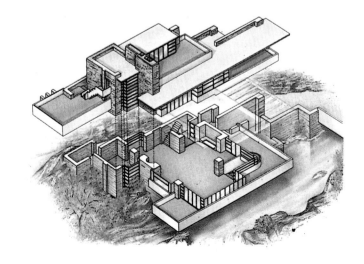

Opposite page, above A VIEW OF THE SKYLINE, MANHATTAN, NEW YORK. The office block is the major building form of the late 20th century.

Opposite page, below FALLINGWATER, BEAR RUN, PENNSYLVANIA, by Frank Lloyd Wright, 1936. Probably the most famous private house of the 20th century, and still an "ideal" home.

This page, left THE CHRYSLER BUILDING, NEW YORK, by William van Alen, 1930. European purism was not much liked in America between the Wars; it was taken up only after World War II. The Chrysler is jubilantly Art Deco in its ornament.

MODERNIST AND POST-MODERN

Shortly after World War II America took over leadership in modernist art with a new, world-beating style (or theory), Abstract Expressionism. For a time it seemed that the only creditable art must be abstract. There was a comparable situation in architecture: the world's leading new buildings apparently had to be strict, pure, slab-like, enormous, like the Lever or the Seagram skyscrapers in New York.

Then came Pop, which was figurative, satiric and much more up-to-date than modernism. So, too, in architecture, at first rather joyfully, things began to fragment. A good example is Paul Rudolph's Art and Architecture Building in New Haven, Connecticut, a building of seven storeys divided, one way or another, into 39 levels. According to the architect, "All Hell breaks loose", which was also a favourite expression of Pop artists. In the 1970s, such buildings were in their turn regarded as excessive, but now there was no return to an orthodoxy, and no new avantgarde: Pop had killed it. However, there was a continued taste for sleek purism, now manifest in "shaped" skyscrapers, such as Philip Johnson and John Burgee's Penzoil Place in Houston, Texas.

As an alternative, there had always been "organic" architecture and this gained in importance. Frank Lloyd Wright's Guggenheim Museum, a most inconvenient spiral, nevertheless encouraged bolder experiment, for instance by Eero Saarinen at the TWA terminal at John F Kennedy Airport, New York, which has great swooping vaults and shapes. Wright's true heir, however, was Louis Kahn, who was against encasing buildings in formal jackets on the one hand, and on the other had a mystical or intuitive sense of what the building "wanted to be"—something other than a utilitarian structure.

Robert Venturi, writing *Complexity and Contradiction in Architecture* in 1966, distinguished between "exclusive" or doctrinaire and "inclusive" architecture, in which situation, place, user-friendliness, environment and looks are all

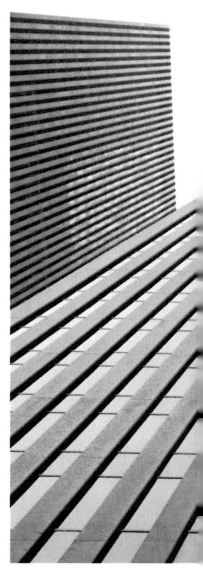

Below THE GUGGENHEIM MUSEUM, NEW YORK, by Frank Lloyd Wright, 1959. Three main factors governed this novel building. Wright himself was interested in complex circular plans. It seemed a good idea to make the view of pictures a kind of procession, induced by the spiral ramp round which they are arranged. And the building was a meeting place. On counts one and three the building is acceptable, indeed successful. On count two it is unfortunate that modern works of art often do not resemble the traditional canvas form Wright had assumed, and cannot be exhibited on a ramp. And the ramp itself bullies the user.
Right VIEW UPWARDS FROM A CONTEMPORARY NEW YORK STREET—clean purity and vast scale in clear air.

considered—an ideal of architecture based on the pragmatic. Venturi went beyond Corbusier, for whom architecture was "a simple response to a problem well stated", and generally speaking the "inclusive" has been favoured: buildings have become both much more interesting and much more considerate since the 1970s. The 1980s felt the touch of the designer, and the transformation of virtually anything banal, including bricks and mortar, into the chic. Fortunately, America has not yet outlived the heritage of Pop.

WELFARE AND WELL-BEING

In Europe, in the aftermath of World War II, housing was a rather more pressing problem than the perfect skyscraper, though plenty of those were built later. Here the standard reference was to Le Corbusier's housing units, and Corbusier himself contributed the Unité block of maisonettes in Marseilles, 1947–52. This extended his influence still further, not so much in housing as in general style—for its exposed concrete (*beton brut*) became the hallmark of European "brutalism"—and in another innovation, the incorporation of shops along corridors of the building. It was an early shopping precinct.

Brutalism neatly answers American purism as European abstract painting of the 1950s, emphasizing texture, answers Abstract Expressionism. In the hands notably of Aldo van Eyck in Holland it was not as brutal as its name suggests, but it soon became dull when compared to Pop. The architect James Stirling was involved from the beginning with Pop artists in Britain, and his buildings reflect their fascination with gleaming junk: today they might very well be called "high-tech". Stirling is also certainly "organic" like Kahn in America. Though it was built so much later, 1972–77, Richard Rogers's Pompidou Centre in Paris is more obviously a Pop building, with its loud, bright colours, its machinery exterior, and not least its (almost satiric) "organic" conception.

The success of this building is due largely to its success as a "lobby", as a place conducive to gathering before the show. This vital quality is difficult to predict and often ephemeral. For instance, the Festival Hall on London's South Bank, felt to be extremely modern and successfully so in 1951, has dated particularly inside. By contrast, the pleasingly "brutalist" National Theatre, opened in 1976, encourages meeting and lingering. But the very similar Barbican arts complex, finished shortly afterwards, is tatty and incoherent inside. Similar criteria will surely determine success or failure—for instance of Ricardo Bofill's housing complexes in France, notably at Marne-la-Vallée, 1979–83, which looks in on a semicircular space for promenaders. Recognition has recently been given to the Viennese Hans Hollein, who is a lobby architect *par excellence*.

These complexes also raise the issue of tact towards the existing environment and of preservation, an issue of great importance in Europe. Preservation carried out in good faith can also destroy, witness Victorianized medieval churches or over-pristine restorations of the 1960s. But Europe consisting entirely of "international modern" buildings would have been a disaster—it already is a disaster in Communist Europe. So it is presumably better that modern architecture should be diverse and "inclusive", or responsive to the individual, and not "modernist", which is doctrinaire.

Opposite page, above and below
THE BEAUBOURG CENTRE,
PARIS, by Renzo Piano and
Richard Rogers, 1972–77.
Above THE NATIONAL THEATRE,
SOUTH BANK, LONDON, by
Denys Lasdun, Redhouse and
Softley, begun 1969 and
completed 1977.
Left VIEW OF A RECENTLY
CONSTRUCTED HOUSING ESTATE
OUTSIDE PARIS.

THE REST OF THE WORLD

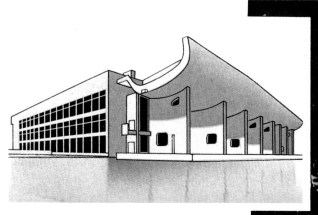

Above THE COURT OF JUSTICE, CHANDIGARH, INDIA, by Le Corbusier, 1956. Certainly a spectacular building.
Right THE OPERA HOUSE, SYDNEY, by Jorn Utzon, designed 1956. The design won the international competition because of its eye-catching forms.
Far right THE 1964 OLYMPIC STADIUM, TOKYO, by Kenzo Tange. An amazing space and shape created in steel and concrete on a vast scale.

In the Third World architecture is for the most part something practised by foreign architects, whose stance is likely to be difficult. Their response to local needs and local traditions is likely to be heavy-handed. However, they are often able to create on a grand scale and perhaps with fewer constraints than at home. Le Corbusier's government buildings at Chandigarh in north India are a case in point.

In Latin America, Corbusier's invitation to Rio de Janeiro in 1936 resulted in the emergence of a local school of which the most famous member is Oscar Niemeyer. His handling of concrete in curved shapes on a large scale, creating highly interesting and eye-catching buildings, was emphatically modern and quite individual—but such exuberance can seem sinful in the midst of social problems. It seems more appropriate in Sydney, Australia, where the Opera House, designed by the Danish Jorn Utzon, is certainly the scenic landmark it was intended to be. Louis Kahn's Sher-e-Banglanader Hotel in Dacca, again a brilliant showcase, is justifiable just because it is a hotel.

It was through a commission to Frank Lloyd Wright for a hotel that modern Western architecture was introduced into Japan, as early as 1916. When the hotel, the Imperial in

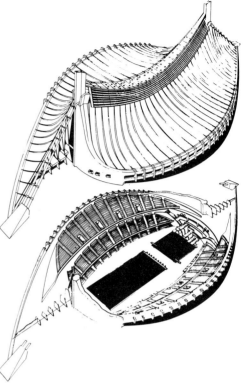

Tokyo, now demolished, withstood an earthquake in 1922, "modernism" was vindicated. It was practised at first by a pupil of Wright's, Antonin Raymond, who set as its goal a synthesis of industrial materials and the traditional Japanese house. Large-scale modern buildings followed after World War II; Kenzo Tange made an international name with his dramatic Olympic Stadium for the Tokyo Games of 1964, vaulting vast oval and circular spaces in virtuoso fashion. He and others were then designing buildings entirely modern—even "brutalist"—in their materials, but oscillating between references to historic Japanese "styles" and complete abstraction. Complete abstraction came out the winner in the next generation, for instance in Arata Isozaki's or Tadao Ando's architecture, though both seek an equivalent to old values in modern forms—which is not the same as returning to them. For instance, they might seek to induce an atmosphere conducive to contemplation, without directly recalling the dimly lit recesses usual in traditional houses. The maturity of modern Japanese architecture, corresponding to the country's industrial status, is evident in Isozaki's invitation to design the Museum of Contemporary Art in Los Angeles.

INDEX

206

INDEX

INDEX

CREDITS